LAW AND PROCEDURE OF
THE STOCK EXCHANGE

LAW AND PROCEDURE OF THE STOCK EXCHANGE

BY

GEOFFREY COOPER, LL.B. (Lond.),
of Lincoln's Inn
and the North Eastern Circuit, Barrister

AND

RICHARD J. CRIDLAN,
Member of the Stock Exchange, London

LONDON
BUTTERWORTHS
1971

ENGLAND: BUTTERWORTH & CO. (PUBLISHERS) LTD.
             LONDON: 88 Kingsway, WC2B 6AB
AUSTRALIA: BUTTERWORTH & CO. (AUSTRALIA) LTD.
             SYDNEY: 586 Pacific Highway, Chatswood, NSW
             2067
             MELBOURNE: 343 Little Collins Street, 3000
             BRISBANE: 240 Queen Street, 4000
CANADA: BUTTERWORTH & CO. (CANADA) LTD.
             TORONTO: 14 Curity Avenue, 374
NEW ZEALAND: BUTTERWORTH & CO. (NEW ZEALAND) LTD.
             WELLINGTON: 26–28 Waring Taylor Street, 1
             AUCKLAND: 35 High Street, 1
SOUTH AFRICA: BUTTERWORTH & CO. (SOUTH AFRICA) (PTY.) LTD.
             DURBAN: 152–154 Gale Street

A/346. 42'092

©

ISBN 0 406 56675 5

FILMSET IN PHOTON IMPRINT 11 PT. BY RICHARD CLAY (THE CHAUCER PRESS), LTD.,
BUNGAY, SUFFOLK
PRINTED IN GREAT BRITAIN BY FLETCHER & SON LTD., NORWICH, NORFOLK

Preface

The law and procedure of the Stock Exchange is a subject which has experienced serious neglect over the years. No comprehensive work has appeared since 1914, when Butterworth and Company published the second and last edition of *A Treatise on the Law of the Stock Exchange* by W. S. Schwabe, K.C., and G. A. H. Branson. The learned authors had appeared as counsel in many of the late nineteenth- and early twentieth-century cases upon which a considerable part of Stock Exchange law is founded, and their work is still regarded as authoritative in many highly respectable quarters.

The subject has changed and expanded in the interval, which has seen many important additions to the pre-1914 case law and numerous amendments to the Rules and Regulations—also, *inter alia*, the Prevention of Fraud (Investments) Acts 1939 and 1958, the Exchange Control Act 1947, the Trustee Investments Act 1961, the Stock Transfer Act 1963, the Monopolies and Mergers Act 1965, the establishment of the Federation of Stock Exchanges and the setting up of the City Panel on Takeovers and Mergers. Only a new book can fill this enormous gap, and we have attempted to provide a really comprehensive guide—not only to Stock Exchange law in the strict sense but also to its Rules and working procedures. For the latter we have drawn freely upon the Rules and Regulations of the Stock Exchange, and its own publications such as *The Admission of Securities to Quotation*, the *Code of Dealing* and *The New Transfer System*.

We turn to the layout of the book. Chapters 1–3 are in a sense introductory. They explain the existence of the Stock Exchange and its history and constitution. Chapters 4–10 contain the meat of the subject; they trace in logical sequence the admission of securities to quotation and the procedures for dealing in them; the formation of bargains; the procedures for settlement and transfer; and finally the remedies for breach of contract and default. We finish the book with chapters on business with provincial and foreign stock exchanges and Exchange Control. In adopting this structure, we have taken the syllabus for the Federal Examination on Stock Exchange Practice as a rough guide—partly because we think the syllabus is divided on a logical basis and partly in the hope that the book will be useful to candidates.

We are particularly indebted to C. D. Morley, Esq., C.B.E., Secretary General of the Stock Exchange, London, for his permission to adopt passages from the Rules and Regulations and other Stock Exchange publications and for his interest and advice in many other respects. We would also like to acknowledge the advice of Mr R. A. Thompson, Official Assignee, of Mr M. E. Fidler, Stock Official, and of Mr K. Gillies, Mr C. W. Jaffé, Mr J. C. Kimmerling, Mr P. J. Lambert and Mr R. W. Penney—all of the Stock Exchange, London. Mr N. S. M. Kemp, Secretary to the Committee of the Federation of Stock Exchanges has provided prompt and helpful answers to all our queries. Our thanks go also to the Bank of England for their advice on Exchange Control, and to the Public Relations Office of the Stock Exchange for their general assistance.

We thank our publishers for preparing the Tables and Index.

We believe that this book is an accurate expression of the law, usages, rules, regulations and procedures of the Stock Exchange as they stood on November 1st 1970.

2 Harcourt Buildings, Temple, E.C.4.	G. W. C.
The Stock Exchange, London, E.C.2.	R. J. C.

February 1971

Contents

Table of Statutes

References in this Table to '*Stats.*' are to Halsbury's Statutes of England (3rd Edn.) showing the volume and page at which the annotated text of the Act will be found.

Table of Cases

In the following Table references are given to the
English and Empire Digest showing where the case
appears in that work.

F

M

W

CHAPTER 1

Introduction

The expression "The Stock Exchange" is generally taken to refer to the Stock Exchange, London. Most of the principal provincial cities have their own stock exchange; they are known collectively as the Associated Stock Exchanges. In addition there are associations of stock and share dealers such as the London Discount Market Association, and the Provincial Brokers' Stock Exchange, which has its headquarters at York but whose members do business in numerous cities and towns which do not have their own exchange. The Stock Exchange, London, is however the leading stock exchange in the United Kingdom. Its practice, usages and customs are, in general, followed by other stock exchanges. In 1965 the various stock exchanges established a Federation and made some rules which are binding on all members. But at present the Federal Rules only cover certain aspects of stock exchange practice. Until all stock exchanges are governed by a comprehensive code, this account of the law and procedure of the Stock Exchange will, unless otherwise indicated, be confined to the law and procedure, the Rules and Regulations of the Stock Exchange, London.

A. THE FORMATION AND DEVELOPMENT OF THE STOCK EXCHANGES

1. The growth of stock and share dealing

The history of stockbroking and the economic and social conditions which led to the formation and development of the London and other stock exchanges are described in fascinating detail elsewhere,[1] and for the purposes of this book a short résumé will suffice.

A stock exchange is a market for the sale and purchase of shares stock and other securities.[2] The first prerequisite for its existence is

1. See in particular E. V. Morgan and W. A. Thomas, *The Stock Exchange, its History and Functions* (2nd Edn., 1969).
2. When it is not specially defined (e.g., by Act of Parliament) the word "securities" includes shares, debentures, government stock and units under a unit trust scheme.

a ready supply of securities suitable for transfer among members of the public. Another vital prerequisite is sufficient persons of means who wish their property to include financial investments as well as business enterprises, houses and land. Given these factors, a stock market will develop, provided there are simple workable procedures for the transfer and payment of securities. In England, all these conditions were present in a rough and ready form by the end of the seventeenth century.[3]

The idea of separating *capital management* (for example the running of a company) from *capital ownership* (the holding of its securities) began to take root about 1550 with the formation of joint-stock companies for the purpose of trade and exploration. Lenders would put up money to finance the explorers and merchant adventurers, and an agreement would be made whereby the money subscribed became a permanent loan and the lenders participated in profits and losses. Sometimes the Crown would grant such a concern a charter of incorporation. The charter had the effect of converting the enterprise into a legal entity distinct from its members; the legal result was that the *company* became liable for *all* its debts —and its members' liability was restricted to the amount they had put into it. The most celebrated of these Charter Companies were the East India Company and the Hudson's Bay Company.

Very soon lenders formed the habit of selling their holdings to other people by private negotiation. But there was no market to which intending buyers had access, nor did they have any means of knowing the fortunes of the enterprises in which they were purchasing "adventures" (i.e., stock), since most of them kept their capital structure a secret and many operated overseas. About 1680 a class of specialist dealers, called "brokers", began to emerge; they arranged transactions in the "stocks" which the public were looking for, and were not backward in giving advice as to their profitability. Brokers generally did business in the coffee houses of the City of London; they had to have a licence from the Lord Mayor and Aldermen to do so, take an oath and enter into a bond of good behaviour. A separate class of dealers, called jobbers, who held company stocks and sold them as principals on their own behalf began to develop contemporaneously. Jobbers were regarded as a lower form of life altogether since there were no rules of dealing and most of the opportunities for rigging the market and other sharp practices lay in their hands.[4]

In 1697 an Act was passed to regulate dealings in stocks and

3. See E. V. Morgan and W. A. Thomas, *The Stock Exchange, its History and Functions, supra.*
4. Defoe's exposé, *The Villainy of Stock Jobbers Detected,* reflects the unpopularity of jobbers during this period.

shares, introducing stiff penalties for brokers who did not have a licence, and having as its principal aim the control of market rigging. But the Act lapsed in 1707 and was never revived. Barnard's Act of 1733 attempted to prohibit stock jobbing. It was effective for a time, but proved in the end to be unenforceable.

2. The Bank of England

In the last two decades of the seventeenth century many banking and commercial companies were formed as trade began to flourish. The Government conceived the idea of raising money for State purposes; in 1694 a syndicate raised over a million pounds which it lent to the Government in return for perpetual interest secured by ship and liquor duties. The syndicate became incorporated under charter as the Bank of England. It was the largest company promotion of the day and its stocks were subscribed for by the public and dealt in by brokers.

In the eighteenth century the Government began for the first time to raise money in large quantities by the issue of loan capital. The National Debt rose from £44 million in 1739 to £709 million in 1816, and by the end of the eighteenth century most of it was under the management of the Bank of England. Stockbrokers were often involved in both the issue of loan stock to the public, and in the subsequent dealings.

3. The South Sea Bubble. Reform of Company Law

With the growth of commerce, the joint-stock company, which required a special Act of Parliament or a charter for its formation, was considered too expensive to form and too clumsy to run. Traders began to form partnerships instead, the terms of which were all contained in a comprehensive deed. Such partnerships did not have charters of incorporation, and so the liability of its members was unlimited. Dishonest promoters and share dealers took advantage of this situation to commit large-scale frauds upon the public, the most notorious of which was the South Sea Bubble. The Bubble Act 1720 dealt with that situation by providing that all companies formed without a charter or under a charter given for another purpose would be illegal, and all transactions in their shares would be void. But unfortunately, one of its effects was to discourage joint-stock enterprises in general; in the result not many new companies were formed in the century that followed the Bubble Act. There was, however, an active market in Bank of England stock, and shares in the older trading companies.

The Industrial Revolution made the reform of Company Law a matter of urgency. The Joint Stock Companies Act 1844 replaced the old system of a charter or grant by the Crown with the new system of company registration, which was developed in subsequent Acts.[5] The Limited Liability Act 1855 provided that in the case of registered companies a member's liability was limited to the amount unpaid on his shares. The introduction of the two principles of registration and limited liability enabled the public to invest with much greater confidence, and therefore in much greater amounts, than hitherto. The business of stock and share dealers grew in proportion.

4. Formation of the Stock Exchange, London
Throughout the eighteenth century brokers and jobbers did business in the coffee houses of 'Change Alley in the City of London. In 1762 some of the more prosperous brokers decided to make their company more exclusive. They formed a club of their own, and made an agreement with the proprietors of Jonathan's Coffee House under which only members of the club were to be admitted. This arrangement did not survive for long, however, because a broker who could not gain admittance to Jonathan's because he did not belong to the club sued the proprietor; the judge, Lord Mansfield, declared that since Jonathan's had been a dealers' resort from time immemorial, the broker could enter and do business as he pleased.

In 1773 another group of brokers, which presumably included some of the original members of the Jonathan's Club, acquired a building in Threadneedle Street which they called "The Stock Exchange". For a time anyone could enter the premises on payment of sixpence a day, but in 1801 its Committee of Proprietors and its General Purposes Committee closed the House to the public and drew up rules for the election of members. In 1801 several of the newly elected members agreed to acquire new and more spacious premises in Capel Court. After negotiations between themselves and the proprietors of the Threadneedle Street premises, an agreement was made whereby the Capel Court building should be purchased by the proprietors and members of the old Stock Exchange. The purchase price was met by a capital sum of £20,000, and the new building was opened early in 1802.

On March 27th 1802 the constitution of the new society was drawn up in the form of a deed of settlement. Under the deed, the new Stock Exchange building was vested in nine Trustees and Managers who held office for life: they were to manage the

5. See the Companies Act 1862 which prohibits alterations in a company's objects clause, and the Companies Act 1907 which established private companies (which were prohibited from inviting the public to subscribe for their shares).

Exchange in the interests of the proprietors (i.e., the members) each of whom held no more than four of the £50 shares into which the purchase money had been divided. This Deed was revoked in 1875 and replaced by the Deed of Settlement which (as subsequently amended) is the constitution under which the Exchange operates to this day.

5. The Development of the Stock Exchange, London

The Stock Exchange, London, now functions as an efficient and well-regulated market which is the end-product of a continuing process of development beginning in 1801. The most important developments are listed in chronological order below:

1802 First Deed of Settlement appointed the Trustees and Managers of the undertaking and the same persons together with others to be a Committee for General Purposes.

1812 Publication of the first Rule Book. This governed admissions, dealings, failures and the general conduct of members. Under it new members were forbidden to engage in other forms of business.

1847 Partnerships between brokers and jobbers prohibited by the rules.

1854 Stock Exchange rebuilt in an enlarged form.

1870 Brokers Relief Act abolished the powers of the Lord Mayor and Aldermen to regulate the conduct of brokers.

1872 Introduction of a settling room for the checking of bargains.

1875 New Deed of Settlement which provided that all proprietors must also be members.

1882 Deed altering the capital structure of the Exchange to 20,000 shares of £12 each.

1884 New Stock Exchange building completed in Threadneedle Street.

1904 New rule requiring candidates for membership to acquire a nomination from a retiring member. Abolished in 1969.

1908 New rules provide that all members must declare whether they are brokers or jobbers.

1912 Scale of minimum commissions introduced.

1939 Private unlimited companies allowed to become corporate members.

1939 Prevention of Fraud (Investment) Act which had the effect of limiting competition from outside the Stock Exchange.

1945 Trustees and Managers and Committee for General Purposes amalgamated to form the Council.

1948 The 20,000 shares written down to one shilling each (the existing holders being compensated with two cumulative annuities

of £4). Each member to hold at least one share. Each member to have one vote, regardless of shares held.
1950 Compensation fund established, to compensate the clients of a defaulting member.
1962 Sureties for candidates abolished.
1969 Member firms permitted to become limited liability companies.

6. The development of provincial stock exchanges

With the growth of commerce and industry during the nineteenth century, many local exchanges were formed. A very high proportion of their business involved the buying and selling of securities in companies which operated locally and had a local head office. The Manchester Stock Exchange had a large market in the shares of cotton and railway companies, Liverpool in insurance shares and American securities, Glasgow in ships and iron, and Cardiff in collieries. The Stock Exchange, London, and the various provincial stock exchanges were established and developed independently of each other. In 1890, however, on the initiative of the Liverpool Stock Exchange, the provincial exchanges formed an association which became known as the Council of the Associated Stock Exchanges. The Associated Exchanges comprised the stock exchanges in Belfast, Birmingham, Bradford, Bristol, Cardiff, Cork, Dublin, Greenock, Halifax, Huddersfield, Leeds, Liverpool, Manchester, Newcastle upon Tyne, Nottingham, Sheffield and Swansea, together with the Scottish Stock Exchange with trading floors in Aberdeen, Dundee, Edinburgh and Glasgow.

In 1912 stockbrokers who carried on business in smaller towns and did not belong to the London or the Associated Exchanges formed an organisation called The Provincial Brokers' Stock Exchange which eventually established its headquarters at York.

7. The Federation of Stock Exchanges in Great Britain and Ireland

The twentieth century has seen a vast increase in the volume of stock exchange business, and while the London and Associated Stock Exchanges, and the provincial brokers, remained independent of each other, "events emphasised the necessity of co-operation, and for many years common practices in dealing and settlement and common rates of commission were accepted in the transaction of business".[6] From time to time negotiations to attain greater unity and to establish a common policy took place, and liaison between

6. See the Prospectus of the Federation of Stock Exchanges, p. (i).

the three bodies became very much closer after the Second World War. The Company Law Committee which reported in 1962 recommended the rationalisation of the existing exchanges. In October of that year a Co-ordination Committee set up by the exchanges reached the unanimous decision that this rationalisation was best achieved by the setting up of a Federation of Stock Exchanges with executive powers on specific matters exercisable by a Federal Committee. The Federation came into being on July 1st 1965. It has made a number of rules on matters in which the federated exchanges have surrendered their individual autonomy and which are binding upon them all.

The Federation's Prospectus[7] sets out the initial minimum requirements to which all member exchanges have to conform:

(i) to provide standard compensation funds for members of the public who have suffered loss from the default of one of their members.

(ii) to conform with common requirements for the quotation of securities.

(iii) to permit and control the use of branch offices within the Federal area.

In addition the prospectus[8] contains rules which member exchanges must adopt unless, in the case of a particular rule, an exchange can satisfy the Federal Committee that it has already adopted a more stringent rule. These are rules providing for the training and qualification of candidates for membership, the control of partnerships, the preparation of balance sheets by member firms and the minimum capital requirements to be met before a member firm may do business.

The Federal Rules cover only certain aspects of stock exchange activity, but the logical and intended result of the Federation's activities is the establishment of a National Stock Exchange with a uniform code regulating all the activities of its federated members.

B. CONSTITUTION AND FUNCTION
OF THE STOCK EXCHANGE

A passage from the opinion of Lord Buckmaster in *Weinberger* v. *Inglis*[9] provides a clear exposition of the character and status of the Stock Exchange:

"The London Stock Exchange is in reality a building vested in certain proprietors and used for the purpose of carrying on a market for stocks

7. Appendix C of the Prospectus.
8. Appendix D of the Prospectus.
9. [1919] A.C. 606 H.L., at pp. 617–619.

and shares. It is not regulated in any way by charter or statute. The management owes no duties to the public and the business is subject to no regulations except those which from time to time (the Council) think right to impose on those whom they choose to admit. The prestige and authority of the institution depend entirely upon the reputation it has established for honest and efficient business methods. Any group of people who so desired could start another Stock Exchange tomorrow. It is not a public market—it is a private market and access to it is only obtained through membership."

1. Constitution

In law the Stock Exchange, London, is an unincorporated company or association of persons, styled its "proprietors", who hold its issued share capital, which now consists of 20,000 shares of one shilling each. Every member must hold one share,[10] and it follows that every member is a proprietor. The Society was originally constituted under the Deed of 1802; the constitution under which it now works is the Deed of Settlement dated December 21st 1875, the terms of which have been altered from time to time as provided in the Deed. In fact the Deed is an indenture between trustees and proprietors under which arrangements are made for the use by members of certain premises which the proprietors had acquired for the carrying on of Stock Exchange business. Under clause 31 of the Deed (as amended) the management and control of the premises and of the society is vested in the Council of the Stock Exchange, London,[11] which (*inter alia*) makes, repeals, amends and alters the Rules and Regulations of the Stock Exchange and publishes them in book form. The premises of the London Stock Exchange are known colloquially as "The House".

2. Function of providing a fair market

Shortly stated, the function of any stock exchange is to provide a fair, orderly and efficient market for dealings in stocks and shares and other securities. When company stocks were first dealt in during the seventeenth century there were no rules of dealing and the opportunities for dishonesty were many. After its formation the London Stock Exchange gradually evolved usages and customs, and made rules for the protection of the public no less than for the benefit of its members. The present Rules and Regulations, revised and reissued on June 23rd 1969, make comprehensive provision for every aspect of its work.

10. Deed of Settlement 1875, Cl. 8(c).
11. For the constitution and powers of the Council, see Chapter 2.

3. Prevention of a false market

The Rules of the Stock Exchange, Common Law and Statute, are all concerned to prevent rigging or the creation of a false market.

A. UNDER THE RULES

The Rules provide that no member shall *knowingly or without due care* deal in such a manner as shall promote or assist in the promotion of a false market.[12] A false market is defined as "a market in which a movement of the price of a share is brought about or sought to be brought about by *contrived* factors, such as the operation of buyers and sellers acting in collaboration with each other, calculated to create a movement of price which is not justified by assets, earnings or prospects".[13]

B. AT COMMON LAW

Where more than one person is engaged in market rigging, that conduct is a criminal conspiracy at common law. So, in *R.* v. *De Berenger*[14] it was held that to conspire on a particular day to raise the price of Government securities by false rumours, with intent to injure those who should purchase on that day, was an indictable offence. In *R.* v. *Aspinall*[15] several persons obtained a quotation for securities in the Stock Exchange's Official List by making false statements. They led persons dealing in the securities to believe that the requirements of the Committee on Quotations had been properly complied with; and in the result the securities obtained an artificial and inflated market value. It was held that this amounted to a criminal conspiracy even though it was not proved that anyone had acted upon that erroneous belief. In *Scott* v. *Brown Doering McNab & Co.*[16] it was held that people who had been parties to an agreement which amounted to a criminal conspiracy could not enforce it in civil law.

Not all market-making is illegal, however. Dealers may combine to "pool" shares, and then arrange for another member of the exchange to buy them at a certain price; this is a perfectly legitimate device for regulating the market.[17] Similarly, combinations are permitted to "corner" the market, i.e., to buy up all available securities of a particular kind so as to drive speculative sellers into a "corner";[18] this will compel them to buy from the combination—at a price dictated by the combination—in order to obtain the securities which they have agreed to acquire for their clients. Where,

12. Rule 73*b*(1).   13. Rule 73*b*(2).   14. (1814) 3 M. & S. 67.
15. (1876) 2 Q.B.D. 48, C.A.   16. (1892) 2 Q.B. 724, C.A.
17. *Sanderson and Levi* v. *British Mercantile Marine and Share Co. Ltd.* (1899), *The Times*, July 19th.
18. *See R.* v. *Bishirgian*, [1936] 1 All E.R. 586, C.C.A.

however, the instigators of pools and corners resort to fraudulent methods, then clearly they bring themselves within the law of conspiracy.

C. BY STATUTE

Two Acts of Parliament help to prevent a false market. The Prevention of Fraud (Investments) Act 1958 made it a criminal offence, to make statements, promises or forecasts designed to induce another to purchase securities if such statements are misleading, false,[19] deceptive or reckless.[20] It is also an offence to distribute investment circulars containing inducements which are misleading, false or deceptive.[1]

The Companies Act 1948 determines the contents of company prospectuses. A prospectus (which is an invitation by a company to the public to purchase or subscribe for its securities) must disclose a wide range of information which will enable an intending shareholder to judge the merits of investing in it.

D. THE PROTECTION OF BARGAINS ONCE MADE

Allegations of market rigging must be substantiated before they can be allowed to annul a bargain; otherwise the Stock Exchange could not function smoothly. The Rules and Regulations provide that the Council will not entertain an application to annul a bargain except upon a *specific* allegation of fraud or wilful misrepresentation, or upon *prima facie* evidence of some material mistake in a bargain.[2] The Council are in the unavoidable position of having to reconcile fairness with efficiency.

E. THE PROHIBITION OF ADVERTISING

Members of the Stock Exchange are in competition with one another in the sense that an investor will tend to choose a broker who he thinks will make him a good bargain. In a fair market, his choice should be influenced by brokers' reputations or his own experience. Accordingly the Stock Exchange prohibits a member or firm from advertising for stock exchange business, or for this purpose to issue circulars or business communications to persons other than their own principals (i.e., clients),[3] nor may they be interested directly or indirectly in any concern which sends adver-

19. In *R.* v. *Lord Kylsant*, [1932] 1 K.B. 442, it was held that falsehood could consist in a material omission.
20. Prevention of Fraud (Investments) Act 1958, s. 13. In *R.* v. *Grunwald*, [1963] 1 Q.B. 935; [1960] 3 All E.R. 380, it was held that reckless meant rash and unsupported by any real basis of facts. *Cf., Shawnigan Ltd.* v. *Vokins and Co. Ltd.,* [1961] 3 All E.R. 396 at pp. 401–403.
 1. Prevention of Fraud (Investments) Act 1958, s. 14.
 2. Rule 74   3. Rules 78 (1).

tisements for stock exchange business to such persons.[4] A broker
may, however, with the consent of the Council issue on behalf of a
client a circular to the holders of a security offering to acquire their
securities, provided that he does not treat any such security holder
so circularised as his client by reason of the issue of the circular.[5]
Members of the Stock Exchange may also, with the consent of
the Council, join the management or advisory board of a unit
trust.[6]

C. THE PRINCIPLE OF
LIMITED LIABILITY

**1. The separation of capital management from capital owner-
ship**

The fundamental principle of company law is that a company
registered under the Companies Act 1948 is a legal person *in its own
right*. So although the shareholders own a company, the company's
money and assets belong to the company and not the shareholders.
As an independent legal person the company makes contracts in its
own name, and the debts which a company incurs are the debts of
the company itself.[7]

But while a company is a legal person it is also a legal abstraction.
Human beings are required (*a*) to manage its affairs (otherwise it
would be incapable of doing business), and (*b*) to belong to it
(otherwise it would not exist in the first place).

The former are called directors, they manage the company's
capital on its behalf; the latter are called shareholders, they own
shares in the capital without which the company would not be able
to operate. The directors are the agents through whom the company
acts. First directors may be appointed by the company's articles of
association (its constitution); subsequent directors are appointed in
the way laid down by the articles (e.g., by a general meeting of the
company). They must exercise their powers honestly and in the
interests of the company and its shareholders, and must not put
themselves in a position where their duties and interests are likely to
conflict.[8] They may receive remuneration in return for their services.

Every shareholder will own one share or more, and his ownership

4. Rule 78 (2).   5. Rule 78 (1).   6. Rule 78 (2).
7. *Salomon* v. *Salomon and Co. Ltd.*, [1897] A.C. 22.
8. *Regal (Hastings)* v. *Gulliver*, [1942] 1 All E.R. 378; *Boston Deep Sea Fishing Co.*
v. *Ansell* (1888), 39 Ch. D. 339; *Eden* v. *Ridsdales Railway Lamp and Lighting
Co., Ltd.* (1889), 23 Q.B.D. 368.

may carry the right to a dividend and the right to vote at general meetings to determine the company's constitution or policy. His rights *vis-à-vis* the company are regulated by the Companies Acts, and the memorandum (defining its powers) and articles of association which it must register with the Companies' Registrar under the Companies Act 1948, and which are available for public inspection at the Registry.

The price of his shares is the only debt which the shareholder owes to the company. In other words, his liability is limited by his shares. Normally he need not pay the full price at once; but he may be required to pay the balance by instalments at fixed dates, or "as and when called on". The latter event is known as a call. If a company is wound up and its assets are not sufficient to pay its debts, shareholders whose liability is limited by their shares are liable to contribute to those assets up to the amount, if any, unpaid on their shares. Their liability extends no further than that.

2. Classes of capital

A company's memorandum will state the amount of share capital which the company is authorised to issue, and its division into shares of a fixed amount. The expression "capital" is often used in a loose and general sense. In fact, a company's capital includes:

(*i*) *Its nominal or authorised capital*

This is the amount of share capital which the company is authorised by its memorandum to issue. The company may increase or reduce the amount, but must do so in a manner which conforms with the Companies Act 1948.

(*ii*) *Its issued or equity share capital*

I.e., that part of the company's nominal capital which has already been issued to shareholders.

(*iii*) *Its paid-up capital*

I.e., that part of the issued capital which the shareholders have paid for.

(*iv*) *Its reserve capital*

I.e., that part of the unpaid capital which a limited company has by special resolution decided it shall not call upon the holders to pay except in the event of the company going into liquidation. In that event, the reserve capital is available for the benefit of the company's creditors.

D. SECURITIES DEALT IN ON THE STOCK EXCHANGE

1. Company securities

A. SHARES

Normally a company's articles gives a company power to issue shares in different classes. The two principal classes are ordinary shares and preference shares.

(*i*) *Ordinary shares*

A share has been described as a bundle of rights in a company. Its holder is *ipso facto* a member, and he has all the rights conferred on shareholders by the Companies Act and the company's memorandum and articles. He can vote at company meetings; he is entitled to receive the company's accounts and he will receive a profit dividend if and when it is declared by the directors.

(*ii*) *Preference shares*

A preference share is entitled to preference as to dividend at a fixed rate (e.g., 5 per cent) over an ordinary share. The exact nature of the preferential rights depends, however, on the articles or the terms on which the preference shares were issued. But if the articles do not provide to the contrary,

(*a*) While the company is a going concern:

(i) Preference shares are *cumulative*, i.e., arrears of dividend are carried forward.[9]

(ii) Preference shares are *non-participating*, i.e., they give no right to participate in *surplus* profits after payment of a dividend on the ordinary shares.[10]

(*b*) When the company is in liquidation:

(i) Arrears of dividend are not payable out of assets[11] (in practice, the articles usually provide that they are).[12]

(ii) Preference shareholders have no priority in the repayment

9. *Webb* v. *Earle* (1875), L.R. 20 Eq. 556.
10. *Will* v. *United Lankat Plantations Co. Ltd.*, [1914] A.C. 11.
11. *Re Crichton's Oil Co.*, [1902] 2 Ch. 86; *Re Catalinas Warehouses and Mole Co. Ltd.*, [1947] 1 All E.R. 51.
12. *Re Springbok Agricultural Estates, Ltd.*, [1920] 1 Ch. 563; *Re Wharfedale Brewery Co. Ltd.*, [1952] Ch. 913; [1952] All E.R. 635.

of the company's capital (in practice, articles usually provide for such priority).[13]

(iii) Surplus assets are divisible rateably among all classes of shareholders. But if the articles give the preference shareholders priority in the repayment of capital, they are not entitled to share in surplus assets as well—unless the articles otherwise provide.[14]

The Companies Act 1948[15] allows companies to issue redeemable preference shares (e.g., redeemable in 1990). The terms on which they can be redeemed depend on the articles, but redemption can only take place:

(*a*) if they are fully paid;

(*b*) out of profits of the company available for dividend or out of the proceeds of a fresh issue of shares made for the purpose of redemption.

The main advantage of preference shares is that they are a comparatively safe investment. Their main disadvantage is that while ordinary shares give their holder full voting rights, the preferential shareholders can usually vote only when their special rights are being varied or the dividend is in arrear. Effective control of the company therefore lies in the hands of the ordinary shareholders.

(*iii*) *Non-voting ordinary shares*

Occasionally companies issue ordinary shares which do not carry the right to vote, when they wish to raise money but do not intend to give new shareholders power to alter company policy. In its requirements for quotation the Federation of Stock Exchanges requires non-voting shares to be designated as such.[16]

B. LOAN CAPITAL

Once a company has commenced business[17] it may borrow money for the purposes of the business,[18] and give security for the

13. *Re Walter Symons Ltd.*, [1934] Ch. 308; *Re Wood Skinner and Co. Ltd.*, [1944] Ch. 323; *Re E. W. Savory Ltd.*, [1951] 2 All E.R. 1036; *Re Wharfedale Brewery Co. Ltd.* (*supra*).
14. Where the articles contain no reference to further rights after giving the preference shareholders priority in a liquidation, they have no right to participate in the surplus; *Scottish Insurance Corpn. Ltd.* v. *Wilsons and Clyde Coal Co.*, [1949] A.C. 462; [1949] 1 All E.R. 1068; *Dimbula Valley (Ceylon) Tea Co.* v. *Laurie*, [1961] Ch. 353.
15. Section 58.
16. See the Admission of Securities to Quotation (issued by the Federation of Stock Exchanges) p. 90.
17. I.e., when it has issued a prospectus inviting the public to subscribe for shares, see the Companies Act 1948, s. 109.
18. Subject to any resolutions in the memorandum and articles, and possible Treasury control under s. 1 of the Borrowing (Control and Guarantees) Act 1946.

loan by creating a mortgage or charge of its property. Loans may be secured by either:

(a) a fixed mortgage (legal or equitable) which fastens on to a specific asset such as a factory. Here the company cannot realise the asset without the consent of the lender; or

(b) an equitable floating charge, which fastens on to a *class* of assets, present and future (such as the company's undertaking) which class is, in the ordinary course of business, changing from time to time. Until some step is taken to enforce the charge, the company can carry on business in the ordinary way and deal with the class of assets as it pleases. But when the lender decides to realise his floating charge (e.g., by appointing a receiver), or when the company goes into liquidation, the floating charge *crystallises* into a fixed charge, and the assets charged are no longer freely disposable.

C. DEBENTURES

A debenture is a document acknowledging a loan to a company, usually under seal and giving a charge on the company's assets [19] as security. Debentures are generally secured by a trust deed which gives trustees for the debenture holders a *legal* mortgage over the company's freeholds and leaseholds, and a floating charge over the rest of its property; this ensures, so far as is possible, that persons who subsequently lend money to the company cannot gain priority over the debenture holders. The deed will specify times and events in which principal and interest become payable, and contain a covenant by the company for payment via the trustees. Where the debenture trust deed confers a charge, and the company defaults in payment of principal or interest, the debenture holder may exercise any of the powers conferred upon him by the debenture or trust deed, e.g., of appointing a receiver; if he is given no such power he can apply to the court for the appointment of a receiver or manager, or for an order for sale or foreclosure. Besides these extra remedies he has the ordinary creditor's remedies of (a) an action to recover principal and interest or (b) a petition to the court for the winding-up of the company.

Usually the company will be given power to use the property charged (e.g., to lease it) to the advantage of itself and of the debenture holders. All charges must be registered in the company's own register,[20] and with the Registrar of Companies.[1] If the debenture is secured by a trust deed, the document which its holder will receive is known as a registered debenture, issued as one of a series.

A company may also issue bearer debentures. These are expressed

19. Sometimes only *part* of a company's specific assets are charged.
20. Companies Act 1948, s. 104.
1. *Ibid.,* s. 95.

to be made payable to bearer, and coupons for the interest are attached. Some bearer debentures are negotiable instruments (as for example cheques) and a *bona fide* transferee for value takes them free from any defects in the title of a prior holder.[2]

Sometimes a company issues a convertible debenture, or unsecured loan stock, giving the holder an option to exchange it for ordinary shares. The rate of conversion and the days on which the option may be exercised are fixed when the debenture is issued.

The debenture *may* give its holder *no* charge over the company's assets. In this case the holder is an ordinary unsecured creditor. If the company defaults in payment of principal or interest he has the remedies of other ordinary creditors. He can either (*a*) sue for principal or interest, or (*b*) petition for the winding-up of the company.

D. STOCK

Stock is simply a collective expression for a number of shares or debentures lumped together. A company cannot issue stock directly, but if issued shares are fully paid up it has power to convert them into stock.[3] Loan capital is usually consolidated by the trust deed, and becomes debenture stock in the process.

While shares can only be transferred in multiples of one, and the majority of debentures only in multiples of £100, stock, and in particular Gilt-Edged stock, can be transferred in multiples of one new penny.

2. Other securities

A. GOVERNMENT STOCKS

The National Debt came into being in 1694, when certain subscribers lent £1,200,000 to the Crown at 8 per cent, and were incorporated under charter as the Bank of England. The National Debt is divided into the External Debt (which consists of money borrowed from overseas countries), and the Internal Debt. The latter consists of the Funded Debt, which is made up of loans provided by the public for which Government securities have been issued, and the Unfunded Debt, which is made up of loans the principal of which must be repaid at a definite date. For example, Defence Bonds and savings bonds (including Premium Savings Bonds) are part of the Unfunded Debt.

The Treasury's power to issue new securities is now regulated by the National Loans Act 1968. For the purpose of raising money the

2. *Bechuanaland Exploration Co.* v. *London Trading Bank,* [1898] 2 Q.B. 658.
3. Companies Act 1948, s. 61.

Treasury may create and issue such securities at such rates of interest and subject to such conditions as to repayment, redemption and other matters, including provision for a sinking fund, as they think fit.[4] In fact there are four types of Government (or "Gilt-Edged") Securities issued under this and previous Acts.

(i) Securities which the Government can redeem at any time (e.g., $2\frac{1}{2}$ per cent Consols).

(ii) Securities which the Government can redeem at any time after a certain date (e.g., $2\frac{1}{2}$ per cent Treasury Stock 1975 or after). The Government need not redeem these stocks at all so long as it continues to pay interest on them.

(iii) Securities which are redeemable between two dates at the Government's choice—but which must be redeemed at the latest by the second date (e.g., $5\frac{1}{2}$ per cent Treasury Stock 2008-12).

(iv) Securities redeemable on a fixed date (e.g., $5\frac{1}{4}$ per cent Conversion Stock 1974).

Government stock can be bought and sold in units as small as a new penny. It is transferable by an instrument in writing (i.e., a stock transfer) in accordance with the Stock Transfer Act 1963 [5]; the transfer must be delivered to the Bank of England, which may retain it.[6] Most Government stocks are entered in registers kept by the Bank; but under the National Debt Act 1870 the Treasury may issue Stock Certificates to bearer, delivery of which is sufficient to transfer the stock in question.

Securities issued by the Government are now charged upon an account of the Treasury at the Bank of England called the National Loans Fund.[7] Before April 1968 Government securities were charged on the Consolidated Fund, i.e., the financial resources of the State *in toto*. But now the Consolidated Fund is balanced daily. If it has a surplus, the surplus is paid into the National Loans Fund; if there is a deficit, a payment to meet the deficit is made out of the National Loans Fund into the Consolidated Fund. It is clear therefore that the holders of Government stock are in as secure a position as they were before the passing of the National Loans Act 1968.

Often, when a particular stock becomes due for redemption, the Treasury gives the holder the choice of redemption in cash or in the form of new stock.

B. DOMINION COLONIAL AND FOREIGN STOCKS

The securities of Dominion and Colonial Governments have been dealt in extensively on the Stock Exchange for many years; foreign

4. National Loans Act 1968, s. 12 (2).   5. See pp. 206–207, *post*.
6. Government Stock Regulations 1965 (S.I. 1965 No. 1420), reg. 4.
7. Established by the National Loans Act 1968.

stocks have been dealt in on a smaller scale. Many overseas loans were raised and made repayable in alternative currencies at the option of the investor; this was to encourage investors who, if the loan were expressed to be in one currency, might have been put off by the difficulty and expense of obtaining it. Certain overseas loans (mainly of Commonwealth governments) have been guaranteed by the United Kingdom Government.

c. LOCAL AUTHORITY LOANS

The powers of local authorities to borrow money for their general purposes depends almost entirely on statute, and principally upon the Local Government Act 1933. Under Section 195 of that Act local authorities are permitted to borrow for any purpose for which they are authorised under any statute or statutory order to borrow. The local authorities securities which are transacted on the Stock Exchange are:

(1) *Local authority stock*

Local authorities enter stocks in their registers and the holder receives a stock certificate. Transfer is effected by a written instrument, and must be recorded in the register. The date for redemption must be not later than sixty years after issue. Before issuing stock local authorities must obtain the consent of the Minister of Housing and Local Government,[8] who may make regulations for their creation, issue and transfer, and for dealing in them.[9]

(2) (*more rarely*) *debenture and debenture stock issued under the Local Loans Act 1875*

These must be redeemed either:

(i) by the annual appropriation of a fixed sum to the discharge of a certain portion of the loan, and then drawing lots as to which holders shall be repaid; or
(ii) by means of a sinking fund; or
(iii) by annual repayment of a fraction of the nominal amount of each debenture.[10]

The other methods by which a local authority may raise money are a mortgage of its revenues, under the Local Government Act 1933,[11] or the issue of bonds (in denominations of £5 or its multiples, and for at least one year) under the Local Government (Financial Provisions) Act 1963. In both cases ownership and the transfer of ownership must be registered by the local authority.

8. Local Government Act 1933, s. 196 (1) (*b*).   9. *Ibid.*, s. 204 (1).
10. Local Loans Act 1875, ss. 13–15.   11. See s. 196.

D. SUB-UNITS OF A UNIT TRUST

Unit trusts, which have been steadily gaining prominence in the United Kingdom since about 1930, cater for the small investor who wishes to spread his risk between a number of companies, but wants to be able to realise his investment, if need be with the minimum of trouble and expense.

Normally a unit trust is constituted as follows. A manager, or managers [12] purchase a block or portfolio of securities in a number of carefully selected companies. A trust deed is drawn up under which the portfolio is divided into sub-units and transferred to trustees (often a bank or insurance company) who are responsible for their safe custody and the collection and distribution of income. The managers then offer the sub-units to the public at a price which is based on the value of the portfolio at the date of the offer. Purchasers of the units become unit-holders, and therefore beneficiaries under the trust. They will be entitled to dividends calculated by dividing the total net dividends received by the trust by the number of sub-units issued.

The trust deed will provide for the creation and issue of further units, and set out a formula for calculating their price based on the market value of the securities and the amount of cash comprised in the trust fund at the date of issue or sale. In addition, the deed will cover the re-purchase of units by the managers and fix a minimum price for such re-purchase; it will deal with the liquidation of units, the collection and distribution of income to unit-holders, the transfer of units, the remuneration of the manager and trustees, accounts, meetings of unit-holders and the duration of the trust.

The distribution of circulars relating to unit trusts is prohibited by the Prevention of Fraud (Investments) Act 1958 [13] unless distribution is by the manager and the unit trust scheme has been authorised by the Board of Trade. A scheme may become an Authorised Unit Trust if the following conditions are satisfied: [14]

(1) The manager and the trustee must be companies incorporated under the law of some part of the United Kingdom, and each must have a place of business in Great Britain at which notices and other documents are received on its behalf.

(2) Effective control over the manager must be exercised independently of the trustee (i.e., by the unit-holders).

12. Occasionally the manager is a company formed by stockbrokers or jobbers.
13. Section 14.   14. Section 17.

(3) The trust must be expressed in a deed which provides, to the satisfaction of the Board, for certain matters which include: [15]

(a) for determining the manner in which the manager's prices for units on a sale or purchase, and the yield from the units, are to be calculated, and for entitling the holder of any units to require the manager to purchase them at a price calculated accordingly;

(b) for regulating the mode of execution and the issue of unit certificates;

(c) for audit of accounts relating to the trust;

(d) for requiring the manager to retire from the trust if the trustee certifies that it is in the interests of the beneficiaries that he should do so.

(4) The trustee must have (or four-fifths of the issued share capital must be held by another company which has) an issued share capital of at least £500,000, of which at least £250,000 has been paid up. Further, it must have assets sufficient to meet its liabilities (including liabilities in respect of the repayment of capital).

Under section 12 of the Prevention of Fraud (Investments) Act 1958 the Board of Trade may appoint one or more competent inspectors to investigate and report on the administration of any unit trust scheme, if it appears to the Board:

(a) that it is in the interests of the unit holders so to do; and

(b) that the matter is one of public concern.

Unit trust investors do not have as much scope for controlling the management of their capital as, say, the holders of ordinary shares in a public company. This is particularly so now that most unit trusts are of the "flexible" variety, usually giving the manager wide powers to vary the securities in the portfolio in the interests of profitability. On the other hand, most unit trusts are run on behalf of a large number of small investors who would have difficulty in making collective decisions with the speed that modern business requires. The managers are invariably experts in investment, and if a unit holder is dissatisfied with the performance of the portfolio, he can always resell his units to the trust.

E. THE DIFFERENT TYPES OF INVESTORS

Although there is no legal definition of investors, they fall naturally into four non-legal categories.

15. See Prevention of Fraud (Investments) Act 1958, Sched. 1.

(i) Individual or private investors
There are no restrictions on the legal powers of an individual adult to invest his money as he pleases. He may not, however, invest in an illegal undertaking, and if he does so his investment is a nullity and cannot be realised. In addition, Exchange Control [16] may limit the amount of foreign currency which he may acquire for the purchase of foreign securities.

(ii) Trustee investors
Where individuals hold money and other property on trust for others, or for the public benefit as trustees, the law allows them to invest the trust funds, but only in certain comparatively safe investments. A trust might continue for a very considerable time and it would be unjust if the trustees were to dissipate the interests of later beneficiaries by making a risky investment for the immediate beneficiary which subsequently turned out to be unprofitable. Trustees are given statutory powers of investment which are contained in the Trustee Investments Act 1961. The powers which that Act confers are exercisable in addition to and not in derogation from any other power of investment conferred (by the trust instrument or otherwise) upon a trustee. The Act divides the authorised trustee investments as follows:

(a) Narrower-range investments:

(1) Where the trustee may invest without taking advice. These investments are—

(i) Defence Bonds, National Savings Certificates, Ulster Savings Certificates, Ulster Development Bonds, [17] National Development Bonds [18] and British Savings Bonds; [19]

(ii) Deposits in the Post Office Savings Bank, ordinary deposits in a Trustee Savings Bank and deposits in a duly certified [1] bank, or duly certified department thereof.

(2) Where the trustee must obtain advice. [2]
These include fixed or guaranteed interest securities issued by the Government of the United Kingdom, Northern Ireland or the Isle of Man, fixed interest securities of United Kingdom public authorities, nationalised industries, and of Commonwealth Governments

16. See Chapter 12, *post*.
17. Trustee Investments (Additional Powers) (No. 2) Order 1962, S.I. 1962 No. 2611.
18. Trustee Investments (Additional Powers) Order 1964, S.I. 1964 No. 703.
19. Trustee Investments (Additional Powers) Order 1968, S.I. 1968 No. 470.
1. I.e., certified under the Finance Act 1956, s. 9 (3): Trustee Investments Act 1961, s. 1 (1), Sched. 1, Part I, para. 2.
2. For definition of advice see p. 22, *post*.

and local authorities being securities registered in the United Kingdom; stock of the Bank of Ireland; loans by United Kingdom local authorities; debentures issued and registered in the United Kingdom by a company incorporated in the United Kingdom; also debentures and preference stock of certain public undertakings such as water companies.

(*b*) Wider-range investments.

Here too the trustee must obtain advice. Wider range investments are as follows:

(1) stocks and shares issued and registered by a company incorporated in the United Kingdom. Under section 1 (2) and 1st Sched., Part IV of the Trustee Investments Act 1961 these securities must comply with the following requirements:

(i) They must be issued in the United Kingdom by a company incorporated in the United Kingdom;

(ii) The company must have a total issued and paid-up share capital of at least £1,000,000;

(iii) In each of the five years preceding the calendar year in which the investment is made the company must have paid a dividend on all its shares which ranked for dividend for that year;

(iv) The price of the securities must be quoted on a recognised stock exchange; and

(v) The securities must be fully paid up, or by the terms of their issue they must be required to be fully paid up within nine months of the date of issue.

(2) shares in any building society designated under the House Purchase and Housing Act 1959.

(3) Units or other shares of an authorised unit trust scheme.

A trustee has no power to make wider-range investments unless the trust fund had been divided into two parts equal in value at the time of division and known as "the narrower-range part" and "the wider-range part" (the investments of each part being confined to the appropriate range). Once such a division has been made, no subsequent division is allowed except under a statutory order of the Treasury.[3]

When the trustee is obliged to seek advice, he must take it from a person whom he reasonably believes is qualified by his ability in and experience of financial matters. This would obviously include stockbrokers, and banks which include investment advice among the services which they provide.

3. Trustee Investments Act 1961, s. 13.

(iii) *Corporate* (or *institutional*) *investors*

Corporate investors include companies registered under the Companies Acts, building societies, co-operative societies, friendly societies and trade unions.

So far as registered companies are concerned, their activities (including their investments) are limited to carrying out their objects as set out in the memorandum, and they are entitled to do everything which is reasonably necessary to that end. But if a company makes a contract which is inconsistent with its objects clause, the transaction is said to be *ultra vires* and does not bind the company. Although companies have no implied power to purchase shares in other companies, they normally circumvent the difficulty by naming "investment" among the objects stated in the memorandum.

Building societies' powers of investment are limited by the Building Societies (Authorised Investments) Order 1962, made under the Building Societies Acts of 1960[4] and 1962.[5] Not less than $7\frac{1}{2}$ per cent in value of a society's assets must be invested in marketable fixed interest securities maturing for repayment within five years and issued by the Government of the United Kingdom or Northern Ireland, Commonwealth Governments, public authorities, nationalised industries, river and water boards in the United Kingdom, and securities issued by the International Bank for Reconstruction and Development. Subject to the investment of that $7\frac{1}{2}$ per cent, provision is made for investment in marketable securities and loans of the same description maturing in up to 25 years.

Industrial and provident (e.g., co-operative) societies registered under the Industrial and Provident Societies Acts[6] must provide in their rules whether and by what authority and in what manner their capital may be invested.[7] In addition, and if their rules do not direct otherwise, societies may invest in trustee securities (i.e., as permitted under the Trustee Investments Act 1961), local authority securities, other registered industrial or provident societies, registered building societies, and limited companies registered under the Companies Acts.

The trustees of friendly societies may, under the Friendly Societies Acts 1896[8] and 1908,[9] purchase any securities in which the law currently allows trustees to invest. At present, therefore, they must take the Trustee Investments Act 1961 as their guide.

4. Section 11 (1).   5. Section 58.
6. I.e., 1893–1954, consolidated in the Industrial and Provident Societies Act 1965.
7. Industrial and Provident Societies Act 1965, s. 1, Sched. I.
8. Section 44 (1) (*b*).   9. Section 4.

The rules of every registered trade union must contain a provision for the investment of its funds.[10] The Trade Union Acts do not restrict the classes of investment which the rules of a trade union may authorise, but unless the rules provide otherwise the trustees are governed by the general law as to the securities in which trustees may invest.[11]

(iv) Public investors

The Government departments and local authorities which invest their money on the Stock Exchange are known as public investors. Most public investment is made by the Government, which borrows from the public by the issue and sale of Treasury securities.[12] The Government Departments always hold some of their own securities themselves; when they feel the need to raise money they sell them on the Stock Exchange through the Government Broker. Conversely the Government may replenish its supply of Treasury securities by taking them up when not subscribed for by the public, or going into the market and purchasing them from existing holders.

By offering or withholding a supply of its own securities the Government can influence interest rates and manage the economy in other ways. If the Government gives the public scant encouragement to purchase Treasury securities, by issuing them on uncompetitive terms, the public will prefer to invest in industry. On the other hand, the Government may take the view that there is an overriding necessity to raise money for its own purposes, and will do everything it can to stimulate Gilt-Edged investment. At this point the subject travels into the realm of economics.

F. INVESTMENT SPECULATION AND GAMING

The Gaming Act 1845,[13] rendered all contracts by way of gaming and wagering null and void and made it impossible to recover money won on such contracts or deposited with any person to abide the event upon which the wager had been made.[14]

In one sense, any stock exchange transaction is a gamble, because the purchaser does not know how the value of his investment will fluctuate. The investor may be a *bull*, who has bought securities to be paid for at a later date, in the hope that he can sell them at a profit before that date arrives; or he may be a *bear* who has sold securities

10. Trade Union Act 1871, s. 14 (1) and Sched. I.
11. See 38 Halsbury's Laws (3rd Edn.) pp. 987 *et seq.*
12. See pp. 16–17, *ante.*   13. Section 18.
14. The Gaming Act 1892 makes it impossible for (e.g.) a broker to recover commission or indemnity on a gaming transaction.

which he has not got for delivery at a later date, in the hope that he can pick them up at a lower price in the interval. Although such dealings are speculative in character, it is only in very rare cases that a contract between a broker and his client is void at law as a wager. The broker makes the bargain with a jobber or other member of the Stock Exchange, and both upon general principles and under the Rules and Regulations of the Stock Exchange, the broker, as agent, is entitled to indemnity from his client against liabilities incurred by the broker in executing his client's orders. The obligation of the client to accept or deliver the shares ensures that the broker is not faced with a liability of which he is not the author.

The client, on the other hand, has made an ordinary commercial transaction, and if it turns out to be unprofitable that is a misfortune which he alone has to bear. So provided that a stock exchange transaction is a real and genuine one, the mere fact that it is speculative does not nullify it in the eyes of the law. [15]

On the other hand a stock exchange bargain will be void as a wager if it is a mere sham in which there is no obligation on either party to sell or deliver. This is the case when the bargain amounts to nothing more than a reciprocal agreement, or secret understanding,[16] that buyer and seller will merely pay or receive the *difference* between a share's price on one day, and its price at some future date.[17] Such a transaction is a bet, and void under the Gaming Acts because both parties stand to win or lose.

In practice it is almost impossible to make a wagering contract on the Stock Exchange. The broker acts as agent for his client, and whether the shares rise or fall, the broker's only reward is his commission. The fluctuation of the market will affect his client, but not himself, and in the words of Lord Atkin: "It takes two parties to make a bet." [18] Bets and wagers on the price of stocks and shares are frequently made outside the Stock Exchange, but they do not fall within the scope of this book.[19]

---

15. *Thacker* v. *Hardy* (1878), 4 Q.B.D. 685, C.A.; *Forget* v. *Ostigny,* [1895] A.C. 318, P.C.
16. See *Universal Stock Exchange* v. *Strachan,* [1896] A.C. 166.
17. See *Thacker* v. *Hardy, supra,* at p. 694 *per* Brett, L.J.
18. *Cooper* v. *Stubbs,* [1925] 2 K.B. 753, at p. 771, C.A.
19. For a full and very lucid discussion of wagers made on and off the Stock Exchange, see W. S. Schwabe, K. C. and G. A. H. Branson, *Law of the Stock Exchange* (2nd Edn., 1914), pp. 243–258.

CHAPTER 2

Constitution

In 1948 the Deed of Settlement of the Stock Exchange, London was amended to vest exclusive control in the Council.[1] The Council has general control over (*a*) the activities of the members and (*b*) membership itself.

A. THE COUNCIL AS GOVERNING BODY

1. Composition of the Council

The Council's members (exclusive of the Government Broker who is *ex officio* a member of the Council) must number not less than thirty nor more than thirty-six.[2] Members must be natural[3] persons who have completed five years' membership of the Stock Exchange; and if a member of the Council ceases to be a member of the Exchange, *ipso facto* he vacates his seat on the Council.[4]

A. ELECTION TO THE COUNCIL

Members of the Council are appointed by ballot and hold office for a term of three years.[5] At the end of that period they retire, but are eligible for immediate re-appointment.[6] The ballot is held on June 20th in every year, or if that day is a Saturday, Sunday or Bank Holiday, the next following business day.[7] Notice of the ballot must be publicly exhibited in the Stock Exchange 21 days in advance, and six business days prior to the ballot a further notice must be displayed containing the names of the retiring members of the Council willing to be re-elected, and of all new candidates and their proposers and seconders.[8]

---

1. Clause 31.
2. Deed of Settlement Clause 19 and Rule 1 (1).
3. I.e., not corporate bodies with legal personality.
4. Deed of Settlement Clause 20 and Rule 1 (2).
5. But a member appointed to fill an occasional vacancy holds office only for the unexpired term of the vacant office. See Rule 2 (1).
6. Rule 2 (2) (*b*).   7. *Ibid.*   8. Rule 2 (2) (*b*).

Notice of intention to propose a candidate for the Council, who is not a retiring member willing to be re-elected, must be given to the Secretary in writing seven days before the ballot is held. It must be signed by two members of the Stock Exchange.[9] The ballot papers, which are printed, set out the names of the retiring members willing to be re-elected and the names of the proposed new members. They must distinguish the former from the latter.

There is a provision for postal voting,[10] but members who take advantage of it must act in accordance with the other provisions of the Rules and Regulations made by the Council.[11]

Ballots are not held where the number of candidates does not exceed the number of vacancies on the Council. Where that is the case, all the candidates who were proposed are deemed to have been duly appointed as members, and they hold office as if the ballot had been held and they had been appointed by it.[12] Apart from this rule, if a ballot is not held on the day appointed by the Rules, or the appointments purported to be made on any ballot duly held are for any reason invalid or ineffective, then:

(i) the Council may forthwith or at any time prior to the next ordinary yearly ballot hold a ballot, on a date fixed by themselves, for making the appointments which should have been made on the yearly date when a valid ballot failed to be held. This ballot must be conducted in accordance with the general provisions, *mutatis mutandis*, relating to Council ballots. It will be deemed to be the yearly ballot, and the members of the Council appointed by it will hold office for the terms for which they would respectively have held office had they been appointed by a valid ballot on the proper yearly date.

(ii) the retiring members of the Council continue in office until the ballot has been held and valid appointments made.[13]

If on the yearly ballot there are not enough candidates to fill all the vacancies, the Council may, within one calendar month after June 24th, appoint members of the Stock Exchange (being natural persons not already members of the Council) to be Council members to fill all or any of the vacancies.[14]

Vacancies normally occur by reason of the expiration by lapse of time of a member's term of office. But they can occur abnormally, for example, on the death of a Council member. Such vacancies are referred to as "occasional vacancies", and as to these the Rules make special provisions. When the yearly ballot is held, the member appointed by the *fewest* number of votes is deemed to fill the occa-

9. Rule 2 (2) (c).   10. Rule 2 (2) (d).
11. Rule 2 (2) (e).   12. Rule 2 (2) (f).
13. Rule 2 (2) (g).   14. Rule 2 (2) (j).

sional vacancy left by the vacating member with the *shortest* unexpired term of office.[15] If no ballot is held (e.g., where the number of candidates exceeds the number of vacancies), the new members are deemed to fill the occasional vacancies; and if the number of new members exceeds the number of occasional vacancies, or the terms of office of the vacating members expire on different dates, the question of which of them is to fill the occasional vacancies or (as the case may be) each occasional vacancy will, failing agreement between them, be decided by lot.[16]

If a ballot results in a tie between two or more members who are to fill the last vacancy on the Council, then as between those members the issue must be decided by lot.[17]

The continuing members of the Council may act notwithstanding any vacancy in the Council.[18]

B. CHAIRMAN AND DEPUTY CHAIRMEN

At its first meeting on or after June 25th in every year the Council elects one of its members to be its Chairman, and two to hold office as Deputy Chairmen until the corresponding meeting in the next succeeding year. If a casual vacancy occurs in either of these offices it may be filled when necessary by the Council. The Chairman and Deputy Chairmen so appointed bear the titles of Chairman of the Stock Exchange and Deputy Chairmen of the Stock Exchange respectively.[19]

The Chairman of the Stock Exchange, or failing him one of the Deputy Chairmen,[20] presides at every meeting of the Council at which he is present. If at any time there is no Chairman or Deputy Chairman of the Stock Exchange, or if at any meeting of the Council none of these officers is present within five minutes of the time appointed for holding it, the members of the Council may choose one of their number to be chairman of the meeting.[1]

C. COUNCIL MEETINGS

The quorum necessary for the transaction of Council business may be fixed by the Council. Unless the Council fixes it at any other number, the quorum is nine.[2] The Council may meet together for the dispatch of business, adjourn and otherwise regulate their meet-

15. Rule 2 (2) (*i*) I.   16. Rule 2 (2) (*i*) II.
17. Deed of Settlement Clause 22 and Rule 2 (2) (*k*).
18. Deed of Settlement Clause 9 and Rule 9.
19. Deed of Settlement Clause 23 and Rule 4.
20. A presiding Deputy Chairman must be selected by the meeting in the absence of agreement between the Deputy Chairmen, should both be present.
 1. Deed of Settlement Clause 25 and Rule 5.
 2. Deed of Settlement Clause 26 and Rule 6.

ings as they think fit. Each member of the Council (other than the Government Broker who, while entitled to attend and speak at meetings of the Council, does not have a vote) has one vote. Questions which arise at any meeting are decided by a majority, but if there is an equality of votes the Chairman of the meeting has a second or casting vote. The Chairman of the Stock Exchange or a Deputy Chairman, or any *three* members of the Council may (and the Secretary on their requisition must) summon a meeting of the Council. If a member of the Council is absent from the United Kingdom, it is not necessary to give him notice of a meeting.[3]

The Rules require that certain particular resolutions of the Council must be *confirmed*,[4] that is to say they must be:

(1) (*a*) passed by a majority of not less than three-quarters of those members of the Council who are present at a meeting of which special notice has been given and at which not less than twelve members are present; and (unless the resolution requires urgent confirmation, as to which see (3) below);

(*b*) confirmed by a majority of those members of the Council who are present at a subsequent meeting of which special notice has been given.

(2) If a resolution specified in (1) above is not so confirmed and another such resolution is passed in substitution for it, the substituted resolution must be confirmed in the same way.

(3) In cases which do not admit of delay the Council may with the concurrence of not less than two-thirds of those members who are present proceed to consider the question of the confirmation of a resolution, *and to confirm* such resolution at the meeting at which it is passed.[5]

In all matters brought under the consideration of the Council, their decision whether expressed by a resolution or otherwise, is final, and must be carried out by every member of the Stock Exchange concerned. Where the Rules require a resolution to be confirmed, that resolution is not valid and may not be put into force before such confirmation.[6]

D. POWERS OF THE COUNCIL GENERALLY

Since the Council has exclusive control over the running of the Stock Exchange its powers are extremely wide and cover every

3. Deed of Settlement Clause 28 and Rule 8.
4. Resolutions that must be confirmed include the expulsion or suspension of a member of the Council (Rule 3) or the Exchange (Rule 18), the dispensing with the strict enforcement of the Rules (Rule 20) and the postponement or extension of a Settlement Period (Rule 96 (6)).
5. Rule 12.   6. Rule 12*a*.

aspect of its affairs. Clause 31 of the 1875 Deed of Settlement (as amended) states the range of these powers in general terms. It provides that, subject to the provisions of the Deed, the Council may make, and from time to time repeal, amend or alter rules and regulations as to the admission, expulsion or suspension of members and their clerks, and as to the mode and conditions on and subject to which business on the Stock Exchange should be transacted, the conduct of the persons transacting that business, and as to the better management and conducting of its affairs and concerns.

It is of course pursuant to that power that the rules contained in the book entitled *The Rules and Regulations of the Stock Exchange* have been made, and it is from that power and other provisions of the Deed of Settlement that they derive their force.

The Rules and Regulations are classified, and deal with particular matters under appropriate headings. In every class of matter the powers of the Council are clearly defined. These powers will be stated at the appropriate place in this book. But the following powers are in a sense introductory and fall to be considered here:

(i) Power to appoint committees

The Council must appoint a Property and Finance Committee and may at any time appoint other committees, with power to appoint sub-committees consisting of such members or member of their body as they think fit. They may delegate to any committee so appointed any duties and powers of the Council. The aggregate number of members of the Property and Finance Committee must never be less than nine nor more than twelve.[7]

(ii) Power to alter the Rules

The power subsists under Clause 31 of the Deed of Settlement. Written notice of any proposal to alter or add to the Rules must be given, and a copy of that proposal sent to every member of the Council.[8]

(iii) Power to obtain evidence

The Council may require members and their clerks to attend before them and give such information as may be in their possession relative to any matter under investigation, including such accounts and information as to their firm's finances as the Council may consider necessary.[9]

The power to obtain evidence is in addition to the Council's power to require the periodic submission of information relating to

7. Deed of Settlement Clause 27 and Rule 7.
8. Rule 13.   9. Rule 15 (1).

the minimum margin of solvency required to be maintained under the provisions of the Rules.[10] Moreover, the Council may themselves appoint an accountant to report upon any matters relating to a firm's finances as they may consider necessary.[11]

The Council may receive written communications on matters generally, but they have no power to act upon anonymous letters.[12]

(iv) Powers over members

The Council may *censure, suspend or expel* any member who:

(*a*) violates any of the Rules and Regulations,[13] or

(*b*) fails to comply with any of the Council's decisions,[14] or

(*c*) is guilty of dishonourable, disgraceful or discreditable conduct,[15] or

(*d*) has been found by the Panel on Takeovers and Mergers [16] (including where reference has been made to it, the Appeal Committee of the Panel) to have acted in breach of the City Code on Takeovers and Mergers. The findings of the Panel (subject to any modification by the Appeal Committee) may not be re-opened in the proceedings before the Council.[17]

The Council may *censure or suspend*, but not expel:

(*a*) any member who in his conduct or business acts in a manner detrimental to the interests of the Stock Exchange, or unbecoming the character of a member.[18]

(*b*) any member who conducts himself in an improper or disorderly manner, or wilfully obstructs the business of the House.[19]

Where a member is *suspended* under any of the above Rules he will, according to the discretion of the Council, forfeit his right to enter the trading floor of the Stock Exchange, and/or in the alternative to trade in any manner whatsoever.[20]

A resolution for the expulsion or suspension of a member must be passed *and confirmed* in the same manner as other resolutions which require confirmation.[1]

The Council may, in their absolute discretion, and in such manner as they think fit, notify the public that any member has been expelled, or has become a defaulter (when he automatically forfeits his membership),[2] or has been suspended, or has ceased to be a

---

10. I.e., under Rule 79*a* (10) and (11). See pp. 66–67, *post.*
11. Rule 15 (2).   12. Rule 14.   13. Rule 16 (1).
14. Rule 16 (2).   15. Rule 16 (3).
16. For the functions and powers of the Panel see pp. 91–98, *post.*
17. Rule 16 (4).   18. Rule 17 (1).   19. Rule 17 (2).
20. Rules 16 (5), 17 (3).
1. Rule 18 and see Rule 12, p. 29, *ante.*
2. For default see pp. 245–258, *post.*

member.[3] The notification may name the member concerned, and the Rules provide that no action or other proceeding will under any circumstances be maintainable by that member against any person who publishes or circulates it. Indeed the Rules give the public express leave to publish and circulate the notification.[4]

(v) Power to dispense with strict enforcement of the rules [5]

The Council may, by a resolution passed and confirmed[6] in accordance with the Rules, dispense with the strict enforcement of any of the Rules and Regulations. But it is provided that no confirmation is required when the Council resolves to dispense with the strict enforcement of any of the Rules and Regulations relating to the following matters:

(a) The admission of candidates for membership and clerks, the re-election of members and the re-admission of defaulters or insolvents.[7]

(b) The authorisation of a member to carry on arbitrage business.[8]

(c) The registration of agents and overseas representatives.[9]

(d) The fixing of account days.[10]

(e) The making of securities ex-dividend.[11]

(f) The granting or refusing of quotation.[12]

The Council have in addition, general power to waive compliance with all or any of the requirements for quotations stipulated by the Rules.[13]

B. MEMBERSHIP OF THE STOCK EXCHANGE

Candidates for membership have to submit a Form of Application to the Council. For 66 years up to March 1970 an applicant for membership of the Stock Exchange could not be balloted for until he had obtained a nomination. Forms of nomination were very simple, and consisted of a short letter addressed to the Council, signed by an outgoing member or the personal representatives of a deceased member, and nominating the applicant as his successor. The right to nominate was personal to members and non-transferable, but nominations themselves were commonly dealt in by dealers in nominations. The price of a nomination fluctuated

---

3. Rule 19.   4. *Ibid.*   5. Rule 20.
6. For confirmation see Rule 12, p. 29, *ante.*
7. For admission see pp. 32–36, *post.* For re-admission see p. 37, *post.*
8. For arbitrage see pp. 262–264, *post.*   9. Rule 199 (2).
10. Rule 96 (1). For the account system see pp. 120–122, *post.*
11. Rule 111. For dividends see pp. 190–193, *post.*
12. For the granting of quotation see pp. 72–84, *post.*
13. I.e., in Appendices 34, 34a and 35 of the Rules. See Chapter 4, *post.*

according to supply and demand, and in the past it was "as high as £2,000 and as low as a pint of beer".[14] The nomination system arose out of a need to restrict the total number of members, which fell steadily during the years after its introduction. By 1969 it was felt that this need was no longer present; moreover, abolition of the system was a necessary step towards bringing the London Stock Exchange into line with the provincial stock exchanges before a unified National Exchange could be set up.[15] Accordingly the nomination system was abolished as from March 1970. A nomination redemption fund was set up to compensate existing members when they retired—the compensation being fixed at £1,000. The fund is financed by payments of £1,000 from new members, and it will be wound up when it is no longer required.

1. Requirements for membership

A. RE-ELECTION AND ADMISSIONS

(i) Generally

On and after the first Monday in March of every year the Council proceeds to re-elect such members and admit such candidates as they think proper. Every such re-election or admission is for *one year only*, commencing on March 25th.[16] The power of re-electing members and admitting candidates is purely discretionary. There are no fetters on the discretion, which must be exercised for the benefit of the Stock Exchange as a body,[17] and the decision of the Council in any case cannot be challenged by any individual affected. The Council are not bound to give reasons for their decision to anyone whose application they have rejected; and the Rules forbid the Council to disclose those reasons to any court or tribunal.[18] It seems that the only duty of the Council in this connection is to exercise their discretion honestly,[19] but otherwise that discretion is probably as wide as it could possibly be.

In Weinberger v. Inglis: [20]

The appellant was born at Nuremburg in the state of Bavaria in 1866. He came to England at the age of twenty, and in 1892 he became a naturalised British subject, taking the oath of allegiance. In 1894 he became a clerk on the London Stock Exchange, and in 1895 he was elected a member. He was re-elected in every succeeding year until 1917. In 1896 he married an Englishwoman, and by 1917 they had two sons who were members of their schools' Officers' Training Corps, and two

14. *The Times*, October 8th 1969. 15. See *ibid.*
16. Rule 21 (1). 17. Rule 21 (3). 18. *Ibid.*
19. See *Weinberger* v. *Inglis*, [1919] A. C. 606. *Cassel* v. *Inglis*, [1916] 2 Ch. 211.
20. *Ibid.*

daughters who, with their mother, had been engaged in patriotic work since the outbreak of war. In March 1917 the appellant applied for re-election to the Stock Exchange. Certain members, who had formed an organisation called The Stock Exchange Anti-German Union, lodged an objection under what is now Rule 32 against his re-election, the ground for the objection being enemy birth. At the invitation of the Stock Exchange Committee (as it then was) the appellant showed cause against the objection by letter and by interview, and he stated various facts in proof of his loyalty with a view to displacing the objection. The committee however refused his application. Of 107 members of enemy birth, 50 were re-elected and 57 were rejected. The appellant brought an action to impugn the decision on the ground that it was arbitrary and capricious and based on irrelevant considerations. The committee by their defence alleged that they did not re-elect the appellant because they did not deem him eligible to be a member of the Stock Exchange for the year in question and for no other reason.

The House of Lords held that, assuming the committee owed a duty to its members as regards re-election, the proper inference from the facts was that the refusal of the committee had proceeded solely on the ground of enemy birth, as to which the appellant had been heard; nevertheless the committee had the discretion conferred upon them by the Deed of Settlement and the Rules, and since they had not been proved to have acted arbitrarily or capriciously the House held that it had no jurisdiction to interfere with their decision.

It is clear from their Lordships' opinions in *Weinberger* v. *Inglis* that if the committee *had* been shown to have acted arbitrarily or capriciously, or (possibly) without giving the member a chance to be heard, then their decision would have been much more vulnerable to judicial intervention.[1] And although the Rules[2] provide that "the decision of the Council upon any application for re-election or admission shall not be liable to be brought into question before or controlled by, and shall not be controlled by, any court or tribunal", this cannot, it is submitted, prohibit an aggrieved member from exercising his ordinary common law right of bringing an action in the courts; nor can it deprive the courts of the jurisdiction which they already have.

(ii) Candidature

A candidate for membership must:[3]

(a) Be at least 21 years of age at the date of the posting of his application in the Stock Exchange.

---

1. For a more recent view of the position, see *Nagle* v. *Fielden*, [1966] 2 Q.B. 633 *per* Lord Denning, M. R., at pp. 646–647.
2. Rule 21 (2).   3. See Rule 31.

(*b*) Have completed three years training with a firm or firms of a federated exchange, unless the Council otherwise permits in the case of a candidate with commercial experience or holding a suitable professional qualification. Three months of such training must be served on the floor of the House. When the Council so directs, candidates must comply with the Federal Examination Regulations and attain a minimum standard in a written federal examination.

(*c*) Be a British born subject. Nevertheless in any particular case and after considering the circumstances, the Council may admit as a member an applicant who is not a British born subject who has been naturalised for not less than five years immediately preceding the date of his application for membership. The Council's discretion so to admit naturalised subjects is unfettered.[4]

(*d*) Not have been bankrupt or had a receiving order in bankruptcy made against him, been proved insolvent, or made a composition with his creditors, unless he has paid 100p in the £ and obtained a full discharge.[5] A candidate is ineligible who has more than once been a bankrupt or insolvent or compounded with his creditors.[6]

(*e*) Be separately proposed and seconded by members of at least four years' standing who have known him personally for not less than two years (such knowledge includes knowledge of the candidate's past and present circumstances). Neither the proposer nor seconder may be a partner in or associated with the firm in or with which the candidate will when elected become a partner or associated member.[7]

(*f*) Submit a form of application accompanied by the required statements.[8]

(*g*) Make a declaration whether he proposes to act as a broker or jobber, or that he is not engaged in active business, and whether he is associated with a firm.[9]

(*h*) Make a declaration giving (*inter alia*) personal details, directorships, partnerships, bankruptcy and any convictions involving dishonesty.[10]

Application for membership must be posted in the Exchange at least eight days before the ballot for election.[11] Objection may be made by letter to the Council.[12] When the ballot is held, a new member's election must be carried by a majority of not less than three-quarters of those members of the Council present at a meeting of which

4. Rule 21 (3).　　5. Rule 30 (1).
6. Rule 30 (2).　　7. Rule 31 (2).
8. Rule 31 (3). See Appendix 2 of the Rules for the form.
9. Rule 22.
10. Rule 33. See Appendix 56 of the Rules for the form.
11. Rule 31 (4).　　12. Rule 32.

not less than twelve members are present. [13] If an applicant (whether for admission, re-election or re-admission) is rejected, he may not be voted on or balloted for again until March 25th in the following year. [14]

(iii) Procedure for re-election

The re-election of members takes place in March every year, and the Council's discretionary power regarding both re-election and admission has been examined in the case of *Weinberger* v. *Inglis*. [15] Candidates for re-election must make the declaration of intended status in (g) above, and submit a Form of Application for Re-Election [16] so as to reach the Secretary not later than February 17th in the year in which the application is made. A member not intending to apply for re-election must give notice of that fact in writing to the Secretary not later than that day. [17] Members when re-elected, admitted or re-admitted become liable for the entrance fees (if any), subscriptions and other payments fixed by the Council. [18]

If a member (or his wife) wishes to engage in business, [19] other than that of the Stock Exchange, whether such business involves dealing in securities or not, he must obtain the prior consent of the Council. [20] Candidates must obtain such consent at the time of the application.

Within one month [1] of their election members must each acquire one share in the Stock Exchange. The Council will, if requested in writing by any member to do so, take all necessary steps, by notices to proprietors who are not members or to the personal representatives of deceased or bankrupt proprietors, or by directions to the share trustees, to enable him to do so. Any member failing to acquire a share within the specified period will, at its expiration, cease to be a member. [2]

(iv) Termination of membership

A member who does not apply for re-election by March 24th is deemed to have terminated his membership on that date. [3] He will be required to transfer his share or shares as directed by the Council and to return the transfer duly executed to the Secretary within such period, not being less than seven days, as the Council may determine. [4] However, the Council may in their absolute discretion up to and including June 30th immediately following, re-elect a

13. Rule 34. 14. Rule 35. 15. See *ante*, pp. 33–34.
16. See Appendix 1 of the Rules. 17. Rule 23. 18. Rule 21 (4).
19. There are certain important exceptions to the Rule: see Rule 27.
20. Rule 27.
 1. Or such extended period as the Council may allow.
 2. Rule 36 and Deed of Settlement, clause 8 (c). 3. Rule 24 (1).
 4. Rule 24 (2).

former member who ceased to be a member on not applying for re-election. The former member must satisfy the Council as to the reason for his delay.[5] Subject to this right of extension, a former member who ceased to be a member must, if he seeks re-election, apply as a *new* candidate.[6]

2. Re-admission

When a member is unable to fulfil his stock exchange engagements he is "hammered", i.e., publicly declared a defaulter, and he automatically ceases to be a member. The requirements and procedure for the re-admission of a defaulter are described in their proper place.[7] Once defaulters have applied for re-admission, they must, besides showing they are solvent, observe the other Rules which apply to candidates for admission. For example, a defaulter asking for re-admission must again declare whether he proposes to act as a broker or jobber, or that he is not engaged in active business, and whether he is associated with a firm.[8]

Not all applicants for re-admission are defaulters. A member may have forfeited his membership on a resolution of the Council when he has failed to pay entrance fees, subscriptions and other payments due to the Council.[9] Or he may have failed to pay an amount assessed upon him by the Stock Official,[10] or failed to discharge a debit note or assessment issued to him by the Central Stock Payment Office,[11] or had a receiving order in bankruptcy made against him, or otherwise proved to be insolvent.[12] Any of the above would entitle the Council to pass a resolution terminating his membership. When the ex-member has paid 100p in the £ he may apply for re-admission without being subject to the additional Rules which apply to the re-admission of defaulters.[13]

Notice of application for re-admission must be posted in the Stock Exchange 21 days in advance, whether the applicant is a defaulter,[14] or not.[15]

3. Resignation of membership

A member wishing to resign his membership must forward to the Secretary a letter tendering his resignation. Notice of the intended resignation will be reported to the Council at their next ordinary meeting; they will then wait four weeks before deciding whether to

5. Rule 24 (3). 6. Rule 24 (4).
7. For default see Chapter 10, *post*. 8. Rule 22. 9. Rule 176.
10. For functions of the Stock Official, see pp. 246–247, *post*.
11. For Central Stock Payment Office see pp. 201–202, *post*.
12. Rule 176. 13. I.e., Rules 37–42. 14. Rule 37 (1).
15. Rule 43 (2).

accept it. During that time a notice of the intended resignation will remain posted in the House.[16]

C. EXTERNAL MEMBERS

Membership of the Stock Exchange does not depend upon, or necessarily include, the right to enter the House and transact business therein. Members who do not have that right are referred to as external members. Generally speaking, all the Rules and Regulations which apply to ordinary members, including member firms [17] apply, insofar as they can be applied to their peculiar position, to external members as well.[18] But there are certain matters in which an external member is in a different position.

A. DISABILITIES

An external member is not eligible for appointment as a member of the Council. He may not act as proposer or seconder of a candidate for such appointment, nor is he entitled to vote in any ballot for appointment to the Council.[19] Similarly an external member may not propose or second a candidate for membership of the Exchange.[20]

B. ADMISSION AND MEMBERSHIP

The ordinary Rules with regard to admission apply to external members, also, but commonsense (and the Rules) ordain that some of them are necessarily inapplicable to external members.[1] The following Rules are inapplicable:

(i) Every new member to declare whether he intends to act as a broker or jobber.[2]

(ii) The Rules governing members who engage in non-Stock Exchange business.[3]

(iii) The qualifications required of a candidate for membership.[4]

In addition a few special rules apply only to external members:

(i) A candidate for external membership may be a male or female over the age of 21, or a corporate body incorporated in the United Kingdom.[5]

(ii) A candidate for external membership must be proposed and

---

16. Rule 44.   17. See Chapter 3, *post.*   18. Rule 47.
19. Rule 48.   20. Rule 49 (4).   1. Rule 49 (1).
2. Rule 22.   3. Rule 27.   4. Rule 31 (1) (*a*), (*b*) or (*c*).
5. Rule 49 (2). The council reserve to themselves the power to restrict the operation of this Rule.

seconded by the general partners of the firm of which he must, if elected, be a limited partner.[6]

(iii) A candidate for external membership must, whether an individual or a corporate body, apply in the forms provided for external membership.[7]

(iv) An external member which is a corporation must supply the Council with such information about its constitution, activities or membership as the Council may from time to time request.[8]

C. RE-ELECTION

An external member is bound by the ordinary Rules with regard to re-election. But he is not allowed to take advantage of Rule 24 (3) which enables an ordinary member who has not applied for re-election in time to obtain it on providing the Council with a satisfactory reason for his delay.[9] Furthermore, an external member's application for re-election must be in the special form provided for in the Rules.[10]

D. EXTERNAL MEMBERS AS PARTNERS

An external member may enter into a stock exchange partnership only as a limited partner. He may not be a member of an unlimited corporate member,[11] nor may he be simultaneously a shareholder of a limited corporate member.

Where an external member is a partner in a jobbing firm, the firm is forbidden to transact stock exchange business for his private account.[12] Similarly, where a corporate body is a limited partner in a jobbing firm, the firm may not deal in its securities, or in the securities of any holding or subsidiary company.[13]

E. EMPLOYMENT

An external member may not be employed by an ordinary member.[14]

F. COMMISSIONS

When business is transacted on his account, an external member must be charged commission in the same way as if he were a member of the general public.[15] An external member may share commissions only if he is a limited partner in the broking firm transacting the business in question.[16]

6. Rule 49 (5). An external member may not become a general partner: see Rule 50 (1).
7. Rule 49 (6). For forms of application see Appendices 2a and 2b of the Rules.
8. Rule 49 (7).   9. Rule 49 (1).
10. Rule 49 (3). For term of application see Appendix 1b of the Rules.
11. Rule 50 (1).   12. Rule 50 (2).   13. Rules 50 (3).
14. Rule 51 (1).   15. Rule 51 (2).   16. Rule 51 (3).

G. DEFAULT

An external member is immune from the provisions under which an ordinary member is declared a defaulter. But if the general partners of the firm of which he is a limited partner are declared defaulters, he is affected by the Rule [17] that partners assume joint and several liability for *all* their firm's stock exchange debts and obligations. [18]

17. Rule 46 (6).   18. Rule 52.

CHAPTER 3

Member Firms

INTRODUCTION

Under the Rules of the Stock Exchange no member may carry on business in the capacity of a broker or jobber as a sole trader.[1] In other words, he must belong to a firm. All bargains must be booked *in the name* of a firm,[2] and the Council may refuse to allow a firm to carry on business under a name which they consider misleading.[3] Brokers' and jobbers' firms must be comprised of members of the Stock Exchange; moreover, they may only do business in one of the three legal forms permitted by the Rules, namely:

(1) as a partnership, or
(2) as an unlimited company or
(3) as a company limited by shares.

1. Partnerships and companies contrasted

Partnership is by far the most common legal form taken by member firms. The law of partnership is to a great extent governed by the Partnership Act 1890, section 1 of which defines a partnership as:

"the relation which subsists between persons carrying on a business in common with a view to profit".[4]

In a stock exchange context it is always useful to consider partnerships in comparison with registered companies, since member firms can take either form. Moreover, the most important legal attributes of both emerge from the comparison.

The outstanding advantages of a partnership over a registered company are as follows:[5]

1. Rule 86 (1).   2. Rule 84 (1).   3. Rule 80.
4. But companies registered under the Companies Acts or formed or incorporated under an Act of Parliament, letters patent or Royal Charter are not partnerships: Partnership Act 1890, s. 1 (2).
5. See *Charlesworth's Company Law* (9th Edn.), p. 438.

(1) A partnership, being a private contract between the partners, does not require so many formalities. A partnership need not be registered,[6] for example. On the other hand a company *must* be registered; in addition, it must file a memorandum and articles with the Registrar of Companies.

(2) A partnership's accounts are its own private affair. But (excepting certain unlimited companies) a registered public company's accounts are open to public inspection.

(3) A partnership is less expensive to form and run, partly because there are fewer statutory documents.

(4) A partnership's business activities are not confined in any way, but under the doctrine of *ultra vires* a company must act within the objects clause of its memorandum.

(5) A partnership can reduce its capital as it pleases: but a company cannot do so without obtaining the consent of the court.

(6) In general, a partnership can make any arrangement it wishes: but a company is restricted by the provisions of the Companies Acts.

The *disadvantages* of a partnership compared with a registered company are more numerous, though on the Stock Exchange not necessarily more important:[7]

(1) A registered company's debts are borne by the company's assets and not by the members whose liability is limited.[8] But a partnership's debts are borne jointly and severally by each partner.

(2) A registered company, not its individual members, is liable on the contracts which it makes. But each partner is personally liable on the partnership's contracts.

(3) A registered company has perpetual succession: i.e., its legal continuation does not depend upon the capacity or survival of its members. But if a partner dies, is made bankrupt, suffers mental disorder or retires, the partnership is dissolved so far as he is concerned. If the partnership deed allows it, the remaining partners can carry on without him. But they must release his share in the partnership assets—perhaps with serious financial embarrassment to themselves.

(4) A registered company can contract with its members: a partner cannot contract with the partnership firm.

(5) A registered company cannot be bound in contract by its members (except by directors acting within the powers given to them in the articles). But a partnership is normally bound by a

---

6. Only a partnership's *name* must be registered. See Registration of Business Names Act 1916.

7. See further, *ibid.*, pp. 436–438.   8. See pp. 11–12, *ante.*

partner who acts *qua* partner, because in that role he is an agent for the firm.

(6) Shares in a registered company can generally[9] be transferred without the consent of the other shareholders; but a share in a partnership cannot be transferred without the consent of *all* the other partners.

(7) If a registered company is limited by shares, the liability of a member to contribute to its assets (e.g., when it is wound up) is limited to the amount unpaid on his shares; but the members of a partnership are usually *each* liable for *all* the debts of the partnership.

(8) A registered company can raise money by creating a floating charge[10] on its assets; but a partnership cannot do this.

The above comparison clearly demonstrates that a company limited by shares is a more flexible organisation than a partnership. In addition, limited companies generally have more capital than partnerships, since they raise it by public subscription; their very size, together with the principle of limited liability, tends to protect its members against the effects of its misfortunes. But if one of (say) six partners "lets the firm down" in a financial sense, the other five are directly affected. Since it is only they who stand between the firm and its dissolution, they must make good the losses which he has incurred.

Stock Exchange partners, like other business partners, have to find their working capital out of their own pockets, and their difficulties in raising large sums for this purpose were not eased by the provision of the Companies Act 1948, which limits the members of a business partnership to twenty.[11] However the Companies Act 1967[12] provided that members of a recognised[13] stock exchange were no longer limited in the number of partners that their firms may contain. The position of small but ambitious firms wishing to expand quickly was not noticeably assisted by the Act: their position was greatly improved in July 1969 when new Rules[14] of the Stock Exchange enabled firms to convert themselves into limited companies for the first time in its history.

2. Limited partnerships

The Limited Partnership Act 1907 established the concept of a two-tier partnership consisting of:

9. I.e., unless the articles provide otherwise. 10. See p. 15, *ante*.
11. See ss. 429, 434. 12. Section 120 (1) (c).
13. I.e., recognised for the purposes of the Prevention of Fraud (Investments) Act 1958: see the Companies Act 1967, s. 120 (3).
14. See pp. 51–55, *post*.

(*a*) the general partners, who are liable for *all* the debts and obligations of the firm, and

(*b*) the limited partners, who at the time of entering into the partnership contribute thereto sums of capital or property valued at a stated amount, and whose liability does not extend beyond the amount of their contribution.

All limited partnerships must be registered at the Board of Trade.[15] The Act made several modifications in the general partnership law, to adapt it to the new concept. The general tenor of the modifications is that the *management* of the partnership, and its winding up, rest with the *general* partners alone, and the death, bankruptcy or mental incapacity of a limited partner do not dissolve the partnership.[16]

Although the Limited Partnership Act restricted the number of limited partners to twenty,[17] that restriction no longer applies in the case of members of a recognised stock exchange.[18]

A. STOCK EXCHANGE PARTNERSHIPS

1. General rules

(*a*) Partnership lists

In every year, as soon as possible after March 25th, a list of partnership and corporate members must be made out by the Secretary of the Stock Exchange.[19]

(*b*) Notices

All notices relative to partnerships must be signed by all the partners concerned, unless the Council otherwise allow.[20]

(*c*) Formation and dissolution

Before entering into partnership with another member, a member of the Stock Exchange must obtain the written consent of the Council.[21] Application for such consent must be made in writing not later than 28 days before the proposed commencement of the partnership. The member must submit such evidence as to his and his intended partner's ability—as at the commencement of the partnership, to comply with the minimum capital requirements of the Rules and Regulations;[1] and he must give, whether verbally or in writing, such other information as the Council may require.

15. Limited Partnership Act 1907, s. 5.
16. *Ibid.,* s. 6.   17. *Ibid.,* s. 4 (2).   18. Companies Act 1967, s. 121 (1) (*c*).
19. Rule 45 (1).   20. Rule 45 (2).   21. Rule 45 (3).
 1. Rule 45 (3) (*a*). For the minimum capital requirements see Rule 79*a* and pp. 65–67, *post*.

Except where the Council otherwise permit, and except where the partnership is dissolved by the death of one of the partners, a member must give at least 28 days' notice in writing of his intention to dissolve a partnership with another member. The Council may require both continuing and retiring partners to attend before them.[2]

(*d*) The posting of notices

A notice must be officially posted in the Stock Exchange as follows:

(*a*) not later than 14 days before the intended commencement of a partnership; and

(*b*) as soon as possible after the receipt by the Council of any notice of dissolution of partnership.

So far as the Rules and Regulations are concerned an entry into partnership, or dissolution, will take effect on the date specified for that purpose in the notice.[3]

(*e*) Undisclosed partnerships

A member who lends securities or cash to another member, on terms contingent on or varying with the profits of his business, *ipso facto* becomes a partner of his borrower, and he must obtain the Council's consent for such a partnership.[4]

(*f*) Liability of partners

A member entering into partnership with another member or members will, for the purposes of the Rules and Regulations, be deemed to assume joint and several liability for all his partner's Stock Exchange debts and obligations existing *immediately prior* to his entry into partnership, and for all debts and obligations of the partnership incurred during the time that he remains a partner.[5] This Rule does not apply to a member who enters into a partnership as a limited partner.[6]

(*g*) Failure of partnership

If a partnership fails (i.e., defaults) it is automatically dissolved. Should the members of the firm, when re-admitted as members, desire to renew the partnership, they must obtain the Council's consent as on a formation.[7]

2. Limited partnerships

A partnership between members of the Stock Exchange may be a limited partnership under the Limited Partnership Act 1907[8] provided that there are at least two general partners.[9]

2. Rule 45 (3) (*b*).   3. Rule 45 (3).   4. Rule 45 (4).
5. Rule 45 (5).   6. Rule 46 (5) (*a*) overriding Rule 45 (6).
7. Rule 53.   8. See pp. 43–44, *ante*.   9. Rule 46 (1).

(*a*) Returns

Every partnership having a limited partner must lodge at the Council Offices a copy of each return or statement registered, and the Certificate of Registration issued, pursuant to the Limited Partnership Act 1907. In each case lodgment must be made not later than seven days after the registration or issue as the case may be.[10]

(*b*) Assignment

A limited partner may not without the Council's written permission assign the whole or any part of his share in the firm of which he is a limited partner.[11]

(*c*) Conduct of business

A limited partner may not take any active part in the conduct of the firm's business.[12]

(*d*) Contract notes and correspondence

The Rule[13] that on all contract notes and correspondence all members shall state (*inter alia*) the name of the firm, of which they are members and the names of the partners applies to limited partnerships; but the names of the limited partners must be shown separately from the names of the general partners, and they must be described as "limited partners".[14]

(*e*) Censure, suspension and expulsion of a limited partner

A limited partner will not be liable to censure, suspension or expulsion by reason of any act or omission of the firm, its associates, attachés, employees or of any of its general partners, unless in the Council's opinion he has, *while a limited partner*, taken an active part in the conduct of the business of the firm, or has been a party to the act or omission in question.[15]

(*f*) Default of a limited partner

A limited partner is not liable to be declared a defaulter on the Stock Exchange unless there are outstanding obligations arising out of Stock Exchange transactions effected at a time when he was a general partner, or unless, in the Council's opinion, he has, *while a limited partner*, taken an active part in the conduct of the business of the firm, and he is not an external member.[16]

If all the general partners of a limited partnership have been declared defaulters, the whole of the firm's assets (notwithstanding the interest therein of any limited partner) will be applicable for the payment of the firm's Stock Exchange creditors *as if* those assets belonged to the defaulters alone, and were unencumbered by any limited partners' interests.[17] To give effect to this provision such

10. Rule 46 (2).   11. Rule 46 (3).   12. Rule 46 (4).   13. Rule 79.
14. Rule 46 (5) (*b*).   15. Rule 46 (5) (*c*).   16. Rule 46 (5) (*d*).   17. Rule 46 (6).

limited partner must at the request of the Official Assignee execute and deliver a deed of assignment in the form set out in the Rules.[18]

3. Prohibited partnerships

(a) With a non-member
A member may not, without the consent of the Council, enter into a partnership with any person who is not a member.[19] The Council may at any time revoke its consent so given and the member concerned must thereupon dissolve the partnership.[20]
An undisclosed partnership with a non-member is prohibited by the Rule that a member may not borrow money or securities from a non-member on terms that the lender shall receive a rate of interest varying with the profits, or receive a share of the profits, arising from the carrying on of the borrower's business.[1]

(b) Between brokers and jobbers
Partnerships between brokers and jobbers are prohibited.[2]

4. Market partnerships between jobbing firms

(a) Permitted market partnerships
Market partnerships are only permitted between firms who otherwise deal and settle bargains *in their own name*.[3] A market partnership may not consist of more than two jobbing firms, and it may not do business in any markets other than those in which both parties deal.[4]

(b) Notification of a market partnership
All market partnerships must be notified to the Secretary of the Stock Exchange immediately upon their formation in accordance with the following form of notice set out in the Rules[5] (or in such other form as the Council may accept):

The Council of the Stock Exchange.
Gentlemen,
We, the undersigned, who otherwise deal and settle in our name, beg to inform the Council that from 19 , we hold ourselves jointly responsible to the Stock Exchange for all transactions entered into by either of us in

(*Name of security*) ....
....
....
Yours faithfully.

18. For the form of deed see Appendix 37a of the Rules. For deed of arrangement generally, see pp. 245–246, 251–253, *post*.
19. Rule 54 (1).   20. Rule 54 (2).   1. Rule 54 (3).   2. Rule 54 (4).
3. Rule 55 (2).   4. Rule 55 (3).   5. See Appendix 17 of the Rules.

Notification of every market partnership must be posted in the Stock Exchange, and objections may be submitted to the Council during the seven days following such posting. The Council must, after the expiration of the seven days, consider whether to permit or refuse a market partnership. If they refuse, such a partnership must be discontinued by such time as the Council will order.[6]

(c) Failure to notify

Unless they have given the notification required above, jobbing firms dealing generally in any particular securities, and participating in the result, will be held responsible for the liabilities of each other. This responsibility extends not only to the securities in which they are jointly interested, but also in any other description of securities in which either of them may transact business.[7]

(d) Dissolution of a market partnership

The Secretary must be informed immediately of the dissolution by the parties concerned of a market partnership in any security.[8]

5. Interpretation

The decision of the Council as to what constitutes a partnership or a market partnership within the meaning and intention of the Rules is final.[9]

B. CORPORATE MEMBERS

1. Unlimited companies

A firm of partners may convert itself into an unlimited company by registering under the provisions of the general Companies Acts for the time being in force a company with unlimited liability. The sole object of the company must be the carrying on of business as a broker or a jobber (but not both) on the Stock Exchange, and the memorandum and articles must be in a form prescribed or approved by the Council. In particular they must effectively restrict membership of the company to natural persons who are themselves members of the Stock Exchange, and who have given to the Council a joint and several undertaking that they will be answerable for all the transactions of the company in the same manner and to the same extent as if its transactions had been their own transactions.[10]

(a) Notice of conversion to an unlimited company

Notice in the prescribed form [11] of a firm's intention to convert itself into a company together with a draft of its proposed memo-

6. Rule 55 (1).   7. Rule 55 (4).   8. Rule 55 (5).   9. Rule 55 (6).
10. Rule 56 (1).   11. For the form see Appendix 46a of the Rules.

randum and articles must be laid before the Council not less than ten days before its registration. At the expiration of that time, and unless the Council otherwise directs, the firm is at liberty to register the company.[12]

(b) Application by an unlimited company for membership of the Stock Exchange

As soon as the new company has been registered, notice of its registration and an application for its admission as a member, signed on its and their behalf by all the members of the firm who form it, must be given to the Council.[13]

No other proposals nor nomination nor any election by ballot will be required for the admission of a company so formed. At the next meeting of the Council after the application is received the company will be admitted as a member, unless the Council in the exercise of their discretion decide otherwise.[14]

(c) An unlimited member company may carry on business in partnership with a firm

As from the date of a company's admission to membership, the business previously carried on by the firm by which the company was formed must, so long as the company continues to be a member, be carried on exclusively by and for the account of either

(i) the company or

(ii) a partnership between the company and other members (all the general partners of such partnership being members of the company). The members of the company may not make bargains except for such account. In the case of such a partnership the company must remain in partnership for not less than six months. Where any such partnership is to be formed from the date of the company's admission to membership, notice of the intended partnership must be given at the same time as the company applies for membership on registration. Where a partnership is to be formed at a subsequent date, the ordinary notice of partnership formation[15] must be given.[16]

(d) Unlimited company deemed to be a partnership for the purposes of the Rules

For the purposes of the Rules and Regulations, an unlimited company admitted to membership is deemed to be a partnership of all the members who are for the time being members of that company.[17]

12. Rule 56 (2).
13. Rule 56 (3).
14. *Ibid.*
15. I.e., under Rule 45 (3), *supra.*
16. Rule 56 (4).
17. Rule 56 (5).

(*e*) Liability of the members of an unlimited company

All the transactions, bargains, debts and liabilities of any unlimited company which is a member of the Stock Exchange are, for all the purposes of the Rules and Regulations, and of all documents executed or entered into pursuant thereto, deemed also to be the *joint and several* transactions, etc., of its individual members at the time when they were entered into or incurred.[18]

(*f*) Re-election of an unlimited company

Where all the individual members of an unlimited corporate member apply for re-election or re-admission to membership of the Stock Exchange, those collective applications are deemed to include an application for re-election or re-admission by the corporate member itself, which is not required to make a separate application of its own.[19]

(*g*) Resignation of an unlimited company

The resignation of an unlimited corporate member operates as the formation of a new partnership between its individual members,[20] who must comply with the Rules governing the formation of general partnerships.[1]

(*h*) Failure of an unlimited company

The failure or declaration of default of an unlimited corporate member is deemed to be the failure and declaration of default of all its individual members.[2]

(*i*) Discipline of an unlimited company

The censure, suspension or expulsion of an unlimited corporate member operates also as the censure, suspension or expulsion of all its individual members.[3]

(*j*) Bankruptcy of the members of an unlimited company

When an order is made, or a resolution is passed, for the winding up[4] of an unlimited corporate member, that is the equivalent of a natural person's bankruptcy for all purposes of the Rules and Regulations. If such an order is made, or resolution passed before the corporate member has by resignation or otherwise ceased to be a member, all its individual members are deemed for the purposes of the Rules and Regulations to have become, and proved to be, insolvent on the date on which the order was made or resolution passed.[5]

18. Rule 57 (1).   19. Rule 57 (2).   20. Rule 57 (3).
1. Rule 45, *supra*.   2. Rule 57 (5).   3. Rule 57 (6).
4. Other than a resolution for a member's voluntary winding-up.
5. Rule 57 (7).

2. Limited companies

A. MEMBERSHIP OF THE STOCK EXCHANGE

Before July 1st 1969 it was not open to member firms to raise outside capital by inviting the public to subscribe for their own shares. Generally a firm had to run itself on the money which its partners or members could put up. In the case of smaller firms this involved a considerable personal risk for the partners or directors, and a corresponding risk for the persons with whom they dealt. In the case of all firms, the fact that they could not raise outside capital acted as a brake on their expansion, which tended in turn to limit the quality and extent of the services which they were able to provide.

(*a*) Introduction

On June 30th 1969 the Council of the Stock Exchange approved new Rules which permit all its member firms to turn themselves into limited companies, and issue shares in themselves to the public at large.[6] The Council were careful to provide safeguards against the consequences of this radical step. A most important example is that while the principle of limited liability has been let in so far as a firm's ordinary shareholders are concerned, the concept of unlimited liability has been preserved by a provision that *the directors* will be held personally liable for all its debts and obligations in the same way as the partners of a partnership firm. In other words, if a limited corporate member is declared a defaulter, the shareholders' liability will not be brought into play unless the directors are unable to pay off its debts at 100p in the £.

(*b*) Notice of registration as a limited company

When members intend to register a company limited by shares under the general Companies Acts for the time being in force they must obtain the prior consent of the Council after giving not less than 28 days' notice on the prescribed form,[7] or in such other form as the Council may accept. At the same time they must supply to the Council the proposed name of the company, and two copies of its draft memorandum and articles.[8]

(*c*) Name, memorandum and articles

Neither the name nor the memorandum nor the articles when they have respectively been approved by the Council may be changed without the Council's prior consent. If any such change is made

6. Rule 71 (1) (*a*).
7. For prescribed form of notice, see Appendix 3 of the Rules.
8. Rule 71 (1) (*b*).

without that consent, or if any provision of the articles is contravened, the limited corporate member will, if the Council passes a resolution to that effect, cease to be a member.[9]

(*d*) Election of a limited corporate member
When the company has been registered it must apply forthwith to the Council to be elected as a limited corporate member. Until so elected, it may not commence business.[10]

(*e*) Capital
The company may not issue any shares unless they are fully paid or credited as fully paid on or before allotment.[11]

(*f*) Bargains
No director or employee of a limited corporate member may make bargains except in that member's name.[12]

(*g*) Right to vote
A limited corporate member is not entitled to act as proposer or seconder of a member for appointment to the Council. Nor may it vote in any ballot for such an appointment.[13]

(*h*) Annual re-election
A limited corporate member which wishes to be re-elected must comply with the rules affecting natural persons who apply for re-election.[14] Unless otherwise permitted by the Council its application must be made on the prescribed form,[15] which confirms that there have been no changes in shareholdings or directors in the last year since the company was elected or re-elected other than those approved by the Council.[16]

(*i*) Re-registration of unlimited corporate member
An unlimited corporate member may not apply to be re-registered as a limited company under the Companies Acts except with the prior consent of the Council. After becoming re-registered it will be subject to the provisions of the Rules which apply to limited corporate members.[17]

B. DIRECTORS

(*a*) Eligibility and notice
No person may be appointed, or act, as a director of a limited corporate member unless he is himself a member of the Stock

9. Rule 71 (1) (*c*).   10. Rule 71 (1) (*d*).   11. Rule 71 (1) (*e*).
12. Rule 71 (1) (*f*).   13. Rule 71 (1) (*g*).   14. See Rule 23.
15. For the prescribed form, see Appendix 1 (*c*) of the Rules.   16. Rule 71 (1) (*h*).
17. Rule 71 (1) (*i*).

Exchange. If the Council do not otherwise permit, 28 days' written notice must be given to the Council before a member is appointed or resigns as a director of a limited corporate member.[18]

(b) Liability of directors

Each director of a limited corporate member will be personally liable for *all* its debts and obligations incurred prior to the date of his resignation or removal. A director's liability includes debts and obligations arising *prior* to his becoming a director.[19]

(c) The assumption by members of personal liability

Its directors' liability may be insufficient to meet all a limited corporate member's general liabilities, or there may be other reasons for shifting the onus of responsibility on to other shoulders. Accordingly it is provided that any member who is not a director in the *service* of a limited corporate member may, by giving to the Council 28 days' notice,[20] accept liability for all the debts and obligations [1] of the limited corporate member.[2] No such provision is made in respect of ordinary shareholder members, whose liability is, of course, limited to the amount unpaid on their shares.

A serving member who has assumed personal liability may terminate it (with the consent of the Council) by giving a withdrawal notice.[3] But he will remain liable for all debts and obligations incurred *prior* to the date on which his withdrawal notice becomes effective.[4]

(d) Unauthorised directors

If (i) a non-member becomes, or

(ii) a member becomes and remains, without the consent of the Council, a director of a limited corporate member, the Council may pass a resolution whereby the limited corporate member loses its membership.[5]

(e) Directors' service agreements

Where a director has a service agreement with a limited corporate member, that agreement must provide that it shall be terminated forthwith:

(i) if he ceases to be a member of the Stock Exchange;

(ii) if the Council passes of its own accord a resolution terminating it.

In either case no compensation is payable in respect of such termination.[6]

---

18. Rule 71 (2) (a). 19. Rule 71 (2) (b).
20. I.e., by a liability notice in the form of Appendix 4a of the Rules.
1. Including debts and obligations arising prior to his giving such notice.
2. Rule 71 (2) (c) (i). 3. In the form in Appendix 4 (b) of the Rules.
4. Rule 71 (2) (c) (ii). 5. Rule 71 (2) (d). 6. Rule 71 (2) (e).

(*f*) Directors' qualification shares, and other qualifications

Every director of a limited corporate member must at all times:[7]

(i) be the beneficial owner of shares in the company which at the date of his appointment as a director were of a value[8] of at least £10,000; or

(ii) have outstanding a subordinated loan[9] to the company of at least £10,000; or

(iii) be the beneficial owner of shares in the company and have outstanding a subordinated loan to the company the aggregate of—

(*a*) the value of such shares at the date of his appointment as a director, and

(*b*) the amount of such loan being not less than £10,000.[10]

C. FAILURE OF A LIMITED CORPORATE MEMBER

The failure or declaration of default of a limited corporate member is deemed to be the failure or declaration of default of all its directors and those members who have assumed,[11] and not withdrawn, personal liability.[12] Where a court order is made, or resolution passed for the winding-up of a limited corporate member,[13] all its directors and those members who have assumed and not withdrawn personal liability are deemed to have become, and been proved, insolvent at the date of such order or resolution.[14]

D. DISCIPLINE OF A LIMITED CORPORATE MEMBER

Unless the Council decide otherwise, the censure, suspension or expulsion of a limited corporate member operates as the censure, suspension or expulsion of all its directors.[15]

E. NOTICE OF SPECIAL RESOLUTIONS

The Companies Act 1948 allows a limited company to make several important alterations to itself. Because these alterations are so radical in nature, they cannot be made except on the passing of a special resolution passed by a three-quarter majority of the members

---

7. I.e., not merely on his appointment as a director.
8. I.e., as between a willing buyer and a willing seller.
9. I.e., a loan which in the event of a winding-up shall not rank for any distribution until *all* other creditors (except other subordinated loan holders) have been paid in full. To qualify under the Rule it must be a loan in respect of which repayment is to be made at the same rate in the £ as the rate at which repayment of capital is made to ordinary shareholders up to but not exceeding the amount of such subordinated loan.
10. Rule 71 (2) (*f*).   11. For assumption of personal liability, see p. 53, *ante*.
12. Rule 71 (3) (*a*).   13. Other than a member's voluntary winding-up.
14. Rule 71 (3) (*b*).   15. Rule 71 (3) (*c*).

entitled to vote, and voting, at a meeting of which they have been given 21 days' notice. Such alterations are (*inter alia*) changing the company's name; altering its articles or its objects clause; altering the directors' remuneration; increasing or reducing its nominal share capital; initiating a members' voluntary winding-up; and giving authority to the liquidator in a voluntary winding-up to sell the company's business to another company for cash or shares in the other company.

The Rules furnish an important safeguard here. They provide that notice of every meeting of a limited corporate member convened to consider the passing of a special resolution must be sent to the Council at the same time as such notice is sent to the shareholders, or 21 clear days before the date for which the meeting is convened, whichever is the earlier.[16] This provision is designed to prevent limited corporate members from secretly taking the initiative in matters in which a reference to the Council would be required under the Rules and Regulations.

F. THE ISSUE OR TRANSFER OF SHARES IN A LIMITED CORPORATE MEMBER

Limited corporate members issue shares which may be dealt in on stock exchanges in the same way as shares in other limited companies. But to allow members of a particular exchange to purchase and sell, as principals, shares of limited corporate members of the *same* exchange would open the way to market rigging[17] and all sorts of other abuses. Accordingly, no share of a limited corporate member may be issued or transferred to a member who is not:

(*a*) a director, or
(*b*) a member in the service of the company, or
(*c*) a non-active member.

And it is provided that no shares of a limited corporate member may be issued or transferred without the prior consent of the Council.[18]

C. NOMINEE AND SERVICE COMPANIES

1. Nominee companies

A member firm whether a partnership or a company may hold and register companies, limited by shares under the provisions of the Companies Act, whose sole purpose is to accept transfers as

16. Rule 71 (3) (*d*).   17. See Rule 73*b*.   18. Rule 71 (3) (*e*).

nominees of the member firm.[19] Membership of such a nominee company must be confined to the general partners in the member firm.[20] The Rules regulate further the position of member firms' nominee companies,[1] and in particular they provide that the partners in the member (i.e., holding) firm are jointly and severally answerable to the Council for all the transactions of its nominee company.[2]

2. Service companies

The Rules permit a member firm to hold and register, under the provisions of the Companies Act, a service company *with unlimited liability*.[3] Examples of service companies are those whose objects are restricted to:

(*a*) providing for the member firm office accommodation fully furnished and equipped, and all services ancillary thereto such as heating, cleaning and telephone.

(*b*) making available to the member firm services of such staff and employees as the member firm from time to time requires for the conduct of its business as a broker or jobber.

(*c*) acting as an insurer of the member firm against any liability arising from its stock exchange business, other than the liabilities required to be insured under the Rules.[4]

(*d*) performing such other services for the member firm as the Council may from time to time approve.

A service company's memorandum and articles must be in a form prescribed or approved by the Council, and in particular must prohibit it from carrying on business as brokers or jobbers either upon the Stock Exchange or elsewhere.[5] Other Rules make the partners in the member firm responsible for the liabilities of the service company.[6]

D. BRANCH OFFICES

Broking firms may establish and maintain for the purposes of their Stock Exchange business branch offices in Great Britain and Ireland,[7] and overseas.[8] In both cases there are several common requirements. The Council's consent must be obtained, and it expires annually,[9] when a fresh application must be made. The Council can revoke its consent at any time, whereupon the firm must close its branch.

19. Rule 28 (1).   20. Rule 28 (2).   1. See generally Rule 28.
2. Rule 28 (3).   3. Rule 29 (1).   4. I.e., in accordance with Rule 79c.
5. Rule 29 (2).   6. See generally Rule 29.   7. Rule 59.
8. Rule 60.   9. I.e., on March 24th.

The following Rules apply to the ownership and management of branch offices, whether in Great Britain and Ireland, or overseas:

(i) The branch office must be wholly under the control of the firm and operated in the firm's name. But in the case of an overseas branch the Council can permit a departure from this requirement.

(ii) A branch office in Great Britain and Ireland must be under the personal control of a resident member; an overseas branch must be managed by a person approved by the Council.

(iii) All branch offices must be used solely for the conduct of the firm's stock exchange business.

(iv) Branch office business must be conducted in accordance with the Rules and Regulations of the Stock Exchange, London and (in the case of an overseas branch) with the laws of the country in which it is situated.

In addition the following provisions are of special application to overseas branches:

(i) Contract notes for business transactions by an overseas branch must be rendered by the firm in London, or by an organisation under the control of the firm which is a member of an overseas stock exchange.

(ii) The overseas branch may not advertise for Stock Exchange business in Great Britain or the Republic of Ireland, nor for this purpose issue or transmit in those territories circulars or communications respecting such business to persons other than the firm's own clients. The Rules make certain restrictions upon advertisement overseas.

(iii) The prior permission of the Council must be obtained for any change of the overseas branch's address.

(iv) Unless the Council otherwise direct in any particular case, the firm is liable for any failure of its overseas branch to meet an obligation arising out of a stock exchange transaction.

(v) With the prior consent of the Council a broking firm having an overseas branch may allow the business of that branch to be conducted by an organisation which belongs to a stock exchange or stockbrokers' association of the country in which the branch is situated.[10] In that event, the Council may permit not more than two persons who are not partners in or directors of the firm to become partners or to hold directorships or other equivalent posts in the organisation.

10. See further Rule 61. For sharing of commission, see Chapter 7.

E. MEMBER FIRMS' BALANCE SHEETS

Member firms [11] are under a duty to prepare balance sheets from time to time, and to have them audited by an independent qualified accountant who will then make a report for the benefit of the Council. In order to facilitate the preparation of balance sheets, member firms are obliged to maintain comprehensive records of all assets and liabilities, receipts and payments.

1. Maintenance of records

Every firm must maintain records [12] in sufficient detail to show particulars of:

(a) all moneys received or paid by the firm;

(b) all purchases and sales of securities by the firm, and the charges and credits arising therefrom;

(c) all transactions by the firm with or for the account of:

(i) clients, excluding partners in the firm;

(ii) partners in the firm;

(iii) firms of the Stock Exchange, London (including bargains to be settled through the Settlement Office); [13]

(iv) firms of all other stock exchanges in Great Britain and Ireland;

(v) Associated members, attachés and employees;

(vi) each overseas branch, incorporated office or firm in respect of: (a) Stock Exchange transactions, (b) other transactions;

(vii) other persons;

(d) all income from commissions, interest and other sources, and all expenses, commissions and interest paid;

(e) all assets and liabilities, including contingent liabilities of the firm;

(f) all securities which are the property of the firm, showing by whom they are held and whether, if held otherwise than by the firm itself, they are so held as collateral against loans or advances;

(g) all securities which are not the property of the firm but for which the firm or any nominee company controlled by it is accountable, showing by whom and for whom they are held, and

(i) the extent to which they are held for safe custody, in which case they must either be registered in the name of the client or of

---

11. In this context, "firms" include (i) partnerships, (ii) limited corporate members and (iii) unlimited corporate members: Rule 79a (a). The expression "partners" is deemed to include (i) limited partners, (ii) directors of limited corporate members and (iii) shareholders of unlimited corporate members: Rule 79a (b).
12. Rule 79a (1).   13. For the Settlement Office, see pp. 200–201, post.

the firm's nominee company, or be deposited in a specially designated Safe Custody Account with the firm's bankers,

(ii) the extent to which they are deposited with, or otherwise pledged or charged to any *third party* as collateral security available against loans or advances, present or prospective, to the firm or to any company owned or controlled by the firm. In such a case the deposit pledge or charge must be authorised by the client or other person concerned;[14]

(h) all purchases and sales of options by the firm and fees (i.e., option moneys) arising therefrom; also any related covering transactions and all declarations to exercise the options.

2. Balance sheets

A. PREPARATION

The proper maintenance of the above records will enable a member firm to draw up its balance sheet. Every firm must cause to be prepared from time to time a balance sheet showing its assets and liabilities and the partners' capital therein. Its assets and liabilities must be brought into account in such amounts, and must be classified and described in such a manner that the balance sheet gives a true and fair view of the state of the firm's affairs as at the date of the balance sheet. When it has been completed, the balance sheet must be signed as approved by each and every partner[15] in the firm.[16]

B. DATE OF BALANCE SHEETS

A firm may not, without the consent of the Council, prepare a balance sheet for a date more than fifty-four weeks after the date for which its last balance sheet was prepared, or (as the case may be) fifty-four weeks after the date on which the firm began to trade.[17]

Without the prior consent of the Council, no firm may change its practice with regard to the date for which its balance sheet is prepared.[18] Although it is theoretically possible for a firm to keep changing the date for its balance sheet, it is obliged to establish a *regular* date to begin with: it is provided that every new firm must, within one month from the date on which it commenced business, notify the Council of the date for which its balance sheet will be prepared in each year.[19]

14. The authority must be in writing. It must specify the period to which it relates, and be renewed annually.

15. For meaning of "partner" see note 11 *supra*.   16. Rule 79a (2).

17. Rule 79a (3). A balance sheet is deemed to comply with this Rule notwithstanding that it fails to take into account transactions in securities since the close of dealing for the last preceding Stock Exchange account.

18. Rule 79a (4) (a).   19. Rule 79a (4) (b).

C. NON-ELIGIBLE (OR "NON-APPROVED") ASSETS AND NON-RANKING LIABILITIES

The assets and liabilities which the balance sheet must disclose fall into two separate classes. They must appear under separate headings in the balance sheet, as follows:

(i) Assets and liabilities which *must* be taken into account in calculating a firm's margin of solvency.[20] These are known as approved assets and ranking liabilities.

(ii) Assets and liabilities which must appear in the balance sheet but *may not* without the consent of the Council be taken into account in calculating the margin of solvency. Non-approved assets and non-ranking liabilities vary according to the type of firm. A summary will be given in the case of each type:

(*a*) Partnership firms [1]

Balances in the individual capital; stock exchange and all other accounts of each individual partner including debit balances in the case of general partners (a note of contangos done and all transactions closed and re-opened for partners contemporaneous with the date of the balance sheet must be supplied); liabilities to, and amounts due from, firms of any stock exchange in Great Britain and Ireland (including tickets payable and receivable) which relate to transactions in securities undertaken for the account of the general partners; any amount set aside for taxation in excess of ranking tax liability;[2] shares in and amounts owing by incorporated offices of the firm, distinguishing shares from indebtedness; interests in overseas firms, other liabilities as may have been agreed with the Council.

(*b*) Unlimited corporate members [3]

The paid-up capital and the amount thereof registered in the name of each shareholder; capital and revenue reserves; balances due to or from each shareholder in respect of transactions in securities and on other accounts between the company and its shareholders (with a note of contangos and all transactions closed and re-opened contemporaneous with the date of the balance sheet); liabilities to, and amounts due from, firms of other stock exchanges in respect of shareholders' transactions; any amount set aside for taxation in excess of ranking tax liability;[4] shares in and amounts owing by overseas incorporated offices of the company distinguishing shares from indebtedness; interests in overseas firms; other liabilities as may have been agreed with the Council.

20. For the minimum margin of solvency, see pp. 66–67, *post*.
  1. Rule 79a (5).   2. For ranking tax liability, see Rule 79a (9) (*d*), and p. 62, *post*.
  3. Rule 79a (6).   4. For ranking tax liability see note 2 *supra*.

(c) Limited corporate members [5]

The paid-up capital; capital and revenue reserves; balances due to or from each shareholder in respect of transactions in securities and on security accounts between the firm and its directors (with a note of contangos and all transactions closed and re-opened contemporaneous with the date of the balance sheet); liabilities to, and amounts due from, firms of other stock exchanges relating to transactions in securities undertaken for the account of shareholders and directors; any amount set aside for taxation in excess of ranking tax liability; [6] subordinated loans [7] by each director; shares in and amounts owing by overseas incorporated offices of the company, distinguishing shares from indebtedness; interests in overseas firms; other liabilities as may have been agreed with the Council.

D. APPROVED (OR ELIGIBLE) ASSETS AND RANKING LIABILITIES

The assets and liabilities which are taken into account in calculating the margin of solvency are roughly common to all types of firms. When that margin has been arrived at, the accountant will have to work out the particular firm's minimum margin, and see whether it exceeds or falls short of its actual margin.

(i) *Approved assets* [8]

Approved assets consist of:

(a) Money receivable in the ordinary course of stock exchange business from: (i) clients, excluding partners of the firm; (ii) associated members, attachés and employees; (iii) firms of any stock exchange in Great Britain and Ireland (including tickets receivable), excluding amounts relating to transactions in securities undertaken for the account of partners (other than limited partners) in the firm; (iv) other persons, excluding partners in the firm.

(b) Securities in which dealings are permitted, [9] stating by way of note the aggregate market value of such securities.

(c) Payments for or towards the purchase of securities for which a quotation is pending.

(d) Treasury Bills, Defence Bonds, British Savings Bonds, National Development Bonds and Tax Reserve Certificates.

(e) Money on deposit (other than with banks) which is encashable within six months after the balance sheet date. [10]

(f) Cash and stamps in hand and balances on current or deposit account with banks.

5. Rule 79a (7).

7. As defined in Rule 72 (2) (f).

9. I.e., permitted under Rule 163.

6. For ranking tax liability see note 2 *supra*.

8. Rule 79a (8).

10. For the balance sheet date see p. 59, *ante*.

(*g*) In the case of a limited partnership, the amount due from each limited partner in respect of transactions in securities.

(*h*) Such other assets of the firm as may be agreed by the Council.

(*ii*) *Ranking liabilities* [11]

Ranking liabilities consist of:

(*a*) Amounts due to bankers.

(*b*) Any other liabilities which are secured, either by the deposit of securities or otherwise.

(*c*) The aggregate amount due to overseas incorporated offices and overseas firms.

(*d*) A provision for taxation to the following extent:
in the case of a partnership, the total amount of the income tax (or a fair estimate thereof) payable or expected to be payable on the whole of the profits of the firm up to the date of the balance sheet on which the margin of solvency is calculated; or, whichever is the greater of—

(i) the total amount of the income tax (or a fair estimate thereof) outstanding in respect of all years of assessment ended on or before the balance sheet date and, where applicable, the accrued proportion for the year of assessment in which the balance sheet date falls; or

(ii) the total amount of the income tax liability (or a fair estimate thereof) which would be payable if the firm had ceased business at the balance sheet date.

In the case of a company whether limited or unlimited, the total amount of the corporation tax (or a fair estimate thereof) payable or expected to be payable on the whole of the profits up to the balance sheet date.

(*e*) The amount, if any, by which the sum at which securities in which dealings are permitted and owned by the firm are brought into account exceeds their aggregate market value.

(*f*) The amount, if any, by which bear positions in securities in which dealings are permitted [12] are brought into account falls short of the aggregate market value of the securities comprised in the bear position.

(*g*) The amount of any loss which the firm could incur in respect of options granted and outstanding, on the basis of market values.

(*h*) The amount of any accumulated losses, so far as they concern the firm, of any service or other company owned or controlled by the firm.

11. Rule 79*a* (9).
12. I.e., permitted under Rule 163.

(*i*) The amount of any foreseeable losses from bad or doubtful debts or from any other causes.

(*j*) In the case of a limited partnership, the amount due to each limited partner—

    (i) in respect of transactions in securities; and
    (ii) on accounts other than capital account.

(*k*) In the case of a limited corporate member, the amount due to each director otherwise than in respect of subordinated loans [13] and transactions in securities.

(*l*) All other liabilities not specifically classed by the rules as non-ranking.

E. EXAMINATION OF BALANCE SHEETS BY AN ACCOUNTANT

All assets (whether approved or not) and all liabilities (whether ranking or not) must appear on the balance sheet. When it has been drawn up the balance sheet must be submitted to an independent qualified accountant for audit. He must be supplied with all the firm's books and records, and all such explanations and other information as he may require for the purpose of his report. [14]

F. THE ACCOUNTANT'S REPORT [15]

The accountant must provide the firm with three signed copies of a report, [16] addressed to the Council of the Stock Exchange and stating:

(i) whether, subject to any reservations relating to the scope of his examinations or to any other matters, he is of the opinion that the firm had, at the balance sheet date, maintained records in compliance with the Rules and that it gives a true and fair view of the state of the firm's affairs. In the case of securities which are not the property of the firm but for which it is accountable, the report must state whether any such securities have been deposited or otherwise pledged with a third party as collateral for loans or advances to the firm; the accountant must state whether or not any such loan or advance was outstanding at the balance sheet date, and, if so, whether he has inspected the written authorisation to deposit or pledge of the client or other person concerned.

(ii) the minimum margin of solvency referred to below, [17] and

---

13. As defined in Rule 71 (2) (*f*), p. 54, *ante.*
14. As defined by Rule 79*a* (13). He must be in public practice, independent of the member firm, and a member of a specified professional body.
15. Rule 79*a* (12).   16. See generally Rule 79*a* (14).
17. For the minimum margin of solvency see note 20, p. 60, *ante.*

64 MEMBER FIRMS

whether on the evidence of the balance sheet, that margin was present at the balance sheet date.

(iii) except in the case of a limited corporate member, the extent to which assets of individual partners have been utilised [18] with the permission of the Council to attain the margin of solvency.

(iv) whether in the case of a limited partnership the aggregate of the balances on capital current and other accounts of the *limited partners* conforms to the provision [19] whereby that aggregate must not at any time exceed one half (or such larger proportion as the Council may agree) of the net aggregate credit balance represented by the sum at credit on the capital and other accounts of the *general partners*, less any debit balances on capital or other accounts of the general partners.

Additional matters to be reported in the case of arbitrageurs and option dealers

In the case of broker firms engaged in arbitrage business as arbitrageurs [20] on joint account, or conducting option business as option dealers, the accountant's report must also certify that the firm has kept proper records in conformity with the Rules,[1] and that no business has been executed on behalf of any of its clients with the firm's arbitrage or option accounts.[2]

Additional matters to be reported in the case of limited companies

In the case of a limited corporate member the accountant must also state whether, in his opinion and subject to such reservations as he considers appropriate, every director had the required £10,000 shareholding or equivalent stake in the company.[3]

G. NOMINEE COMPANIES, SERVICE COMPANIES, CORPORATE MEMBERS OF A FIRM, OVERSEAS BRANCH OFFICES

The Rules and Regulations make various provisions[4] for the drawing up of balance sheets for a firm's nominee companies, service companies and overseas branch offices. Generally, all the provisions as to the keeping of records and preparation of balance sheets apply to such bodies. Accountants' reports must be prepared at the same time, and submitted in the same way, as the accountants' reports in respect of a parent company or firm.

---

18. Under Rule 79*a* (10) (*b*).   19. Rule 79*a* (10) (*d*).
20. For arbitrage, see Chapter 11, *post*.
1. For a firm's undertakings in the matter of records, see Appendices 32 and 32*c* of the Rules.
2. Rule 79*a* (14) (*b*).   3. As required by Rule 71 (2) (*f*): Rule 79*a* (14) (*c*).
4. Rule 79*a* (17, (18) and (19).

H. INTERIM BALANCE SHEETS OF LIMITED CORPORATE MEMBERS
In the case of a limited corporate member, the directors must
have an interim balance sheet prepared at a date which is not
without the consent of the Council less than twenty-four weeks nor
more than twenty-eight weeks after the date of the company's last
principal balance sheet.[5] The interim balance sheet must comply
with the relevant provisions for balance sheets generally, and must
be submitted to the Exchange Accountant (see below) together with
a directors' report.

I. SUBMISSION OF THE ACCOUNTANT'S REPORTS[6]
When the firm is in possession of the three signed copies of the
accountant's reports it must submit to the Council:

(i) one copy to the Council of the accountant's reports on (a) the
firm (b) nominee and service companies (if any) and (c) overseas
branch offices (if any);
(ii) in the case of a limited corporate member, one copy (as soon
as it is available) of the accounts sent to its shareholders in accordance with the Companies Acts.

Firms must submit one copy of each of the above reports,
together with the related balance sheets, to the Exchange
Accountant (see below) to which they decided to submit their
balance sheets.

All accountant's reports must be submitted to the Council not
later than six months after the balance sheet date.[7]

J. THE EXCHANGE ACCOUNTANT[8]
The Council will from time to time appoint one or more firms of
professional accountants as exchange accountants, and it notifies
firms of the name and address of each exchange accountant so
appointed.

Every firm must select the exchange accountant to which its
balance sheet is to be submitted, and it must inform the Council of
its choice. It cannot alter its choice without the consent of the
Council. Firms may not select an exchange accountant who happens
to be its own independent auditor or tax adviser.

An exchange accountant's task is supervisory in nature. He has a
general power to obtain direct from the accountants reporting on
the balance sheet any information which he may require. If he forms
the view from his enquiries that the firm's affairs require fuller
investigation, he must report to the Council. Except for the purpose

5. Rule 79 (b).   6. Rule 79a (15).
7. Rule 79a (16).   8. See generally Rule 79a (20).

of making his report he must treat all documents coming into his hands as confidential.

F. THE MINIMUM MARGIN OF SOLVENCY

Member firms doing business on the Stock Exchange must not operate below a level of solvency which is specified in the Rules. The Council will be given notice that a firm has fallen below that level on an examination of its accountant's report, for that is one of the matters with which the accountant has to deal.

1. Partnerships and unlimited corporate members

The partners of such firms must at all times maintain approved (or eligible) assets [9] in the firm to the extent that, in the aggregate, they exceed its ranking liabilities [10] by not less than its minimum margin of solvency as defined below. [11] For the purposes of attaining the requisite minimum margin a firm may seek the Council's permission to include certain assets of individual general partners in the computation as if they were assets of the firm. The Council have an absolute discretion in granting or refusing such permission and may impose such conditions as they consider appropriate.

A. CALCULATION OF THE MINIMUM MARGIN [12]

The minimum margin of solvency is the aggregate sum obtained by:

(i) multiplying £5,000 by the number of partners or by the aggregate number of associated members and attachés, whichever is the greater; and

(ii) multiplying £5,000 by the number of branch offices, in Great Britain, Ireland and overseas, not under the control of a resident partner of the London firm.

However, in the case of (a) a jobber firm or (b) a broker firm engaged in arbitrage business on joint account or conducting option business as option dealers, such margin must not in any event be less than £15,000. Where a member continues to carry on the business of broker on his own account (e.g., where he is sole surviving partner and has the Council's permission), [13] the margin must not be less than £10,000.

---

9. As defined by Rule 79a (8), *supra.*
10. As defined by Rule 79a (9), *supra.*
11. Rule 79a (10).
12. See *ibid.*
13. Under Rule 86 (2).

B. RESTRICTION ON THE STAKE OF LIMITED PARTNERS [14]

In the case of a limited partnership the sum of the amounts on the capital and other accounts of the *limited* partners may not at any time exceed one half (or such larger proportion as the Council may agree) of the net aggregate credit balance represented by the sum at credit on the capital and other accounts of the *general* partners less any debit balances on the capital or other accounts of the general partners.

2. Limited corporate members

In the case of limited corporate members the approved assets and ranking liabilities are similar to those of other member firms. The minimum margin of solvency is the aggregate sum obtained by:

(i) multiplying £10,000 by the number of directors or by the aggregate number of associated members and attachés, whichever is the greater; and

(ii) multiplying £10,000 by the number of branch offices in Great Britain, Ireland and overseas not under the control of a resident director of the limited corporate member.

However it is provided that the minimum margin must not, without the consent of the Council, be less than £200,000.

G. ASSOCIATED MEMBERS OF THE STOCK EXCHANGE FIRMS AND CLERKS

1. Associated members

A firm which wishes to employ a member of the Stock Exchange in any business capacity, or to have an arrangement with such member for sharing commission [15] must (unless that member is a retiring partner who gives the appropriate notice) apply for him to become an associated member. [16] Application should be made on one of the appropriate forms [17] depending on whether it is intended that the associated member will act as a dealer or not. The forms include undertakings by the firm to hold themselves responsible for the associated member's conduct in all stock exchange matters, and an assurance that he will abide by and conform to the Rules, Regulations and usages of the Exchange, and directions given by the Council in so far as they affect him.

14. Rule 79a (10) (d).
15. For sharing of commission see Chapter 7.
16. Rule 62.
17. For forms of application see Appendices 22 and 23 of the Rules.

68 MEMBER FIRMS

2. Clerks

There are two classes of clerks employed by stock exchange firms:

(a) Authorised clerks

No clerk may be authorised to transact business (i.e., make bargains) unless he is at least 20 years of age,[18] and until he has been employed by a firm for two years with a minimum service in the House of one year.[19] An application for an authorised clerk that would result in the total number of authorised clerks exceeding the number of partners in the firm must be accompanied by a letter from the firm to the Secretary of the Stock Exchange stating the reason for the application.[20] The appropriate application form[1] states that the firm will hold themselves responsible to the Council for the clerk's business conduct and for his behaviour in all matters affecting the Stock Exchange or its members.

(b) Unauthorised clerks

Unauthorised clerks are not allowed to transact business of any sort, whether it be a purchase sale or contango in the Stock Exchange or elsewhere. They may enter the House, and the Checking and Ticket Rooms. They must be at least 16 years of age, and an application for their admission will be made by their firm in the form provided.[2] Their firm must enter an undertaking similar to that in respect of authorised clerks. When an unauthorised clerk is absent on holiday or ill, his firm may apply for a temporary replacement on an abbreviated and simplified form.[3]

(c) Defaulters and bankrupts as clerks

A firm may apply for the re-admission as a clerk, either authorised or unauthorised,[4] of

(i) a defaulter, even though he has not paid from his resources the minimum dividend of one-third of the balance of losses occurring on his transactions.[5]

(ii) a former member, not a defaulter, who has ceased to be a member upon a resolution of the Council under Rule 176.[6]

The Council has power to order the posting of notice of any such application. A resolution allowing the application must be carried by a three-quarter majority of Council members present.[7]

18. Rule 62 (4).   19. Rule 65 (1).   20. Rule 62 (2).
1. The form is in Appendix 18 of the Rules.   2. See Appendix 19 of the Rules.
3. Rule 63 (1) and see Appendix 21 of the Rules.   4. Rule 64 (1).
5. As provided by Rule 41.
6. Such resolutions may be passed when a member has (*inter alia*) failed to pay subscriptions and other payments due to the Council, or is proved to be insolvent.
7. Rule 64 (3).

(*d*) Clerks of defaulters

Clerks of defaulters are excluded from the Stock Exchange.[8]

(*e*) Clerks of deceased members

Clerks of a deceased trading member may, by permission of the Chairman, a Deputy Chairman, or two members of the Council, enter the House for the purpose of adjusting unsettled accounts.[9]

3. Rules applicable to all associated members and clerks

(*a*) Notice of admission

No clerk may enter the House, nor may an associated member who is a dealer or an authorised clerk do a bargain, until his employer has received from the Secretary notice of his admission or authorisation.[10]

(*b*) Notice of withdrawal

A firm withdrawing an associated member or clerk must give notice on the prescribed form to the Secretary.[11]

(*c*) Re-admission

A firm wishing to obtain the re-admission of an associated member or clerk must apply each year for the permission of the Council.[12]

4. Miscellaneous provisions as to dealers

(*a*) Restrictions on dealing

An associated member who is a dealer, or an authorised clerk to a jobber, is allowed only to deal in a market where one of the partners in the firm employing him is already jobbing.[13]

(*b*) Liability of dealers for unsecured debts

A firm authorising an associated member who is a dealer or an authorised clerk to transact business is not answerable for money borrowed by that member or clerk without security, unless the firm has given him special authority for that purpose.[14]

(*c*) Lists of dealers

A list of dealers, distinguishing those who are associated members, and the names of their employers, is available for inspection in the Stock Exchange.[15]

8. Rule 69 (1).   9. Rule 69 (2).   10. Rule 67.
11. Rule 68. For the prescribed forms see Appendix 30*a* of the Rules.
12. Rule 62 (3). For the form of application see Appendix 1*a* of the Rules.
13. Rule 65 (3).   14. Rule 65 (4).   15. As provided by Rule 65 (2).

(*d*) Badges

The Rules make it compulsory for all who enter the House to transact business, or Checking Room, to wear distinctive badges.[16]

(*e*) Employment of expelled members

A firm may not without the special permission of the Council employ on stock exchange business a former member who has been expelled from the Exchange.[17]

16. Rule 66.   17. Rule 70.

CHAPTER 4

Quotation

INTRODUCTION

The seventeenth-century speculator who purchased an "adventure" [1] in one of the joint stock companies formed for the purpose of overseas exploration and trade was usually taking an enormous risk. It is true that if the company had been incorporated by Royal Charter, he was not liable for its corporate debts: that was a measure of protection. But he had little guidance as to the capital and prospects of the company and did not know whether his investment would be squandered in some risky or ill-advised project. Usually he had to rely on coffee house gossip and his own intuition.

The modern investor is in a much safer position. In the first place he can find out all the most important facts about a company without purchasing, or even being offered its shares. He can read a financial newspaper or take the expert advice of his broker; and he has a legal right of enquiry in that a company's memorandum and articles [2] are public documents and can be inspected by *any person* at the office of the Registrar of Companies. [3]

Secondly, when a company invites the public to subscribe for its shares or debentures, it must issue a document, known as a *prospectus*, setting out the advantages of investing in any class of its securities. A prospectus is defined as "any prospectus, notice, circular, advertisement, or other invitation offering to the public [4] for subscription [5] or purchase [6] any shares or debentures of a company". [7] The Companies Act 1948, stipulates the many and various matters which a prospectus is required to contain. [8] They may be summarised as follows:

1. Who the directors are, and what benefit they will get from their directorships.

---

1. See pp. 2–3, *ante.*   2. See pp. 11–12, *ante.*
3. Companies Act 1948, s. 426.
4. For the meaning of "the public" see *Nash* v. *Lynde,* [1929] A.C. 158.
5. "For subscription" means to be taken for cash when issued.
6. "Purchase" means purchase from an existing shareholder.
7. Companies Act 1948, s. 455.   8. See *ibid.*, s. 38 and Sched. 4.

2. What profit is being made by the promoters.[9]

3. The amount of capital required by the company to be subscribed, the amount actually received or to be received in cash, and the precise nature of the consideration given for the remaining capital.

4. What the company's financial record has been in the past.

5. What the company's obligations are under contracts which it has entered into, and for commission and preliminary expenses.

6. What are the voting and dividend rights of each class of shares.

These requirements are extremely comprehensive and are recognised as providing an ample though not complete protection to intending shareholders. The public protection provided by Parliament has in the past been supplemented and reinforced by the domestic rules of the various stock exchanges. With a specialist knowledge of investment pitfalls, and a concern for their own reputations as markets, they made stringent regulations for the admission of securities to quotation in their own particular exchange. In the Stock Exchange, London, the co-operation of brokers is guaranteed by the Rule that no firm may allow its name to appear as brokers in any prospectus or circular connected with an offer of securities in respect of which no application for quotation has been made; or, if such an application has been made, it has been refused or deferred or quotation has been suspended or cancelled.[10]

The Federation of Stock Exchanges has succeeded in establishing a common policy on quotation, and in June 1966 the Federation produced and published a code for all its member exchanges. This code, called "The Admission of Securities to Quotation",[11] takes the form of six memoranda and an Appendix, and is based on the requirements of the London Stock Exchange. It binds all issuers who apply for a quotation of securities in any member exchange[12] on or after September 1st 1966.

A. THE ADMISSION OF SECURITIES TO QUOTATION

1. Methods of issue

Securities may be brought to the Stock Exchange by any one of the following methods:

9. "Promoters" means the persons who intend to form a company and who take the necessary steps to bring it into existence.

10. Rule 78 (3).

11. The code is issued by authority of the Committee of the Federation of Stock Exchanges, and is available in loose-leaf booklet form.

12. For the member exchanges see pp. 6–7, *ante*.

(*a*) A prospectus issue

An offer is made to the public, by or on behalf of a company or other authority, at a fixed price.

(*b*) An offer for sale

An offer is made *to the public*, by or on behalf of a third party (e.g., an issuing house) at a *fixed* price. The third party purchases or agrees to purchase the securities from the company and then invites the public to buy from it at a higher price. Where the third party has agreed to take up shares not subscribed for by the public, this is known as underwriting.

(*c*) An offer by tender

This is an offer to the public by or on behalf of a company or a third party, at a minimum but no maximum price.

(*d*) Placing

This is defined as the sale by an issuing house or broker to a restricted list of places of securities which have previously been purchased or subscribed.[13] Placings must be distinguished from offers for sale.

(*e*) Introduction

An issuing house or brokers may, *without buying*, act as agents for the company and invite *their own clients* to buy the securities on offer: as agents they receive a commission known as brokerage.

(*f*) Rights offer to holders of existing securities [14]

Sometimes shareholders are offered the right to apply to the company for new shares in proportion to their existing holdings. Such offers are normally conveyed by a renounceable letter, or other negotiable document, which enables the shareholder to renounce the shares offered in favour of another person or persons.

(*g*) Open offer to holders of existing securities

(*h*) Capitalisation issue to holders of existing securities [15]

When authorised by its articles, a company may turn its capital reserves into share capital by issuing "bonus" shares instead of cash dividends. Such shares, credited as fully paid up, are issued to the existing shareholders *pro rata* to their holdings.

(*i*) In consideration of assets acquired, i.e., as a method of paying the vendors.

13. Memorandum on Quotations, para. 9.
14. See further, Chapter 9, Transfer.
15. See further, *ibid.*

(*j*) In exchange for, or conversion of, other securities.

(*k*) In exercise of options
A company sometimes gives its existing shareholders options to purchase additional shares on a *pro rata* basis.

2. General requirements for all quotations

A. PROCEDURE ON APPLICATION

No application for quotations will be considered unless the company has an expected market value of at least £250,000, and any one security for which quotation is sought has an expected market value of £100,000.[16] A company whose assets consist substantially of cash or short dated securities will not normally be admitted to quotation although some relaxation of this principle is afforded in the case of investment trusts.[17]

All applications and documents to be considered or approved by the Council should always be submitted to the Quotations Department at the earliest possible opportunity. When the application is to quote securities of companies and statutory bodies to which the provisions of the Companies Acts relating to prospectuses apply, the "Admission of Securities to Quotation" places the requirements in three categories:

(i) When the quotation sought is for securities of a company *no part* of whose capital is already quoted.[18]

(ii) When the intended quotation is for securities of a company *part* of whose capital is already quoted.[19]

(iii) When the intended quotation is for securities already quoted on another federated stock exchange where no further issue is being made.[20]

The requirements in each case are comprehensive and for the purposes of this book a summary will suffice. All applications (whether in categories (i), (ii) or (iii)) can be regarded as having three stages:

(*a*) An application in the form of Schedule I to the Appendix of the Rules of the Stock Exchange, London, reproduced in the "Admission of Securities to Quotation":

16. Memorandum on Quotations, para. 2. ,
17. For investment trusts see p. 83, *post.*
18. For the full requirements see "The Admission of Securities to Quotation", Appendix A, section I.
19. For the full requirements, see *ibid.*, Appendix A, section II.
20. For the full requirements, see *ibid.*, Appendix A, section III.

TO THE SECRETARY
  THE QUOTATIONS DEPARTMENT
—— 19—

Dear Sir,
    We are instructed by   (name of company) to
make application for permission to deal in and for quotation for
    (1) (The Securities for which application is made)
    (2) (A statement of how it is proposed to issue the securities,
whether by prospectus, offer for sale etc., as above)
    We shall be glad to receive in due course a note of the require-
ments of the Department.
    Application is being made simultaneously to the ————
———— Stock Exchange.
        We are,
            Yours faithfully
                ———————— Brokers.

(b) Applicants must submit for *initial approval* of the stock exchange, at least fourteen days prior to publication or posting, copies
of the stock exchange prospectus[21] (which must comply with the
"Admission of Securities to Quotation" Schedule II Part A. The
requirements of this schedule are wider than those of the Companies
Act). They must also submit copies of abridged particulars, if any, of
a preliminary announcement of public offer (which must not contain any material information not included in the prospectus) for
approval at least four days prior to insertion in the press.
    Where following submission of any document, any amendment is
made, further copies must be submitted for approval, indicating in
red amendments suggested by the Department, and in blue or black
the other amendments.
    (c) Applicants must lodge other specified documents at least two
days prior to the hearing of the application by the Committee on
Quotations. These include the formal application, signed by the
company's broker and supported, in the case of the Stock Exchange,
London, by at least two firms of jobbers in the market who are
prepared to deal, together with payment of the appropriate charge
for quotation. Prominent among the other documents are: copies of
the stock exchange prospectus (see below) signed by the directors;
the certificate of incorporation;[1] specimens of the memorandum
and articles;[2] a specimen of the trust deed or other document

21. There are various requirements as to the publication of the prospectus in
    newspapers.
 1. Not required where part of the share capital is already quoted on that exchange.
 2. Not required where part of the capital is already quoted on that particular
    exchange.

securing or constituting the loan capital;[3] the general undertaking;[4] and copies of the board or company resolutions authorising the issue of all the securities for which quotation is sought.

When reading documents submitted to it for approval and considering applications, the prime concern of the Quotations Department is to ensure that there is sufficient information to enable a fair view to be formed of the worth of the securities involved.[5]

B. THE CONTENTS OF STOCK EXCHANGE PROSPECTUSES

(i) In the case of companies

The stock exchange (as distinct from the Companies Act) prospectus which must accompany a company's application for quotation must be based on either Part A and Part B of the three parts of Sched. II of the Memorandum on Quotations. Part A recites the contents of the prospectus where *no part* of the company's capital is already quoted. Part B recites the contents of the prospectus where *some part* of the company's capital is already quoted.

The matters which both prospectuses must contain are similar. Basically, they are the same type of matter required for Companies Act prospectuses,[6] but the details asked for tend to be more elaborate. Particularly heavy duties of disclosure are imposed in respect of:

(a) The interests of each director, his wife, and children under 18 in the company

These include, for example, trusts of which the director or his wife is a settlor or trustee and in which the director or his wife or any of his children under 18 are beneficiaries or discretionary objects; also companies controlled by the director or his wife or his children, or the trustees of any such trusts in their capacity as such trustees.

(b) Details of directors' existing or proposed service contracts with the company

These include contracts with the company's subsidiaries.

(c) The company's financial and trading position and prospects

The Memorandum on Quotations includes an Accountants' Memorandum, to which accountants making reports for inclusion in prospectuses,[7] must conform. It is emphasised that the Memorandum is not exhaustive and that further information may be

3. See note 2, *supra*.   4. See *ibid.*
5. Memorandum on Quotations, para. 3.
6. For the Companies Act requirements see pp. 71–72, *ante*.
7. *And offers for sale, advertised statements and circulars.*

required, or the required information varied, by the Quotations Department where such a variation is relevant.

A great deal of information has to be supplied about subsidiary companies, i.e., their profits and losses, and how far they are attributable to the interests of the holding company; the nature and extent of the holding company's interest in the subsidiary company if the subsidiary's profits or assets will make a material contribution to the holding company's accounts; and details of the relevant activities[8] in which both the holding company and its subsidiaries are engaged.

The specific requirements for the stock exchange company prospectuses are neatly summarised in the more general requirement:[9]

> "A statement as to the financial and trading prospects of the company or group, together with *any* material information which may be relevant thereto, including, where known to the directors, special trade factors or risks (if any) which are not mentioned elsewhere in the prospectus and which are unlikely to be known or anticipated by the general public, which could materially affect the profits . . ."

(ii) In the case of the Government and local authority quotations

Schedule II, Part C recites the contents of the Stock Exchange prospectus where a quotation is sought for securities of a Government, municipality, local authority or statutory body. This is a much shorter prospectus. Its principal contents are: full particulars of the security for which a quotation is sought; a copy of the last audited balance sheet and profit and loss or income and expenditure account, with a copy of the auditor's report; and a declaration by the directors (or appropriate office holders) that they collectively and individually accept full responsibility for the accuracy of the information given.

C. THE TIMING OF ISSUES

The Bank of England exercises control over the timing of issues where the amount of money to be raised is £1,000,000 or more, in order to maintain an orderly new issue market; in such cases it is necessary for the sponsoring broker to apply to the Government Broker for a date known as "impact day", which is the first day on which the size and terms of the issue may be made known to underwriters, placees and the market.[10]

8. The precise details of the relevant activities are specified in the Schedule.
9. Schedule IIA, para. 18.
10. Memorandum on Quotations, para. 4.

D. INCREASE OF THE AUTHORISED CAPITAL

In all cases where the company desires to increase its authorised but unissued share capital, the directors must state, in the explanatory circular or other document accompanying the notice of the meeting to pass the resolution, whether they have any present intention of issuing any part thereof. If the increase is 25 per cent or more of the authorised share capital, the directors must undertake that the increased capital will not be issued in such a way as to change the control (or nature) of the business without the prior approval of the shareholders in general meeting.[11]

3. Special requirements for particular methods of quotation

A. IN THE CASE OF PROSPECTUS ISSUES, OFFERS FOR SALE AND OFFERS BY TENDER

The Quotations Department must approve the prospectus before it is issued and the prospectus must be advertised in accordance with the Appendix. The card inserted in the Statistical Services is based on the prospectus. Any abridged particulars or preliminary announcement of a public offer must not include any information which does not or will not appear in the prospectus. If none of the company's securities is already quoted on the Exchange, the Quotations Department must also approve the memorandum and articles.

Where the company intends to give shareholders preferential treatment on allotments such treatment must be approved by the Quotations Department prior to publication of the prospectus. The preferential treatment must normally be limited to 10 per cent of the amount offered and then only to employees or shareholders. Prior approval must also be obtained for any part underwritten firm, i.e., which an underwriter has agreed to subscribe for and the company has agreed to allot in full, irrespective of whether the issue is fully subscribed or not. The amount underwritten firm must be strictly limited, depending upon the proportion of the total amount of the security being offered for subscription.[12]

In the case of offers by tender, the Quotations Department must be satisfied as to the procedure for determining the price and basis of allotment.[13]

B. IN THE CASE OF PLACINGS

Approval in principle to a placing must always be sought at an early date. An advertised statement, or other particulars to accord

11. Memorandum on Quotations, para. 6.   12. *Ibid.*, para. 7.   13. *Ibid.*, para. 8.

with the Appendix must be approved by the Quotations Department before it is issued.[14]

When applying to the Committee on Quotations for permission to place equity capital or securities having an element of equity, the broker must normally state the nature of the company's business; its profit record before taxation for the past ten years, or since inception, whichever is the less—also what profit is forecast for the next year; what dividend is expected to be paid and the profits cover therefor; the expected placing price and yield at that price; and the total amount of capital in issue or to be issued.[15]

In all other cases the broker's application should state the total amount of the security to be issued and the proportion to be placed.[16]

If securities are to be placed with a broker member of another federated stock exchange (not being a broker whose name appears in the advertisement) the Federation and sponsoring brokers are asked to ensure that his clients are not given a price advantage as against clients of brokers other than the sponsoring brokers.[17]

When a company is allowed to place securities, at least 35 per cent of the issued amount of equity capital, and at least 30 per cent of the issued amount of fixed income securities must in fact be placed. Of the amount placed at least 25 per cent of equity capital, or securities convertible into equity capital, and at least 20 per cent of other securities must be offered to the market.[18] In placings of fixed income securities of £1,000,000 to £5,000,000, a two-tranche system will apply, whereby 10 per cent of the amount placed must be offered to the market initially, and a further 10 per cent must be at the call of the market until noon on the day after publication of the advertised particulars. In the case of placings of fixed income securities in excess of £5,000,000, special arrangements will have to be made with the Quotations Department.[19]

In the case of the London Stock Exchange, jobbers must decide as to the amount of a security they wish to accept on the same terms (including payment) and in no longer time than is allowed by the sponsoring broker to his own clients. This must be a matter of private negotiation between the sponsor and the jobber, for if the jobber were to consult other brokers before the time of acceptance had expired, it would be possible to rig the market. Accordingly such consultation is prohibited.[20]

Having accepted securities, the jobber will begin to deal. His

14. Memorandum on Quotations, para. 9.   15. *Ibid.*, para. 10.
16. *Ibid.*, para. 11.   17. *Ibid.*, para. 12.   18. *Ibid.*, para. 13 (*a*).
19. *Ibid.*, para. 13 (*c*) (iii).   20. *Ibid.*, para. 13 (*b*).

opening price should be realistic, but the memorandum on quotations does not require it to bear any close relation to the placing price.[1] As for the sponsoring broker, he must (so far as the placings are concerned) drop out of the picture. He may not participate in the disposal of securities reserved for the market, nor may he retain securities which he has agreed to place if there is a demand for them.[2]

It is important to the public as share purchasers, and to the stock exchanges as markets, that demand should, if possible, be met by supply. So the memorandum provides that in the case of both fixed income and equity securities not more than 10 per cent may be retained by the market in the face of public demand for the remainder of a placing.[3] In the case of equity capital, a list for names must be kept open during market hours on the day on which the particulars are advertised in the press.[4]

In the case of loan capital (e.g., debentures) a discount of $\frac{1}{2}$ per cent is allowed to the market on the first or only tranche and $\frac{1}{4}$ per cent on the second tranche; the respective discounts in the case of preference capital is $2\frac{1}{4}$d and $\frac{3}{4}$d per £1 of capital.[5]

Placings in foreign currency securities are permitted. International placing systems whereby underwriting, selling and dealer groups receive commission on a uniform placing price, may be adopted. The memorandum provides guidance for the parties to such placings.[6]

Securities which are the subject of a placing may not be dealt in before the grant of a quotation by the Council of the exchange in which they are intended to be placed.[7]

C. IN THE CASE OF INTRODUCTIONS

Normally an introduction is effected by a broker or issuing house as intermediary, and at that stage the issuer is not committed to sell. An introduction is only permitted when there is no commitment to sell the security and either the security in question is quoted on another stock exchange or is already widely held, and there are no other circumstances, including the disposal of a large block of securities which make special marketing arrangements necessary to ensure an orderly market.[8]

Approval in principle to an introduction must always be sought at an early date. The application should give the number of existing holders of the security, the names of the ten largest beneficial holders, and

1. Memorandum on Quotations, para. 13 (c) (v).
2. Ibid., para. 13 (d).   3. Ibid., para. 13 (c) (i).
4. Or on the first business day thereafter: ibid., para. 13 (c) (ii).
5. Memorandum on Quotations, para. 13 (c) (iv).
6. Ibid., para. 14.   7. Ibid., para. 13 (e).   8. Ibid., para. 16.

the amounts held. No commitment to deal in the securities can be entered into until after permission to deal has been granted. The security must be advertised in the same way as a prospectus issue.[9]

The Committee on Quotations view the introduction of big blocks of securities with suspicion. Their concern is to maintain a fair and orderly market. Accordingly where an equity security, in which there is as yet no market, is introduced, the Committee will prescribe that an interval elapses before the commencement of dealings. This is to allow a realistic price to be established and to allow the market to "assess the level at which buying and selling orders are likely to equate". Normally the interval will be quite short, and the memorandum anticipates that application will become effective from the next business day but one following that on which quotation is granted.[10]

D. IN THE CASE OF RIGHTS ISSUES, OPEN OFFERS, AND CAPITALISATION ISSUES

These issues or offers are in essence internal offers by a company to its existing shareholders. The right to receive such offers is normally an incident to the ownership of shares, or else it is provided for in the company's articles. But although the offer is, initially, an internal one, the prospectus or document of offer must comply with "The Admission of Securities to Quotation", Schedule II, Part B;[11] in particular it must show:

(*i*) *Where the securities for which quotation is sought are offered as a rights issue,*

(*a*) as a heading, the date the offer expires, and that the document is of value and negotiable, and that a stockbroker, solicitor or other professional adviser should be consulted immediately in all cases of doubt; and

(*b*) how shares not taken up will be dealt with, and a time, being not less than 21 days, in which the offer may be accepted; and

(*c*) the *pro rata* entitlement; the last day on which transfers were accepted for registration for participation in the issue; how the new shares rank for dividend; the nature of the document of title and proposed date of issue; and how fractions of shares are to be treated.

(*ii*) *Where the securities are a capitalisation issue.*[12]

The matters in (*c*) above, but "the last day on which transfers were *or will be* accepted for registration".

9. See Memorandum on Quotations, para. 16.   10. *Ibid.*, para. 17.
11. I.e., the prospectus where quotation is sought for the securities of a company some part of whose capital is already quoted: see para. 8.
12. See *ibid.*, para. 9.

Of course an offeree may refuse to subscribe. If that happens the memorandum recommends one of the following courses, whichever is most appropriate: sale of the benefit of the shareholder entitled; or an offer to existing shareholders by the provision of application forms for excess shares; or sale for the benefit of the company. In the case of rights and capitalisation issues the old securities generally are not made "ex" (i.e., without) rights until the first business day following the posting of the document of offer. This is in order to ensure that the shareholder can at all times sell and deliver *the whole* of his stake (i.e., his shares with rights attached) in the company. The memorandum enables companies to make arrangements whereby buyers of securities are not automatically deprived of rights merely because a rights issue was, at the time of purchase, offered to, but not accepted or registered by, the seller.[13]

E. IN THE CASE OF SECURITIES ISSUED IN CONSIDERATION OF
ASSETS ACQUIRED
These securities are referred to as "vendor consideration issues". The requirements and procedure for transfers of assets are set out in the acquisitions memorandum.[14]

If the transaction is very substantial, the company's quotation may be temporarily suspended until accounts showing the effect of the transaction are available. If the company's assets after the transactions are substantially cash, quotation may be suspended until the major part of the assets are permanently invested.[15]

If vendors desire to sell holdings of securities which they are to receive as consideration, a broker may on application be permitted to sell the securities through the market before dealings in the remainder of the securities begin, provided that the securities are identical with securities already quoted.[16]

(*i*) *In the case of share options*
Except with the specific approval of the shareholders in general meeting share options may not be granted other than to shareholders on a *pro rata* basis.

(*a*) Employees' share options
Where a company seeks powers to grant options over its equity capital to its employees (and indeed to any persons other than its equity shareholders), the company's brokers must lodge details of

---

13. Memorandum on Quotations, para. 23.
14. "The Admission of Securities to Quotation", p. 17.
15. Memorandum on Quotations, para. 25.
16. *Ibid.*, para. 26.

the option scheme, the resolution to be proposed and other documents with the Quotations Department for approval.[17]

(*b*) Shareholders' share options

All schemes must be specifically approved by an ordinary resolution of the shareholders and must provide for:[18]

(i) a specified total number of shares subject to the scheme;

(ii) the period during which options granted may be exercised;

(iii) the subscription payable on the exercise of the option;

(iv) the transfer or transmission of rights;

(v) the rights of option-holders on the liquidation of the company;

(vi) variations in the subscription price or number of shares, to take account of further issues of capital by the company.

4. Relaxation of the quotation requirements in the case of investment trusts

When an application is made to quote securities of an investment trust, the normal requirements regarding details of assets and liabilities and profit records may not be insisted upon if the management[19] is known to have had satisfactory experience of the management of investment trusts, and the amount that may be invested in any one security or in unquoted securities is restricted. The company's powers of investment, and the policy it will follow, must be clearly set out.[20]

An investment trust may only be quoted in the investment trust section of the Official List if capital profits cannot be distributed as dividends.[1]

5. The grant of quotation

A. UNDER THE FEDERAL SYSTEM

Where an application is made to one federated exchange only, the committee of that exchange will be solely responsible for ensuring that the Federal requirements are complied with, and for the decision to grant or withhold quotation. When an application is made to more than one exchange, it is the joint responsibility of the exchange committees concerned to ensure that the Federal requirements are complied with before granting quotation.

17. See *in extenso* Memorandum on Quotations, para. 28.
18. *Ibid.*, para. 29.
19. "The management" includes the directors and the investment managers.
20. Memorandum on Quotations, para. 30.
 1. See *ibid.*

If a quotation has been refused by another federated exchange, no exchange committee may grant it without the permission of the Federal Committee.[2]

B. NEW ISSUES PANEL

A New Issues Panel, appointed by the Federal Committee, is responsible for advising exchange committees on quotations policy. Brokers applying for quotations must abide by the Panel's decisions on matters arising from their applications; there is a right of appeal to the federated exchange to which application was made.

C. OFFICIAL LIST

Having granted a quotation, the exchange will publish the security in its Official List. The Council of the Stock Exchange, London, may order the quotation of a security in the Official List before all the requirements for quotation have been complied with; but in that case the entry in the Official List must be printed in italics until the requirements have been fully complied with.[3] Unless the Council orders otherwise, the Official List will contain a record of bargains marked by members[4]—and the Council may make separate provisions for the recording of bargains in inactive quoted securities.[5] Members may not publish or sell lists or records of dealings without the sanction of the Council.[6]

D. SUSPENSION AND CANCELLATION OF QUOTATIONS

The grant of quotation may be suspended or cancelled, or the recording of bargains suspended, on the authority of the Council, or of the Chairman, a Deputy Chairman, or two members of the Committee on Quotations.[7]

The Council's decisions regarding:—

(a) the rejection or deferment of an application for quotation; or
(b) suspension or cancellation of quotation; or
(c) suspension of the record;

must be posted in the House.[8]

2. See Prospectus of the Federation of Stock Exchanges in Great Britain and Ireland, Appendix C, reg. II.
3. Rule 159 (3).   4. Rule 159 (4).
5. Rule 159 (5).   6. Rule 159 (6).
7. Rule 159 (7).   8. Rule 159 (8).

B. AFTER THE GRANT OF QUOTATION:
THE RESPONSIBILITY OF COMPANIES
UNDER THE GENERAL UNDERTAKING

Before the grant of quotation all companies must sign a general undertaking that *after* the grant they will provide promptly certain information about their operations and that they will follow certain administrative procedures. It has been commented that the general undertaking "has been used as a vehicle for safeguards and prohibitions which cannot conveniently be put into articles of association or debenture trust deeds".[9] A number of the requirements in the general undertaking may be varied if a stock exchange's Council are satisfied that any of its requirements should not apply in the circumstances of a particular case; but approval for the variation must be specific.[10]

Under the general undertaking companies are obliged:

1. To notify the Quotations Department of the date of the board meeting at which a dividend will be considered, or at which any announcement of the profits or losses in respect of any financial period or part thereof will be approved for publication.

2. To notify the Department by telex, telegram, telephone or letter immediately after the relevant board meeting has been held of—

(*a*) all dividends and/or cash bonuses recommended or declared, or of the decision to pass any dividend or interest payment;

(*b*) the preliminary profits announcements for the year or half year;[11]

(*c*) short particulars of any proposed cash issue of shares or other securities, or any proposed change in the capital structure.[12]

3. To notify the Department without delay:

(*a*) of such particulars of any acquisition or realisation of assets as are prescribed in the Acquisitions Memorandum;[13]

(*b*) of any information required to be disclosed to the Stock Exchange under the provisions of the City Code on Takeovers and Mergers;[14]

---

9. See R. R. Pennington, *The Investor and the Law*, p. 634.
10. Memorandum on Quotations, para. 5.
11. As required by Sched. VII *c* of the Memorandum on Quotations.
12. Announcement of a new issue may be delayed to avoid prejudicing underwriting.
13. See Memorandum on Quotations, pp. 17–23.
14. See pp. 93–98, *post.*

(*c*) of any changes in its directorate;

(*d*) of any proposed change in the general character or nature of the business of the company, or of the group, or any change in voting control or in beneficial ownership of the securities carrying voting control;

(*e*) of any extension of time granted for the currency of temporary documents of title to shares;

(*f*) of intention to make a drawing of any redeemable securities, intimating at the same time the amount and date of the drawing and, in the case of a registered security, the period of the closing of the transfer books (or the date of the striking of the balance) for the drawing;

(*g*) of the amount of the security outstanding after any purchase or drawing has been made;

(*h*) of any other information necessary to enable the shareholders to appraise the position of the company and to avoid the establishment of a false market in the securities.

4. To forward to the Quotations Department four copies of:

(*a*) proofs for approval (through the company's brokers) of all circulars to holders of securities, notices of meetings (other than those relating to routine business of the annual general meeting), forms of proxy and notices by advertisement to holders of bearer securities;

(*b*) all circulars, notices, reports or other documents at the same time as they are issued to holders of securities;

(*c*) all resolutions passed by the company other than resolutions passed at an annual general meeting for the purpose of adopting the report and accounts, declaring dividends, and re-electing directors and auditors.

5. To circularise to the holders of securities, not later than six months from the date of the notice calling the annual general meeting of the company, a half-yearly interim report.

6. To include in or circulate with each annual directors' report and audited accounts or Chairman's statement:

(*a*) (i) a description of the operations carried on by the company or, if the company has subsidiaries, the group;

(ii) if the company or the group carries on widely differing operations, a statement showing (in percentages) the contributions of the respective differing operations to its trading results;

(iii) if the company or the group trades outside the United Kingdom, a statement showing (in percentages) a geographical analysis of its trading operations.

(*b*) if the company has subsidiaries,[15] a list [16] giving for each—

    (i) its name and country of operations;
    (ii) the percentage of its equity capital attributable to the company's interest (direct and/or indirect)

(*c*) if the company or the group has interests in associated companies,[17] a list giving for each—

    (i) its name and country of operation;
    (ii) particulars of its issued share and loan capital, and the total amount of its reserves;
    (iii) the percentage of each class of share and loan capital attributable to the company's interest (direct and/or indirect)

(*d*) a statement of persons holding or beneficially interested in any substantial part of the share capital of the company and the amounts of the holdings in question. Also particulars of the interest of each director (and, so far as he is aware or can by reasonable enquiry ascertain, of his family interests) [18] in the share capital of the company and, otherwise than through the company, any of its subsidiaries, distinguishing between beneficial and other interests.

(*e*) particulars of any arrangement whereunder any director has waived or agreed to waive any emoluments.

7. (*a*) To prepare and make available for inspection at the registered office or transfer office during the usual business hours on

15. Containing similar information to that required in Sched. VII, Part C of "The Admission of Securities of Quotation". As an alternative to circularisation, interim reports may be inserted as paid advertisements in at least two leading daily newspapers.
16. Subsidiaries which are dormant, or not material, are not included. For this purpose a subsidiary company will be considered material if (*a*) the total investment in it normally represents more than 5 per cent of the assets of the company or group, or (*b*) the interest in its profit or loss normally represents an amount which is more than 5 per cent of the profit or loss shown by the accounts of the company or group.
    The particulars required in 6 (*b*) may (if the Committee on Quotations so adjudicates) be omitted for non-trading companies.
17. For the purpose of the general undertaking an "associated company" means a company which is not a subsidiary but in which 25 per cent or more of the equity is held by the company, or, if the company has subsidiaries, by the group companies collectively (i.e., before excluding any proportion attributable to the interests of outside shareholders in the subsidiaries).
    The particulars required in 6 (*c*) need not given if the associated company is dormant or not material, as to which see note 16, *supra*.
18. "Family interests" are, for this purpose, the same interests as those required to be disclosed in stock exchange prospectuses.

any weekday [19] from the date of the notice convening the annual
general meeting until the date of the meeting, and to make available
for inspection at the place of meeting for at least 15 minutes prior to
the meeting, and during the meeting:

(i) a statement, made up to a date not more than one month
prior to the date on which it is made available for inspection, for the
period from the end of that covered by the last previous statement,[20]
of all transactions [1] of each director [2] in each class of the equity share
capital of the company and any of its subsidiaries since the end of
the period covered by the last published statement of such
transactions.[3] The word "director" includes a person who was a
director *at any time* during the relevant period, but the information
required does not extend to transactions at a time when he was not a
director;

(ii) copies of all directors' service contracts unless expiring or
determinable by the employing company without payment of compensation within one year. Where any such contract is not in writing, a memorandum of its terms;

(*b*) to state in the notice convening the annual general meeting,
or any accompanying circular letter, that the above statement of
director's transactions and copies or memoranda of service contracts will be available for inspection. If there are no such contracts,
that fact must be stated.

8. To insert in the press a notice showing the basis of allotment
in prospectus and other offers, and, if applicable, excess shares. Such
notices must appear not later than the morning after the allotment
letters were posted.

9. To certify transfers of shares against definitive certificates or
temporary documents and to return them on the day of receipt or
(should that not be a business day) on the first business day following their receipt; also to split and return renounceable documents
within the same period.[4]

19. Saturdays and public holidays excluded.
20. Or in the case of the first such statement, not less then 12 months.
1. Including put or call options, whether or not exercised.
2. And also, so far as he is aware or can by reasonable enquiry ascertain, of the
   director's family interests. For the meaning of "family interests", see note 18,
   supra.
3. Or during the previous twelve months if no such published statement has been
   issued.
4. If the company does not maintain its own registration department, appropriate
   arrangements must be made with registrars to ensure compliance with paras.
   9–12.

10. To register transfers and other documents without payment of any fee.[5]

11. To issue, without charge, definitive certificates, within

(*a*) one month of the date of expiration of any right of renunciation;

(*b*) fourteen days of the lodgment of transfers.[6]

12. To arrange for designated accounts, if requested by holders of securities.[7]

13. Where power has been taken under the articles to issue share warrants to bearer:

(*a*) to issue such warrants in exchange for registered shares within fourteen days of the deposit of the share certificates; and

(*b*) to certify transfers against the deposit of share warrants to bearer.

14. To send out with the notice convening a meeting to all shareholders and debenture holders entitled to vote thereat proxy forms with provision for two-way voting on all resolutions intended to be proposed.[8]

15. In the absence of circumstances which have been agreed by the Committee on Quotations to be exceptional, to obtain the consent of equity shareholders in general meeting prior to issuing for cash to other than equity shareholders of the company:

(*a*) equity capital or capital having an equity element;

(*b*) securities convertible into equity capital; and

(*c*) warrants or options to subscribe for equity capital.

16. In the event of a circular being issued to the holders of any particular class of security, to issue a copy or summary of such circular to the holders of all other quoted securities unless the contents of such circular are irrelevant to such other holders.

Summary

The provisions of the general undertaking are diverse, but the thread which links them is quite conspicuous. It is a desire to ensure that companies keep their shareholders (or the Quotations Department which is concerned to protect them) fully informed of all the factors which will or might affect their interests, and to give them the opportunity to take such action as they see fit.

5. See note 4, *supra*.   6. See note 4, *supra*.   7. See note 4, *supra*.
8. Other than resolutions relating to the procedure of the meeting or the remuneration of the auditors.

C. REQUIREMENTS AND PRACTICE
FOR THE ACQUISITION BY
ONE COMPANY OF ANOTHER

One company can acquire a controlling interest in another company in a variety of different ways.

1. By merger

An amalgamation or merger is effected by a contract of sale. The company which is being acquired (the transferor) agrees with the acquiring company (the transferee) to sell to the transferee the whole or part of its undertaking. In return, the transferee company agrees to compensate the members of the transferor company. The transferee company will divide the consideration among them, either in cash or in the form of an allotment of securities in the transferee company itself. The transferor is swallowed up by the transferee and disappears. Section 287 of the Companies Act 1948 provides that the transferor company must:

(i) be wound up voluntarily by its members; and
(ii) pass a special resolution conferring authority on the liquidator to carry out the arrangement.

The sale is binding on all members of the transferor company, whether they voted for the resolution or not. But dissentients can require the liquidator to purchase their interests at prices to be determined by agreement or arbitration.[9]

Mergers are sometimes referred to as "reconstructions", where businesses formerly belonging to the transferor are absorbed under the merger agreement by the transferee, but continue to be managed by substantially the same persons.

2. By a scheme of arrangement

Section 206 of the Companies Act 1948 allows a company to make a compromise or arrangement with its creditors *without* going into liquidation. The arrangement must be agreed by a majority, representing three-quarters in value of the creditors, and be sanctioned by the court. One of the arrangements allowed under section 206 is a scheme whereby the debtor company is merged with another company (the transferee) which takes over its debts and liabilities as well as its assets. Under such a scheme the court has power to approve the dissolution of the debtor company without a formal winding-up.

9. Companies Act 1948, s. 287 (3).

3. By takeover

Both mergers and schemes of arrangement depend upon the companies concerned reaching an agreement. But sometimes companies (and in particular their directors) are fiercely opposed to a merger, which will involve a complete loss of their business identity and their separate legal personality. In that case the intending transferee can resort to a takeover bid. It will make an offer to the transferor's shareholders to purchase their shares at a given price, higher than the stock market price because the transferee company wants to win over the transferor's shareholders. The offer will name a date for acceptance of the offer, and provide for its withdrawal if it is not accepted by a named percentage of the shares held by the transferee's shareholders.

If the offer is accepted, the transferee company may acquire *all* the shares of the transferor *including* the shares of the dissentient minority who did not accept the bid. But notice must be given to the dissentients, who may apply to the court to set aside the takeover. The dissentients must satisfy the court that the takeover is unfair to the body of shareholders as a whole; and it is not enough to show that the takeover is capable of improvement.[10]

A takeover must be distinguished from a merger in that after a takeover the transferor company remains in existence. Its *shares* have been purchased but not its undertaking. Accordingly it becomes a subsidiary of the transferee and does not disappear.

4. The control of takeovers

The control of takeovers is a comparatively recent development, and depends partly on statute and partly on a voluntary code of conduct known as "The City Code on Takeovers and Mergers". In practice stockbrokers do not make takeover bids, for members of the Stock Exchange, London, are forbidden to issue circulars to persons other than their own clients.[11] However, they may with the prior consent of the Council issue *on behalf of a client* a circular to a company's security holders offering to acquire their securities. So although members of the Stock Exchange do not actually make takeover bids, the way in which they are conducted is of close concern to them.

A. BY STATUTE

Section 14 of the Prevention of Fraud (Investments) Act 1958, specifies who may legitimately distribute circulars containing offers to purchase shares—which would include circulars containing take-

10. *Re Grierson, Oldham and Adams Ltd.,* [1968] Ch. 17; [1967] 3 All E.R. 192.
11. Rule 78 (1).

over bids. *Certain* dealers in securities (members of recognised stock exchanges are exempt)[12] must under the Act have a principal's licence—holders of which are *among those* whom the Act allows to distribute takeover circulars.[13]

In 1960 the Board of Trade made the Licensed Dealers (Conduct of Business) Rules[14] under powers conferred on the Board by section 7 of the Prevention of Fraud (Investments) Act. The Rules make certain requirements as to takeover offers which licensed dealers *must* observe:

(i) The terms of the offer must be delivered to the transferor company (i.e., to its directors) at least three days before the offer is communicated to the shareholders.

(ii) the offer must (except insofar as it may be totally withdrawn) remain open for acceptance by every offeree for at least 21 days from the date on which the document was dispatched.

(iii) Where the offer is conditional, a date must be specified as the latest date on which the offeror can declare the offer to have become unconditional.

(iv) The acquisition of the securities offered must not be conditional upon the offerees approving or consenting to any payment or other benefit being made or given to any director of the transferor company as compensation for loss of office, or as consideration for his retirement from office.

(v) If the offer relates to less than the total amount in issue of any class of securities of the transferor company the offer must be open to acceptance by *all* the holders of that class of securities. If acceptances are received relating to a greater number of securities than those in respect of which the offer is made, the number of securities to be acquired by the offeror from each of the offerees will be reduced rateably according to the number of securities in respect of which the offer is accepted by each offeree.

The Licensed Dealers (Conduct of Business) Rules 1960,[15] also specify the contents of takeover circulars.[16] In particular they must state:

(i) the latest available middle market quotation for the securities prior to the date of offer;

(ii) at least six middle market quotations during the period of six months immediately preceding the date of the offer, so as to give a fair view of price fluctuations during that period;

12. Prevention of Fraud (Investments) Act 1958, s. 2 (1) (*a*).
13. *Ibid.*, s. 14 (3) (*a*).   14. S.I. 1960 No. 1216.   15. See p. 92, *ante.*
16. See the Licensed Dealers (Conduct of Business) Rules, 1960, Sched. 1, Part 1, and Sched. 2.

(iii) where there is no quotation, at least six recorded dealing prices during the six months preceding the offer so as to give a fair view of price fluctuations during that period.

Other matters to be disclosed in takeover circulars are the number of shares in the transferor company already held by the offerors, the proposed consideration for the shares bid for, and the terms of the offer generally. Where the directors of the transferor company have recommended acceptance of an offer, the offer must state each director's shareholding in the transferor company, whether they propose to accept the offer in respect of their own shares, and what benefits they will receive as a result of the acceptance.[17]

The Rules for takeover offers and circulars apply only to licensed dealers, but in practice firms of licensed dealers are seldom instrumental in the distribution of takeover circulars. Nevertheless the Rules are generally observed by offerors who are not legally bound by them. The Jenkins Committee on Company Law (which reported in 1962)[18] recommended that the Board of Trade should have power to make similar Rules applicable to *every* takeover offer and *every* takeover circular. The Committee also recommended that circulars should no longer be required to be sent through an authorised channel or approved by the Board of Trade, but that anyone should be free to distribute them. This freedom would of course be subject to safeguards such as those contained in the existing Rules.

B. THE CITY CODE ON TAKEOVERS AND MERGERS

(i) Nature of the Code

This Code,[19] which was published on March 27th 1968, was prepared at the suggestion of the Stock Exchange, London, and the Governor of the Bank of England. It was drawn up by the City Working Party, which contains representatives of the Issuing Houses Association, the Accepting Houses Committee, the Association of Investment Trust Companies, the British Insurance Association, the Committee of London Clearing Bankers, the Confederation of British Industry, the National Association of Pension Funds and the Stock Exchange, London. The Working Party's aim was to devise a system of *voluntary self-discipline* based on the Code and administered by the City's own representatives. The Panel on Takeovers and Mergers is the body which administers the Code. Its role is supervisory, but it is available for consultation

17. *Ibid.*, Sched. 3.
18. Cmnd. 1749.
19. See Introduction to the City Code, p. 2.

at any stage before a formal offer is made to a company, as well as during the course of a takeover transaction. The Introduction to the Code states the belief that the system will "possess a degree of flexibility and speed in action which would be difficult to achieve in any more legalistic procedures imposed by statute".

(ii) The general principles

The Code is divided into general principles of conduct to be observed when takeover bids are made, and rules which in effect exemplify the application of the general principles in practice. The general principles are as follows:

(a) Persons engaged in takeovers and mergers should observe *the spirit* as well as the precise wording of the principles and the ensuing rules.

(b) It is inevitable that the Code will impinge on the freedom of action of boards of directors and other persons involved in takeovers and mergers.

(c) Shareholders must have in their possession sufficient evidence, facts and opinions upon which an adequate judgment and decision can be reached, and sufficient time to make an assessment and decision. *No relevant information may be withheld from them.*

(d) At no time after a *bona fide* offer has been communicated to an offeree company's board, or after it has come within the reasonable contemplation of the board that a *bona fide* offer is likely, may the board take any action in relation to the affairs of the company, without the approval of their shareholders in general meeting, which could effectively result in any *bona fide* offer being frustrated, or in the shareholders being denied an opportunity to decide on its merits.

(e) All parties to the bid or transaction must use every endeavour to prevent the creation of a false market in the shares of either the offeror or offeree company.

(f) A board which receives an offer or is approached with a view to an offer being made should normally, in the interests of its shareholders, seek competent outside advice.

(g) Rights of control must be exercised in good faith and the oppression of a minority is wholly unacceptable.

(h) All shareholders of the same class of an offeree company must be treated similarly by an offeror company.

(i) If, after a bid is reasonably in contemplation, an offer has been made to one or more shareholders of an offeree company, any subsequent general offer made by or on behalf of the *same* offeror or his associate [20] to the shareholders of the same class must not be on less favourable terms.

(*j*) During the course of a takeover or merger transaction, or when such is in contemplation, neither the offeror company, the offeree company nor any of their respective advisers may furnish information to some shareholders which is not made available to all shareholders. But this principle does not apply to the furnishing of information in confidence by an offeree company to a *bona fide* potential offeror company, or *vice versa*, nor does it apply to the issue of circulars by members of a stock exchange to their own investment clients, provided such issue has previously been approved by the Panel.

(*k*) Directors of an offeror or offeree company must always, in advising their shareholders, act only in their capacity *as directors*, and not have regard to their personal or family shareholding or their personal relationship with the companies. It is the shareholders' interests *taken as a whole* which should be considered, together with those of employees and creditors.

(*l*) Any document or advertisement addressed to shareholders containing information, opinions or recommendations from the board of an offeror or offeree company, or its respective advisers, must be treated with the same standards of care as if it were a prospectus within the meaning of the Companies Act 1948. Special care must be taken over profit forecasts.

(*iii*) Sanctions on breach of the Code

The Code does not of course bind the parties to a takeover or merger in the same way as an Act of Parliament. Nor can it be compared with professional rules (such as the Rules of the Stock Exchange) which are binding upon a defined group of people (such as the members of the Stock Exchange) and (so far as *they* are concerned) have the force of law. There is no clearly defined body of persons to whom the Code applies. It does not pretend to be anything more than a *voluntary code* of behaviour governing those who are involved in a certain kind of transaction. Nevertheless, there are many examples of unwritten, but generally accepted trade usages which the courts have recognised as legally binding: *a fortiori*, if a widely representative body of city men agree upon a course of conduct, enunciate it in a written code, and set up a panel to ensure its observance, it is submitted that there is a clear and general intention to establish usages which have the force of law. Further

20. "Associates" include a subsidiary, fellow subsidiary or parent company; bankers or stockbrokers who normally act for the company; its financial advisers; and its directors.

evidence of that intention is contained in the Policy Statement dated April 28th 1969, which invests the Director-General of the panel with a semi-judicial character and demonstrates a readiness on the part of the panel to apply what sanctions it can to deal with a breach of the Code. The following points in the policy statement are examples of the teeth which the panel can show in face of such a breach:

(a) The panel may have recourse to private or public censure, or in the case of a flagrant breach of the Code, "further action designed to deprive the offender temporarily or permanently of his ability to practise in the field of takeovers and mergers". As in many other fields of business it is a great advantage to an offeror to have a *reputation* for honesty; the threat of censure (and in particular of public censure) is therefore a potent one.

(b) The Council of the Stock Exchange, London, agreed to accept the findings of the panel or its appeal committee as proof that the Code has been broken. Under Stock Exchange Rule 16 (4) the Council may censure, suspend or expel any member found by either body to have acted in breach of the Code.

The federated stock exchanges and the Executive Committee of the Issuing Houses Association will take similar action against their members.

(c) Where the panel is of the opinion that public censure would not be an adequate sanction, it will report both exempted and licensed dealers who break the Code to the Board of Trade, and invite the Board to take this report into consideration with a view to the possibility of action under the Prevention of Fraud (Investments) Act 1958. Under the Act, the Board may, in certain circumstances, revoke the exemption of an exempted dealer or the licence of a licensed dealer.[1] The effect of such a revocation would be that the person concerned would no longer be permitted (subject to the exceptions stated in the Act) to carry on the business of a dealer in securities or to circulate any offer to buy or sell securities.

The policy statement of April 1969 states that "the panel has been assured by the Board of Trade that they will take into prompt consideration the facts relevant to the exercise of their powers and disclosed in any such report by the panel".

It will be observed that while the panel makes rulings, it generally recommends the necessary sanctions to others. All the same, the sanctions which it is able to recommend are powerful, and tend to give it the character of a court.

1. In the case of licensed dealers there is an appeal procedure.

(iv) The panel's supervisory role

The panel's role includes the prevention as well as the punishment of mischief. For example:

(*a*) The Director-General or his deputy are available at all times to give rulings on the interpretation of the Code. They will give their rulings as promptly as is necessary to the free functioning of takeover and merger business.

(*b*) During the currency of a takeover bid the panel may request the Council of the Stock Exchange to suspend the quotation of any security—particularly where it is necessary "to prevent dealings in securities ... during a bid situation in the absence of adequate information or clarification of some position or state of affairs".

(*c*) The panel may request the Council to refuse quotation for new securities to be issued in connection with an acquisition, where a breach of the Code has been committed.

(*d*) In the event of a takeover involving exchange control consent, the panel will keep in close consultation with the Bank of England during the currency of the offer, in order that the Bank of England may satisfy itself that the conditions under which such consent is granted are properly observed.

(v) Judicial character of the panel

The status and force of the Code are reinforced by the sanctions which the panel can impose, and the powers which it can exercise to ensure that its provisions are observed. The reputation of the panel, and hence its authority, must depend upon the fact that it acts judicially; it is an important fact that the panel has no power to make findings or recommendations without the alleged offender being present and having the opportunity of a hearing.

There is a right of appeal to the Appeal Committee, which consists of a chairman and three members of the panel who did not sit at the first hearing: one of the three must represent the City body (if any) to which the alleged offender belongs. The decision of the Appeal Committee is in all cases final and publication of the panel's findings will be delayed until after the appeal (if any) has been heard. Both the panel and the Appeal Committee have distinguished lawyers as their chairmen.

(vi) Conclusion

It is to be hoped that the authority of the Code on Takeovers and Mergers, and the panel which supervises its operation will increase with the passage of time. The City's desire for flexibility postulated a voluntary system; but all voluntary systems, if generally accepted and complied with, tend to become binding in the end. The Code may nevertheless retain its flexibility if the widely differing circumstances of each case are looked at on their own, and old cases are not treated as setting an over-rigid body of precedents.

D. AFTER THE ACQUISITION OF ANOTHER COMPANY

1. The Acquisitions Memorandum

After a quoted company has made a substantial acquisition or disposal of its shares or undertaking, it has, in certain circumstances, a duty of disclosure to the Stock Exchange. The Memorandum on Quotations contains a "Memorandum on Acquisitions and Realisations of Subsidiary Companies, Businesses or Fixed Assets" which requires quoted companies to announce specified acquisitions or disposals. The relevant transactions are divided into four categories:

A. CLASS 1

Where the assets dealt in, net profits, or consideration involve the company's assets, or profits to the extent of 15 per cent or more. An announcement must be made to the Quotations Department and the press, and a circular sent to shareholders.[2]

B. CLASS 2

Where 5–15 per cent of the company's assets or profits are involved. An announcement must be given to the Quotations Department and, if desired, directly to the press, giving particulars of the transaction. No circular need be sent to shareholders.

C. CLASS 3

Where less than 5 per cent of the company's assets or profits are involved.

(i) Where the transaction is for cash, no announcement or circular is required.

(ii) Where the consideration includes securities for which quotation is being sought, it will be necessary to announce to the Quotations Department the amount of securities issued, and brief details of the assets being acquired.

2. The contents of the circular are the same as the contents of the prospectus sent to the Quotations Department by a company which already has securities quoted in that particular exchange. See "Admission of Securities to Quotation", Sched. II, Part B.

D. CLASS 4

Where the company acquires or disposes of directors' or substantial shareholders' interests. The Quotations Department should be informed of all details. The Department may on the instructions of the Council require that a circular be sent to shareholders and that their approval of the transaction be sought.

In deciding whether a circular should be sent to shareholders the Council may aggregate acquisitions or realisations that have taken place since either the publication of the last accounts, or the issue of the last circular, whichever is the later. Such aggregate transactions may then be treated as if they were one transaction if they were all completed within a short space of time.[3]

2. The Monopolies and Mergers Act 1965

The Monopolies and Mergers Act 1965 enlarged the Monopolies Commission which was set up under the Monopolies and Restrictive Practices (Inquiry and Control) Act 1948. The Commission consisted of between four and ten members appointed by the Board of Trade, and had a duty to investigate "monopoly conditions" in respect of the supply, processing and export of goods. The 1965 Act widened the Commission's area of investigation to include the supply of services; and the Commission was given power for the first time to examine the effect of a *merger* between business enterprises.

A. MONOPOLIES RESULTING FROM MERGERS; FUNCTIONS OF THE MONOPOLIES COMMISSION

Section 6 of the 1965 Act provides that where it appears to the Board of Trade that:

(i) two or more enterprises,[4] one at least carried on in the United Kingdom by or under the control of a company incorporated here, have within the past six months ceased, or are about to cease to be distinct[5] enterprises; and

3. See the Acquisitions Memorandum, para. 8.
4. Enterprises are defined by s. 7 (2) as "the activities or any part of the activities of a trade or business".
5. By s. 7 (3) two enterprises must be treated as ceasing to be distinct enterprises if at any time they are brought under common ownership or control. By s. 7 (4) the following enterprises are treated as carried on under common control: (*a*) those of inter-connected bodies corporate (i.e., members of the same group) such as a company and its subsidiaries; (*b*) those carried on by any two or more bodies corporate of which the same person or group of persons has control; (*c*) an enterprise carried on by a body corporate together with one carried on by the persons controlling that body corporate.

(ii) either (*a*) as a result, at least *one-third* of certain goods or services are or will be supplied in the United Kingdom by or to any *one* person, or by or to the persons by whom the enterprises are carried on; or (*b*) the value of the assets taken, or to be taken over, exceeds £5 million;

then the Board may refer the matter to the Monopolies Commission for investigation and report within, normally, six months.

B. POWERS OF THE BOARD OF TRADE

If the above conditions are fulfilled, the Commission will decide whether the monopoly condition operates against the public interest. If, according to the Commission's report as laid before Parliament, the monopoly condition does so operate, then the Board may exercise its powers under section 3 of the 1965 Act.[6]

With regard to mergers, the following are the Board's most important powers:

(i) to prohibit or restrict bodies corporate from becoming interconnected bodies corporate;[7]

(ii) to provide for the division of any trade or business by the sale of part of the undertaking carried on by any one person or two or more interconnected bodies corporate, or for the division of interconnected bodies corporate, and for this purpose the Board may order:

(*a*) the transfer or vesting of property, rights, liabilities or obligations;

(*b*) the adjustment of contracts, whether by the discharge or reduction of any liability or obligation or otherwise;

(*c*) the creation, allotment, surrender or cancellation of any shares, stock or securities;

(*d*) the formation or winding-up of a company or other association (corporate or unincorporated), or the amendment of the memorandum and articles or other instruments regulating any company or association;

(*e*) the extent to which, and the circumstances in which, provisions of the order affecting a company or association in its share capital, constitution or other matters may be altered by the company or association; and the registration of the order by companies or associations so affected;

(*f*) the continuation, with any necessary change of parties, of any legal proceedings.

6. Monopolies and Mergers Act 1965, s. 3 (5).
7. *Ibid.*, s. 3 (6).

C. THE BOARD'S RIGHT OF INSPECTION

The Board may appoint an inspector to investigate and report on the affairs or the ownership of a company, for the purpose of obtaining information on which to exercise the powers conferred by section 3 of the Monopolies and Mergers Act 1965.[8]

8. See note 6, *supra.*

CHAPTER 5

Floor Procedure

THE JOBBING SYSTEM IN PRACTICE

The reputation of the London Stock Exchange as a fair market depends upon the ethical standards of its members and the safeguards inherent in its own system of dealing. A crucial safeguard is the division of its members into two classes, brokers and jobbers. The two classes are complementary yet distinct. The broker buys or sells securities as the agent of the public for a commission: the jobber buys and sells securities as a principal on his own behalf and has no relations with the public. No member may do business both as a broker and as a jobber, and there is a custom that the two classes deal with one another at arm's length. So in floor bargaining each member will keep his cards close to his chest by adopting a form of words designed (a) to conceal his intentions, and (b) to avoid committing himself. Prices are made by the jobbers in open competition with each other, and if a jobber is to attract business, he must make a competitive price. If he were not bound by custom to deal with a broker at arm's length, he would be able to collaborate with him in the rigging of prices. The advantage of the London system is not only that the broker is able to deal for his client at the best price ruling at the time, but in addition the client has no grounds for *suspecting* that the price is not the best. Generally, if the client is acquainted with the system, he is confident that the best price has been obtained on his behalf.

A. FUNCTION OF THE JOBBER

A jobber deals only with fellow members of the Stock Exchange, and he deals only on his own behalf. He may be described as a wholesaler in securities. Jobbers nowadays specialise in securities of a particular type (e.g., shares in companies in a particular industry) because of the very great expansion in the number of securities which have sought and obtained a stock exchange quotation during the past fifty years. Physically, jobbers need to remain in the same place on the floor so that they may readily be found by brokers wishing to deal in the securities in which they specialise. Their function is to provide a continuous security market for the public by so adjusting their prices, if necessary in anticipation, as to strike a balance between supply and demand. A jobber does not charge a commission; his profit—known as the "jobber's turn"—consists in the amount by which his sale price exceeds the purchase price or (where he has contracted to sell shares which he has not yet bought) the amount by which his buying price is less than the price at which he originally contracted to sell. Of course, a jobber may make a loss instead of a profit, and in difficult market conditions losses may predominate. "Even so," runs the London Stock Exchange Code of Dealing, "it is the proud tradition of jobbers that they continue to deal and provide a continuous share market for the public in all but the most exceptional circumstances."

The jobber's price, in the case of a company which is a going concern, is for a marketable number of shares, and reflects value put on investment (or disinvestment) of money. But some holdings have a value disproportionate to their size. Suppose, for example, that 500,000 shares are a minority holding, but that 600,000 would be enough to give the holder control over the company. Obviously the 600,000 shares are worth more to the holder than 1·2 times the value of the 500,000: they have a peculiar value of their own. The jobber's price does not normally reflect such a notional special value: it reflects the value of an ordinary holding adjusted to supply and demand. Similarly where there is no prospect of a company going into liquidation, the jobber's price does not reflect their notional value on such a liquidation.

However, where a takeover is thought likely, shares often acquire a special value at the prospect. The jobber's price may reflect this, even though no firm indication of a bid has been given.

B. FUNCTION OF THE BROKER

The broker's function is quite simply to buy and sell securities as the agent of the public. Jobbers may not deal with the public, and so the brokers are the only link between the public and the Stock Exchange. For his agency the broker charges a commission. The minimum scale of commission is governed by the Rules and Regulations of the Stock Exchange, which forbid any reduction not authorised in the Rules.[1] All broker firms dealing in the Stock Exchange have been elected members of it, and every bargain

1. See Chapter 7.

entered into on the floor must be made and executed in a manner which conforms with its Rules. A broker is not, however, bound to deal for his client on the Stock Exchange: instructed to purchase shares, he may be able to acquire them privately instead of in the market. But except as authorised by the Rules relating to business with country brokers,[2] business in overseas stock exchanges,[3] and business in Euro-Currency Bonds,[4] he may not execute an order with a non-member unless he has previously offered the business in the Exchange on the same terms as those proposed to or by that non-member;[5] moreover he retains the agent's general legal responsibility to act in the best interests of his principal—but if he can make as good a bargain on the Exchange as outside it, he is obliged to deal on the Exchange.[6]

It is an increasingly important part of the broker's function to give advice. He is not bound to advise every client. So a broker may be instructed by his client to sell 500 shares in the A company when he (the broker) knows that a takeover bid is imminent, and the value of those shares is liable to rise steeply. He is under no duty to advise the client if he has unequivocal instructions to sell those particular shares. But the position would be different if the client said: "I am considering asking you to sell my 500 shares in the A company. Do you think that this is the right moment to sell?" Clearly this is a request for advice, and the broker would have to give honest advice in the light of all the circumstances of which he knew or ought to have known at the time. In particular, where a broker has access to privileged information about a company, and is aware of circumstances which will affect the value of its securities, he must not allow that knowledge to operate to the disadvantage of his client.[7]

The broker's duty is to his client and to the Stock Exchange

The broker's duties to his client will be extensively described in the next chapter.[8] These duties are mere illustrations of the broker's overriding duty: to deal for his client to the best advantage. Obviously, this means dealing at the best price. Less obviously, the

---

2. Rule 88*a*.
3. Rule 88*b*.
4. Rule 88*d*.
5. Rule 88 (2).
6. Rule 88 (1).
7. And see "The City Code on Takeovers and Mergers", Chapter 4, *ante*.
8. Pages 124–136, *post*.

broker must inform his client when he is acting as a principal (e.g., selling the client his *own* shares), and a broker must not exceed his instructions even if he thinks it would be in his client's best interests for him to do so.

Although a broker has a primary duty to his client, he has in addition a duty to the Stock Exchange and to its individual members. It would be inappropriate to describe this duty as secondary; rather the broker is said to have a double duty. In reality the two duties interlock. The broker must have the confidence of his client if the client is to retain him for further transactions; and this confidence can be gained only if he has a reputation for fair dealing. A client is not likely to retain a broker who conducts his business in such a way that jobbers are reluctant to have further dealings with him in the future. The broker will therefore enhance his own interests by observing his duty to the Stock Exchange which, says the Code of Dealing, "is fulfilled by obedience to the Rules, both in letter and spirit, and by observance of the customs and usages of the House". Of course, clients are nearly always unfamiliar with the Rules, customs and usages of the Stock Exchange, and a client may unwittingly give his broker instructions which conflict with the broker's duty to observe them. The broker must not accept such instructions. If he understands the instructions clearly, he should get in touch with his client, and explain how they conflict with his duty to the Stock Exchange. The client will usually be willing to give alternative instructions which do not meet with the same objection, and it is open to the broker to suggest such an alternative. The important point is that instructions must be acceptable to the client who gave them, to the broker who receives them, and to the Stock Exchange on which they are carried out.

The broker deals with other members as a principal: so that where his client cannot find the money on a purchase, or deliver the securities on a sale, the broker is obliged to arrange the settlement of the contract himself. This obligation is an inevitable corollary to the broker's duty not to disclose his client's identity to the jobber. As a result, the jobber cannot pick and choose the persons with whom he contracts. He does not know whether they are reliable or unreliable. Such a choice is an essential element in the freedom which a contracting party should enjoy: and to compensate the jobber for not having that choice, the broker is bound by the Rules and Regulations of the Stock Exchange to assume personal responsibility for his client's liabilities. It is to the broker alone that the jobber looks for satisfaction.

C. FLOOR PROCEDURE

1. Making a Price

A. WHERE THERE IS A SUBSTANTIAL TURNOVER IN THE SHARES

When a broker approaches a jobber on the floor of the Stock Exchange, the jobber will be ready to quote a price. The broker, in accordance with his duty to his client, is careful not to let the jobber know the name of his client or whether he intends to buy or sell. So the broker's opening words will be, "What are A and Co ordinary?"—meaning, "What price are you quoting for the ordinary shares of A and Co?" Clearly, this is a mere request for information and not an offer.

If there is sufficient supply and sufficient demand, the jobber will quote a double price, e.g., "1·50–1·52". The lower figure is the price at which he will buy, the higher figure that at which he will sell. Quotation of a double price amounts to an undertaking by the jobber to buy (if the broker wants to sell) and an undertaking to sell (if the broker wants to buy). A simple quotation amounts to an undertaking to deal in a reasonable number of shares at the specified prices. What is reasonable may depend on the nature and value of the shares, and the state of the market.[9]

When a broker goes into the market he may have firm instructions, or he may be merely "checking his market" i.e., collecting quotations. In the former case, if he shows his hand, he commits himself to a bargain. The procedures for dealing are set out below:

(*i*) *The broker has no firm instructions. He goes to investigate the price of a particular share and the amount available.*
Broker: "What are A and Co?"
Jobber: "1·50–1·52."
Broker: "I am only quoting. What is the size of the (i.e., your) market?"
Jobber: "I will make that (i.e., 1·50–1·52) in 1,000." Here the broker has not committed himself to a bargain. He may approach other jobbers, discover their terms in the same way, and then report back to his client.

(*ii*) *Broker has firm instructions.*
(*a*) If he has checked the price with a particular jobber as in (*i*), and that jobber's price is better than that of others, he will approach

9. Where the turnover is small, the jobber may take a cautious view, and be unwilling to deal in a very large number of A and Co. If so, he will protect himself by saying "1·50–1·52 in 200", indicating thereby that 200 is the maximum number of shares that he will deal in at the price quoted.

that jobber again (for he is likely to offer the most advantageous price) with the intention of dealing.

(*b*) If the broker has not checked the prices with jobbers before-hand:

Broker: "What are A and Co?"

Jobber: "1·50–1·52."

Broker: "What is the size of the market?"

Jobber: "I will make that in 1,000."

If the broker leaves it at that, he may move on to other jobbers for quotations.

But beyond this point he commits himself, so:

(*iii*) *If the client has limited the broker as to amount, e.g., to sell 500 A and Co (this limit is known as the "way" of a member's business).*

Broker (continuing from (*ii*)): "Is there any way in 500?"

(This commits him to dealing).

Jobber: "Yes. I'll make you 1·50–1·51½."

(*iv*) *If the client has limited the broker as to price, e.g., to buy at 2·38½.*

Broker: "What are A and Co?"

Jobber: "2·35–2·40."

Broker: "I am limited. I am 1½p out in 500" (note that the broker does not disclose in which direction he is 1½p out).

Jobber: "I could deal one way" (meaning that he could make *either* 2·36½–2·40 or 2·35–2·38½).

Broker (hoping for the 2·35–2·38½ which will suit him): "Very well, you may open me."

Jobber: "Give you 1½p" (i.e., he will buy at 2·36½ or sell at 2·40).

Broker: "Sorry, I am a buyer at 2·38½".

Suppose that the jobber had said: "Take 38½." This would indicate that the jobber was willing to sell 500 at 2·38½, and the bargain would have been clinched. If the jobber's offer coincides with the broker's instructions in this way, the broker must not bluff his way out of the bargain by pretending that his instructions were to sell. It would of course be possible for him to do so, because his initial answer, "I am 1½p out" was necessarily ambiguous. However, such a trick is contrary to the recognised codes of the Exchange; and since the only motive for it is to get the opportunity of a better bargain with another jobber, the danger of exposure would be considerable.

B. WHERE TURNOVER IS SMALL

(*i*) *"Negotiation" and "nominal" prices*

The supply or demand for a particular security may be so small that jobbers have difficulty in making a dealing price. Nevertheless, a jobber may still quote a price, and cover himself by expressing it as a basis for negotiation (to show that he regards a bargain as feasible), or as a nominal basis (where he thinks there is little prospect of a bargain: this amounts to an invitation to the broker to make a proposition of his own).

Where a broker has no firm instructions and is investigating the market as in (*i*) above,
the broker will say "What are B and Co ordinary?"
and the jobber may reply "1·90–1·93 negotiation" (if he is hopeful of dealing either way),
or "1·90–1·93 nominal" (if he is less hopeful). The broker may go on to say that he is only quoting, and ask the jobber the size of the market; then, having obtained the information he requires he will move on to other jobbers.

The broker might go to three jobbers, who all quote "negotiation", and then approach a fourth who makes a firm unqualified quotation, wider than the negotiation prices of the other three. The broker then has a right, by custom, to "challenge" the earlier negotiation quotations for a bargain. *The challenge should be in the middle of the jobber's negotiation price if the broker is not to commit himself, so:*

Broker: "What are B and Co?"
Jobber: "1·90–1·93 negotiation."
Broker: "I am a dealer at 1·91$\frac{1}{2}$."
Jobber: "May I open you in 200?"
Broker: "Yes." (If the broker says "No" the challenge ends there.)
Jobber: "Sell."
Broker: "I am a buyer" (and the bargain is made at 1·91$\frac{1}{2}$).

If, however, the broker is also a seller, no business is done. Both he and the jobber are bound in confidence not to disclose the position of the other to the market at large.

Suppose that the jobber is not prepared to open the broker either way. When the broker says: "I am a dealer at 1·91$\frac{1}{2}$", the jobber will reply: "I can't touch you."
If the broker challenges above the middle, e.g.:
    "I am a dealer at 1·92",
ipso facto he discloses his position as buyer. Conversely, if he challenges below it, he reveals himself as a seller. In both cases he commits himself to dealing if the jobber accepts his challenge.

All the above formulae have a common characteristic. It is that brokers and jobbers are doing business at arm's length, and with the minimum of disclosure. Normally disclosure involves a commitment to do a bargain, but there is an exception where a buying broker challenges in the middle, and it turns out that the jobber is a buyer too. In that case the parties' respective positions remain a secret shared only by themselves.

(ii) One way markets

Suppose that jobbers have heavily oversold shares in the C Company. When a jobber is approached by a broker who asks him "What are C and Co?" it seems very likely that the broker has instructions to buy. This is known as a "buyers only" market. The jobber cannot be absolutely certain that the broker is a buyer, however, so he protects himself by quoting a very wide price e.g., "Basis 3·25–3·45, Buyers only." Because C and Co are scarce, the jobber feels that a buyer would be willing to pay a high price. But for all he knows, the broker has instructions to sell; the jobber realises that no one sells C and Co without good reason, and in view of that he will not offer the broker any more than is prudent.

Conversely C and Co may have been overbought by jobbers, so that a "sellers only" market is the result. Here the jobber's phrase might be, "Basis 3·25–3·45. Sellers only." [10]

Where markets are virtually one way, the broker will have great difficulty in getting reasonable terms for his client. Yet he is under a duty to get the best terms he can. A jobber whose bid is a little less wide than those of other jobbers will do a great amount of business. [11] Recognised custom prevents brokers from actually disclosing one jobber's bid to another. They cannot attempt to even out the market in *that* way. In this context the Code of Dealing [12] seems to come to the broker's help, by permitting him, where there is (e.g.) a "buyers only" market, to hint in reply to a jobber's opening that he is in fact a buyer: and *vice versa* where there is a "sellers only" market:

"In such cases, the broker can only give an indication, as loose or as firm as he chooses, in an endeavour to seek the best terms for his client."

2. When a mere quotation becomes binding

A jobber's quotation is intended for the approval or rejection of the broker's client. When a broker is investigating the market, he will receive a number of quotations which he will then consider.

10. The phrase is based on his own position (a bear) or on known buying limits or indications.
11. Here the jobber may be an unwilling bull, having too many shares and reluctant to buy more.
12. See Code of Dealing, p. 21.

A quotation may be varied by the jobber and it does not become binding as a price unless and until both the broker and jobber have agreed to make it so. Such an agreement must be clear in its terms, and specify, for example, times and dates at which a quotation will commit both sides. The agreement must bind both the broker and the jobber. It might bind the jobber, for instance, to sell D and Co shares even if between quotation and bargain he has made other bargains disposing of all his available shares in D and Co. It might bind the broker to deal at the quoted price, even if in the meantime the jobber has made other bargains at a lower price. But unless there is a contrary agreement, a price made by a jobber to a broker for quotation to his client, is subject to alteration by the jobber in the interval.

A quotation is for approval or rejection of the client. So if a broker leaves a jobber saying, "I am on the 'phone," or something like that, the jobber is under no obligation to get in touch with him later to find out his position, nor is the jobber under any obligation to hold his price.

3. Two exceptional cases in which a broker must disclose one jobber's quotation to another

A. WHERE HE IS FINDING HIS CHOICE

Suppose that a broker is checking prices quoted by different jobbers in A and Co and he finds that he can *buy* from Black and Co at £2 and *sell* to White and Co at £2. He is then said to have "found his choice". If he chooses to buy from Black and Co at £2, he may do so. But he must disclose his choice to Black and Co. Although they get this disclosure as of right, there is nothing Black and Co can do about it. They cannot refuse to deal, nor can they insist on altering the price which they have made. However, the information will assist Black and Co in gauging the state of the market; the custom applies to all members, and is clearly for their mutual assistance.

B. WHERE HE IS DEALING ON A BACKWARDATION

Suppose that the jobbers Green and Co quote A and Co at 4·20–4·30, and that the jobbers Blue and Co quote them at 4·05–4·15. A broker checking these prices will readily see that he can *sell* to Green at a price *higher* than that at which he can *buy* them from Blue. Obviously he would prefer to deal with Blue. He must however disclose Green's quotation to Blue, and he cannot deal with Blue without Blue's permission. Their exchanges would run as follows:

Broker: "What are A and Co?"
Blue: "4·05–4·15."
Broker: "That gives me a back, do you want to deal?" [13]

Blue and Co now have two courses open to them. Either they can refuse to deal on a backwardation, and adjust their price to overlap with Green's; or they can deal on their own quotation—there may indeed be sound business reasons for doing so.

4. Limits

Those orders whose execution is subject to conditions are described as "limits". The conditions may be imposed by the brokers at (or sometimes without) the express wish of their client. The conditions may refer to

(i) the price alone; or

(ii) the price in conjunction with the number of shares to be dealt in; or

(iii) the terms of delivery.

There are four main types of limit. Their attributes are set out here as in the Code of Dealing. [14]

A. FIRM LIMITS

A broker may decide to leave a sale or purchase limit at a fixed price with one selected jobber until that order is either completed or cancelled. The limit will be understood as being in force until the close of the House the same day unless a longer or shorter period is clearly specified. The broker must inform the jobber accordingly, and leave him in no doubt. In the event of the stock being bid for by another jobber while the jobber is retaining the limit, the jobber is then obliged either to deal with the broker in a reasonable part of the limit or else to release him. The jobber, having accepted the broker's firm limit must do his utmost to complete all or at least part of the broker's order. A broker may not cancel a firm limit before the expiry of the time originally specified except on terms acceptable to the jobber.

B. CONDITIONAL LIMITS

A broker with a firm order may decide to inform more than one jobber that he has business at a price at which it is not possible to deal at once. It is essential, in this case, for the broker to inform the jobbers concerned directly he has completed the order

---

13. The broker is not required to, and would not, *name* Green. He must merely disclose that he has found a "back" elsewhere, and ask Blue if he still wishes to deal.
14. See Code of Dealing, pp. 30–32.

elsewhere (unless specifically asked not to do so by the jobber with whom he dealt), or as soon as he has been advised that the order is cancelled.

C. INDICATIONAL LIMITS

A broker may indicate to a jobber or jobbers that he might have business in a particular share at a certain bid or offered price. Here again, the broker should inform the market if he has completed his business or if his client now has no interest in the share.

The jobber takes on himself the full risk if he deals against purely indicational limits without first ascertaining their current validity.

D. CONTINGENT LIMITS

A broker may receive an order to buy or sell provided he takes into account other governing factors, conditions or contingencies which are a part of the order. A contingent limit frequently imposed upon the dealer is in the form of an order to sell, or buy, at a price, conditional on another share being offered or bid at another price. The most common example is "swap" or exchange orders in Gilt-Edged securities. The price factors may be arbitrarily set by the client. They may be statistically related to yield, or regulated by reference to the expenses involved, or by technical considerations such as the delivery of the securities to be bought or sold. A broker must always inform a jobber whenever a buying or selling limit is contingent.

It will complicate his task, as well as that of the jobbers, if the order links two shares which are dealt in by different markets. It is, however, possible for one jobber to leave a firm proposition, while the broker attempts to deal in the contingent part of the order with another jobber. Flexibility such as this is possible under the jobbing system, but not equally so in any other form of market.

5. The broker's procedure where the size of his order compels him to deal with more than one jobber

Suppose that a client has instructed his broker, X, to sell 5,000 shares in the A Co, at the best price. Suppose also that the market in these shares is normally 1,000 or less, occasionally 2,000 and exceptionally 5,000. It is clear that X will have to use his judgment and his knowledge of the market to the full if he is to make the best bargain for his client. One particular jobber, Brown and Co, may have quoted him a particularly good price. If so, X will consider how many shares Brown and Co can be expected to deal in. Alternative courses now open before him:

(*i*) *X may decide to ask Brown and Co for a proposition which covers all the 5,000 shares.* He might conceivably get it. If Brown and Co make such an offer, and their proposition is favourable enough, then X may decide to sell all 5,000 in the one transaction.

(*ii*) *Brown and Co might propose an acceptable price in some only of the 5,000 shares (say 2,000).* If X accepts that, he is left with the problem of how to dispose of the remaining 3,000. In accepting Brown and Co's bid for the 2,000, he has *established a price.* He can now do one of three things:

(*a*) he may leave a firm limit as to price in the market with Brown and Co, who will retain that limit for a specified period. If, while Brown and Co retain it, White and Co bid a better price for all or some of the remaining 3,000, Brown and Co must deal with X in a reasonable part of the limit, or release him from it; or

(*b*) he may indicate to Brown and Co the price at which he would wish to do further business. This frees him from the price at which he sold the 2,000; or

(*c*) he may ask Brown and Co for a proposition in relation to the remaining 3,000.

Since it is unusual for bargain shares in A Co shares to be effected in parcels greater than 1,000, it is likely that the balance of 3,000 will be subject to bids from other jobbers, White and Co, Grey and Co, Black and Co *et al.*, not in the *whole* balance, but in smaller parcels. Even so, X has established his price, and he is tied to it in the following ways:

(i) He may not deal in the balance (or part of it) at a better price.

(ii) He may not deal in the balance (or part of it) at a worse price without offering the revised price to Brown and Co.

(iii) Where he has left Brown and Co with a firm limit, he must not attempt to deal with the balance elsewhere unless Brown and Co have bid back at a price agreed to between them.

(iv) If while Brown and Co retain a firm limit, X receives further bids from White and Co, Grey and Co and Black and Co for shares in the A Co, he must direct such business to Brown and Co before attempting to deal elsewhere. Alternatively, he must not accept such offers without the consent of Brown and Co.

(v) If Brown and Co have made a firm proposition, and have not withdrawn it, X may not deal with White and Co, Grey and Co or Black and Co, or elsewhere.

(vi) X and Brown and Co may have agreed a time limit for (a), (b) or (c) (above). If they have not concluded a bargain in the balance of 3,000 (or part of it) on its expiry, new market conditions may compel X to lower his selling price in order to complete the order.

He must give Brown and Co the first refusal at the new price. If Brown and Co are not interested in dealing at the new price, X will have to deal with other jobbers. He is expected to deal with each jobber at a price that is fair having regard to the number of shares they offer to buy, and having regard to the price which he established in his initial sale of the 2,000.

Once X has put the balance of 3,000 on the market, Brown and Co must not "touch" that market without X's permission. They must leave the field open for their competing jobbers. For example, they must desist from offering the 2,000 which they have bought for sale: to do so might spoil X's market for the remaining 3,000. If, however, Brown's are approached by one of their competing jobbers, there is nothing to prevent them from concluding a bargain not made at their own instigation.

Where a broker has a large order he should not split it up and attempt (e.g., through several dealers) to bargain with several jobbers simultaneously. This is not in the best interests of his client, and could easily lead to confusion in the market.

6. Put-throughs

A. ORDERS EXECUTED SIMULTANEOUSLY

It often happens that where there is a two-way market in a company's shares, a broker will receive an order from one client to buy, and an order from another client to sell, and the orders are in the same or a similar number. In this situation the Rules allow a broker to create a matching order so as to put all or part of both buying and selling orders through the market. Before attempting to create such matching orders, the broker must consult a jobber who deals in the security and agree with him fair put-through prices. The jobber then has the right to declare what portion of the broker's business he will take at the eventual put-through price, provided he does not thereby prevent the broker executing the order of his client who initiated the business.

The broker will then buy or sell the agreed portion of his shares to the jobber at the agreed price. This device of putting the shares through the jobber's books enables the broker to execute both his orders simultaneously.

The number of shares which jobber and broker wish to put through the market might coincide exactly. Where this is so, the parties will have little difficulty in arranging the transaction. The jobber is not permitted to make the broker agree to a price lower than that at which he bid when they first came together.

But suppose that the jobber will not agree to put through the entire amount. If he and the broker can devise an equitable basis for putting *some* of the shares through, and the broker's clients will do business on that basis, then everyone will be satisfied. If, however, the agreed put-through price is unacceptable to the broker's clients, he may approach the jobber anew. They may then agree to vary the terms of the put-through provided they can find a price which is fair to both the principals.[15] If the jobber indicates that the price is not fair in this or any other respect, and refuses to accept it for that reason, the broker cannot approach another jobber in the hope that he will accept it.

A jobber who has received a put-through proposition must maintain his previous price however much the broker's confidential disclosures tempt him to alter it. Other business, or market conditions, may force him to alter it in the end, but in that case it is his duty to inform the broker of the fact.

B. ORDERS MADE SIMULTANEOUSLY

In the normal put-through arrangement governed by Rule 90 (1), the jobber has the right to declare what proportion of the business put through his books he wishes to take for himself. But members of the same family, or two subsidiary companies in the same group, to take two examples, may wish to transfer identical blocks of the same shares between themselves. They would not use the stock market if, in the event of the shares being put through the market, the jobber had the option of purchasing some of the shares himself and so breaking up holdings which they wanted to transfer *in toto*. Rule 90 (2) deprives the jobber in those circumstances of his right to declare what portion of the broker's business he will take at the put-through price.

It is extremely important for brokers to be clear in their own minds, and to make it clear to jobbers, whether they are negotiating a put-through under Rule 90 (1) or under Rule 90 (2).

C. THE DIVISION OF PUT-THROUGHS BETWEEN JOBBERS

Where a broker has a very large number of a particular company's shares to put through, he will get the jobber's assistance in arranging a put-through with other jobbers running a book in the particular share. The Code of Dealing notes that where this happens the risk that the broker will default is borne solely by the jobber who dealt with the broker himself. He accepts the liability of a principal for *both* sides of the transaction—at least where he actually books the whole put-through, and agrees to pass to the participating jobbers

---

15. Rule 90 (3).

cheques representing their proportion of the profits. But the participating jobbers have a moral obligation to bear their proportion of the risk, provided they know the price and the identity of the broker. Arguably, they have a legal obligation too. Their put-throughs should be regarded as collateral to the dealing jobber's put-through, because normally it is the dealing jobber alone who is instrumental in bringing them and the broker together.

D. THE MARKING OF PUT-THROUGHS

Rule 90 (4) provides: "All put-through bargains must be marked by the broker and will be recorded unless withheld by the authority of the Chairman, a Deputy-Chairman, or two members of the Council."

E. JUSTIFICATION OF PUT-THROUGHS

Rule 90 (5) provides: "Members transacting business under this Rule must be prepared to justify their transactions to the Council if called upon to do so." For example, a client might claim that his broker had agreed to a put-through which was unfair and unreasonable from his own point of view. The broker might then be concerned to argue that market conditions and other factors prevented him and the jobber from arriving at a more satisfactory result.

D. MISCELLANEOUS RULES FOR THE PROTECTION OF JOBBERS

(*a*) A jobber's unauthorised clerk is forbidden by the Rules to make a price.[16]

(*b*) Firms of country brokers sometimes have a jobbing side. If a London broker negotiates on the London Stock Exchange as agent for that side he must, by Rule 92b, disclose the fact. Otherwise the London jobber would not know that he is negotiating with a competitor.

(*c*) Before he takes up dealing in a share in which he has not hitherto kept a book, a jobber should, as a matter of courtesy, advise other jobbers who already deal in this share.

(*d*) In the absence of special circumstances, a jobber should not temporarily deal in a share in which he has not previously kept a book unless he intends to continue dealing commercially in the share.

16. Rule 65.

E. FLOOR DISCIPLINE

The Code of Dealing states that all broking and jobbing firms must be prepared to justify to the Stock Exchange Council their actions or those of their dealers, if they fail to observe, in letter or in spirit, any of the practices mentioned in the Code. This is a powerful sanction in view of the Council's virtually unfettered discretion to terminate membership.[17]

17. See *Weinberger* v. *Inglis*, pp. 33–34, *ante*, and see Rule 24.

CHAPTER 6

Dealing

A. PERMITTED AND PROHIBITED DEALINGS

1. Permitted Dealings

Rule 163 lists the securities which may be dealt in on the Stock Exchange. These are:

(*a*) Securities for which quotation has been granted by the Council and which are not subject to a Council Notice suspending or cancelling quotation or suspending dealings.

(*b*) Treasury bills and the bills, mortgages and short term securities of local government authorities and public boards of Great Britain and Northern Ireland.

(*c*) Securities arising out of the disposal of fractions of an entitlement on a rights, capitalisation or other issue and in respect of which an application for quotation is being made.

(*d*) Securities which are quoted in the lists or supplementary lists published by stock exchanges affiliated to the Council of Associated Stock Exchanges.

(*e*) Securities which have been granted a primary listing on the Johannesburg Stock Exchange or have been granted a quotation on any other stock exchange or stockbrokers' association recognised by Rule 203a (1),[1] or on a foreign stock exchange.

(*f*) and (*g*) Various Government and other securities issued under the laws of the United States of America and Canada, and Government securities of the Republic of South Africa.

(*h*) Sub-units of unquoted unit trusts if negotiated by brokers with unit trust managements; but dealings between members in unquoted sub-units are not allowed.

Bargains may be made in the securities of public companies or corporate bodies not listed under Rule 163 with the permission of the Stock Exchange Council.[2] Forms of application for such permission are available, and can be obtained in the Quotations

1. These include all the principal Commonwealth stock exchanges.
2. Rule 163 (2).

Department and at the marking boards. In exceptional circumstances an application may be made to the Head of the Quotations Department to dispense with the permission stipulated by the Rule.

2. Prohibited Dealings

Under the Rules, the Council of the Stock Exchange may prohibit dealings in any security for any cause[3] and such decision must be posted "in the House".[4] Some dealings are prohibited in any event: others are controlled as a matter of policy.

A. DEALINGS PROHIBITED IN ANY EVENT[5]

Certain types of dealing are specifically forbidden:

(i) Prospective dividends.

(ii) "Majorities."

(iii) "Results."

(iv) Securities the quotation of which has been suspended or cancelled on the authority of the Council, the Chairman, a Deputy-Chairman or two members of the Committee on Quotations.

(v) Dealings put through by one broker for another broker.[6]

(vi) Long options, i.e., those done for a period beyond the seventh ensuing account day.[7]

(vii) Dealings in unquoted unit trusts.[8]

(viii) Dealings at below the minimum price if specified in the Official List.[9]

(ix) In addition, no bargains for cash to close a transaction done for the current account and no contango shall be made after 6.30 p.m. on the last dealing day of the current account.[10]

B. DEALINGS PROHIBITED OR CONTROLLED AS A MATTER OF POLICY

The Stock Exchange must try to ensure that bargains are honoured if its public standing is to be maintained and its members protected against default. Accordingly, the Council have, as a matter of public and private policy, made rules which prohibit certain types of business:

(i) Speculative business for employees. Members may not transact speculative business directly or indirectly for or with an employee in any public or private establishment without the written consent of his employer.[11]

(ii) Private dealings with individual members of stock exchange

---

3. Rule 165 (1).   4. Rule 159 (8).   5. Rule 165.
6. Rule 90 (6).   7. Rule 110.   8. Rule 163 (1) (h).
9. Rule 166.   10. Rule 96 (5).   11. Rule 82.

firms. Such dealings are prohibited if intended to be concealed from the firm.[12] Nor may a firm deal openly with an associated member or clerk of another firm without first obtaining that member's or clerk's firm's consent.[13]

(iii) Business for or with a person expelled from the Stock Exchange.[14]

(iv) Business for or with a person who has forfeited his membership,[15] either by not holding the obligatory share under the Deed of Settlement, or failing to pay any payment due to the Council.

(v) Business for or with an ex-member who has become a bankrupt.[16]

(vi) Business for the benefit of a defaulter, unless the consent of the creditors and the sanction of the Council has been obtained.[17]

(vii) Business for defaulting principals. This includes all principals who have failed to fulfil their obligations to another firm or member.[18]

(viii) Broker to broker bargains (other than those resulting from the exercise of an option or in Euro-Currency Bonds). These are not permitted unless:

(*a*) they are marked by each broker without delay;

(*b*) the brokers are prepared to justify their actions to the Council if called upon to do so.[19]

In addition the Council have power to prohibit dealings for principals whom they considers generally undesirable. The Rules provide that in *any* case where the Council are satisfied that in the interests of the proper regulation of business it is desirable to do so, the Council may in their absolute discretion and without giving reasons, issue instructions prohibiting members from transacting business, directly or indirectly, for any specified non-member or class of non-member or for anyone acting on his or their behalf.[20]

B. THE ACCOUNT

All stock exchange contracts are made, continued and settled within a time-framework which is fixed by the Council and governed by the Rules and Regulations. The most important unit in this framework is the dealing period generally known as "the account". This period normally consists of ten consecutive *business* days ending on the contango day. The first seven consecutive business days of the

12. Rule 83.   13. Rule 84 (2).
14. Rule 84*a*. In this case permission may be obtained from the Council.
15. See note 14, *supra*.   16. See note 14, *supra*.   17. Rule 84*a* (2).
18. Rule 85.   19. Rule 87.   20. Rule 85*a*.

dealing period are known as the settlement period (i.e., for the previous account): the seventh day is known as settlement (or account) day. There are normally twenty-four account days in each year: it follows that there are normally twenty-four settlement periods.

A settlement period or account is made up as follows:

(1) Preliminary day (the day on which contangos [1] arranged on the last day of the preceding account are confirmed and making-up prices, on the basis of which contangos are settled, are fixed. These prices, based on the middle market price, are the prices on which "differences" [2] on contangos are calculated).

(2) Making-up day.

(3) Ticket day (where shares have passed through more than one pair of hands, the ultimate purchaser's broker must issue a ticket with his name as payer—for transmission, via intermediate dealing members, to the original selling broker). [3]

(4) First intermediate day.

(5) Second intermediate day.

(6) Third intermediate day.

(7) Account day (also known as "settling day" or "pay day").

If the parties to a bargain have not made a carrying-over (or contango) arrangement, their bargain is deemed to be for the *current* account. [4] Every bargain is made during what is known as a "dealing period". There is always a dealing period in progress because such periods run from the preliminary day of one account, beyond the account day for the previous dealing period, and right up to the contango day. A simple diagram makes the system clear:

Business Day (*usually* *a Monday*)	Dealing Period	Settlement Period	
1	Account X	—	
2	"	—	
3	"	—	
4	"	—	
5	"	—	
6	"	—	
7	"	—	
8	"	—	
9	"	—	
10 (*usually a Friday*)	"	Contango Day	Account X

1. For contangos, see pp. 151–155, *post.*
2. For differences, see p. 154, *post.*
3. For tickets, see pp. 182–185, *post.*
4. Rule 96 (4).

Business Day	Dealing Period	Settlement Period	
11	Account Y	Preliminary Day	,,
12	,,	Making-up Day	,,
13	,,	Ticket Day	,,
14	,,	1st Intermediate Day	,,
15	,,	2nd ,, ,,	,,
16	,,	3rd ,, ,,	,,
17	,,	Account Day	,,
18	,,	—	
19	,,	—	
20	,,	Contango Day	Account Y
21	Account Z	Preliminary Day	,,
22	,,	Making-up Day	,,
23	,,	Ticket Day	,,
24	,,	1st Intermediate Day	,,
25	,,	2nd ,, ,,	,,
26	,,	3rd ,, ,,	,,
27	,,	Account Day	,,
28	,,	—	
29	,,	—	
30	,,	Contango Day	Account Z

When in a particular *dealing period* a bargain is done for the *current* account, it must be completed (that is to say delivery and payment must be made) during the next following *settlement period*.

Bargains for earlier settlement

There are, however, certain dealings to which the above general rule does not apply. Unless they are subject to stamp duty,[5] dealings in the following securities must be settled on the business day following the day of the bargain: (i) British funds, (ii) corporation and county stocks in Great Britain and Northern Ireland, (iii) public boards and (iv) dominion, provincial and colonial government securities.[6]

In addition to these Gilt-Edged securities, bargains in new issues passing by delivery in scrip form, or by letters of renunciation, made more than two business days before the application day, are also for settlement on the business day following the day of the bargain. If specially made less than two business days before the application day, such bargains are for immediate settlement.[7]

5. Most dealings are in fact exempt from stamp duty. See Stamp Act 1891, Sched. 1.
6. Rule 97 (1). But contrary arrangements may be made, see Rule 97 (2) and (3).
7. Rule 101 (2).

A grasp of the structure within which stock exchange transactions are conducted is a vital preliminary to a consideration of the
law as it affects these transactions.

C. DEALING RELATIONSHIPS IN LAW

The floor procedures under which brokers and jobbers deal *inter
se* were described in the last chapter. As explained,[8] the jobber does
not know for whom the broker is acting and consequently he treats
the broker *as if* he were a principal. But in the last legal analysis, it is
the broker's *client* with whom the jobber contracts. This section
will examine, firstly, the client's position *vis-à-vis* the jobber with
whom his broker makes a bargain, and secondly the client's position
vis-à-vis his broker.

1. The client's relationship to the jobber

Stock Exchange Rule 73 states that: "The Stock Exchange does
not recognise in its dealings any other parties than its own members." The Stock Exchange is a market, and its Rules must bind all
who use it as a market if they are to be effective. But Rule 73 does
not deprive a broker's client of the right to sue the jobber who dealt
with his broker: conversely the jobber may sue the client. Privity of
contract is said to exist between them, and the client will sue and be
sued in his own, and not the broker's, name.[9]

Suppose that the client is selling securities on the Exchange. The
purchasing jobber assumes a contract of alternative obligations [10] in
that, on the account day, he will either (i) take the shares himself, in
which case he would be bound to accept and pay for the shares and
register a transfer, or (ii) name on ticket day a member firm to
whom delivery must be made and from whom payment must be
received on the account day.

If the jobber chooses the latter course, he *must*, by stock exchange
usage, name the buying member firm on the next ticket day. In other
words he will transmit to the selling broker a ticket bearing the
name of another member firm who will accept and pay for the
security. This will relieve the jobber from further liability provided
that the firm named as willing to accept and pay for the security
does in fact do so. In *Nickalls* v. *Merry*:[11]

8. See pp. 102–105, *ante.*
9. See also *Allen* v. *F. O'Hearn & Co.*, [1937] A.C. 213; [1936] 3 All E.R. 828, P.C.,
   where the Privy Council held that a broker may not bring or defend actions as a
   trustee for his client.
10. *Coles* v. *Bristowe* (1868), 4 Ch. App. 3, *per* Lord Cairns, at pp. 11, 12.
11. (1875), L.R. 7 H.L. 530.

M directed his broker to sell shares. The broker sold them to a jobber, who re-sold them. The shares passed through several hands and eventually the jobber received from his buyer, and passed on to M's broker, the name of L as ultimate transferee. Unknown to the jobber, L was a minor and therefore legally incapable of accepting the shares. Unknown to M, the shares remained on the company's register in M's name, and as L did not pay the subsequent calls, M was required to pay them.

The House of Lords held that despite his ignorance of L's incapacity, the jobber was liable to make good to M the calls which he had been compelled to pay on L's default.

The requirement of an able and willing buyer is not satisfied, obviously, if the person named does not exist: nor, apparently, is it satisfied if the person is a foreigner domiciled or resident abroad,[12] or if he has not sanctioned the passing of his name for the particular account.[13]

When the jobber has named the transferee's brokers, the firm named assumes not only the obligation to accept and pay for the securities, but also to have the transfer executed, and cause it to be registered. If, therefore, the client of the firm named does not assume ownership, and the seller remains on the register and has to pay calls, the seller's remedy is against the firm named and not the jobber.[14]

2. The broker's relationship with his client

A. THE BROKER'S FUNCTIONS

The stockbroker's position, shortly stated, is similar to that of other kinds of agent. Rowlatt, J., described his functions as follows:[15]

"It seems to me that what a stockbroker does is to buy and sell a commodity on the market. It is true he does not expect to have to pay for it himself or to be responsible ultimately to satisfy the contract himself, as he is a buyer and seller in the market for an undisclosed principal to whom he looks to indemnify him from liability . . . The stockbroker is remunerated by a commission which he receives from his principal, the person who takes the liability off his shoulders."

Putting it another way, the broker, as agent, does not carry the liability to pay: but in consideration for his commission, he has other functions to perform.

12. *Goldschmidt v. Jones* (1870), 22 L.T. 220; *Allen v. Graves* (1870), L.R. 5 Q.B. 478.
13. *Maxted v. Paine* (1869), L.R. 4 Exch. 81.
14. *Grissell v. Bristowe* (1868), 4 C.P. 36; *Coles v. Bristowe, supra.*
15. *Christopher Barker & Sons v. Inland Revenue Commissioners,* [1919] 2 K.B. 222, at p. 229. See also *Hart's Law of Banking* (4th Edn.) p. 1043.

(i) The broker and his client's money

(a) In civil law

In the ordinary course of business, a client will place money in his stockbroker's hands for investment. Or he may instruct the broker to sell his securities in the market. In both cases, the broker will hold money on his client's behalf. He is not, in the strict equitable sense, a trustee for his client; but the courts have regarded the relationship as containing an *element* of trust—and it is therefore said to be of a fiduciary character.

Suppose the broker sells his client's securities, and then mixes the proceeds with moneys of his own (e.g., in a bank account). The rule was long established that the client could "follow" the money into the hands of the bankers: that is to say he could recover the money if it could be ear-marked in the accounts. *Re Hallett's Estate, Knatchbull* v. *Hallet,*[16] decided that even if the money cannot be ear-marked, the court will disentangle the account. So long as the broker has money of his own standing to the account, the court will attribute the broker's private drawings to his own private purposes; so that what remains can be charged with the sum owing to his client.

But the broker, having paid his client's money into his own account, might, for various reasons, draw so heavily upon that account as to exhaust it. What will be his client's position then? The account may have been composed of moneys held for several clients or on several trusts. In this situation the rule in *Clayton's Case*[17] applies. The rule has been conveniently summarised by the expression: "first in, first out." In other words, the court will attribute the broker's earliest drawings on the accounts to the earliest deposits; and the first person whose money he deposited with his banker will stand at the head of the queue of claimants against the bank or the trustee in bankruptcy. The client will have to wait his turn in this chronological order.[18]

This part of the law has a weakness from the client's point of view. His right to follow his money depends upon whether the banker has notice, actual or constructive, that the money was in reality deposited on his behalf. A banker who receives money from a stockbroker is not bound to enquire into its source; so even if he knows that the money is held by the broker on account for his client, he may retain the money against a debt owed by the broker to

16. (1880) 13 Ch. D. 696, and see *Re Diplock, Diplock* v. *Whintle,* [1948] Ch. 465; [1948] 2 All E.R. 318. For a full discussion of the rule, see *Lewin on Trusts* (16th Edn.) pp. 650–663.
17. (1816) 1 Mer. 572.
18. *Re Halletts' Estate* (1880) 13 Ch. D. 495; *Re Diplock (supra),* at pp. 550–564.

the bank.[19] The same principle applies when a broker holds securities for his client and pledges them with a bank to secure a loan. The bank may treat them as the broker's.[20] But there is a limit beyond which a bank is not exempt from enquiry; in *Selangor United Rubber Estates, Ltd* v. *Cradock (No. 3)*:[1]

> A successful bid for the stock of the S company was made by B & T Ltd, acting for an undisclosed principal C. C attended a board meeting of the S company, and through his instrumentality a resolution was passed that the S company's credit of £232,764, on current account with the N bank, should be transferred to a branch of the D bank where C had a small account of his own. The board also resolved to draw a cheque for £232,500 on the new account with the D bank to lend to W T Ltd. W T Ltd lent that amount to C who applied it for his own, rather than the S company's purposes.

Ungoed-Thomas, J., held that the D bank had been negligent and awarded damages to the company. The D bank had assisted C in a fraudulent disposition of the S company's assets, of which he as a director was trustee. The bank had constructive knowledge of the fraud, because there were circumstances which would indicate to an honest reasonable man that fraud was being committed, and it was held that the transfer of the S company's account to the D bank, followed by payment by endorsement of a cheque to C of almost the total account, was a circumstance which put a reasonable banker on enquiry.

It is difficult to lay down a hard and fast rule as to when a bank has a duty to enquire whether a broker acts for himself or another. Each case will depend on its own circumstances; so, in another case,[2] it was said that the mere fact that a broker has pledged securities for a considerable time, is not sufficient to merit the banker's attention.

Although a broker is in a fiduciary position where he holds money or securities on behalf of his client, a difference arising in favour of the client when a bargain is carried over[3] into another account is not impressed with the nature of a trust. It is merely a debt due to the client. So in *King* v. *Hutton*,[4] where a broker was declared a defaulter on the Stock Exchange, his trustee in bankruptcy and not the client was entitled to a difference in the hands of the Official Assignee. The client was left to prove for the difference in the broker's bankruptcy.

19. *Thomson* v. *Clydesdale Bank, Ltd.*, [1893] A.C. 282, H.L.
20. *London Joint Stock Bank* v. *Simmons*, [1892] A.C. 201, H.L.
 1. [1968] 2 All E.R. 1073.
 2. *Fuller* v. *Glyn, Mills, Currie & Co.*, [1914] 2 K.B. 168, *per* Pickford, J., at p. 174.
 3. For carrying over, see Contangos, pp. 151–155, *post.*
 4. [1900] 2 Q.B. 504.

(b) In criminal law

A broker who holds money or shares for his client, and contrary to his instructions misapplies or converts it to his own use was formerly guilty of the offence of fraudulent conversion under the Larceny Acts.[5] But the offence did contain an unfortunate flaw. It was necessary to prove that the defendant had been *entrusted* with the property either for safe custody or for a specific purpose;[6] this created difficulties where he had been given money to hold *until an opportunity for investment should arise,* but had converted the money before that event.

The difficulty was swept away by the Theft Act 1968. The Act abolished the old offences of larceny, fraudulent conversion and embezzlement, and replaced them with the new offence of theft. Section 1 (1) provides that a person

"is guilty of theft if he dishonestly appropriates property belonging to another with the intention of permanently depriving the other of it."

The expression "belonging to another" is defined in the Act, section 5 (3) of which is particularly relevant to members of the Stock Exchange:

"Where a person receives property from or on account of another, and is under an obligation to the other to retain and deal with that property or its proceeds in a particular way, the property or proceeds shall be regarded (as against him) as belonging to the other."

The new offence therefore covers all the ground formerly covered by fraudulent conversion. But it travels further, in that the expression "dishonestly appropriates" should, it is submitted, be interpreted as including a misappropriation where the offender has *not* been *expressly* entrusted with the property concerned,[7] and the loophole which appeared in *R.* v. *Newman*[8] now seems to have been finally closed.

(ii) The broker must act as an agent

It is a most important rule, fundamental to the existence of the Stock Exchange—and to its status and reputation as a market—that a broker who has been instructed to make a bargain for his client on the Stock Exchange must make the bargain with another member

5. See *R.* v. *Christian* (1873), L.R. 2 C.C.R. 94; Larceny Act 1861, ss. 75, 76; Larceny Act 1916, ss. 20–22.

6. *R.* v. *Newman* (1882), 8 Q.B.D. 706, C.C.R.

7. For a discussion of the expression "appropriates", see Griew, *The Theft Act 1968*, pp. 24–35.

8. See note 6, *supra.*

and not with himself. Without such a rule, the confidence which the client traditionally reposes in his broker would have no basis. The matter was settled by the House of Lords as long ago as 1831 in the leading case of *Rothschild* v. *Brookman*.[9] Lord Wynford placed his finger on the rationale:

> "If I live in Dorsetshire, and I write to my broker in London to sell my stock, I fancy that I have the advantage of that broker's assistance as to the day on which it is proper to sell; I fancy that, living in London, he has a knowledge of the facts which will act on the market. If the broker in London, instead of going to the stock market, or instead of exercising a discretion as to the period when he should sell any stock, is to take that stock to himself, he deprives me of the security I have, and the confidence I repose in his skill and intelligence; and if there is a loss to me, he is the person who takes advantage of that loss."

The House of Lords were satisfied that the broker (Mr Rothschild) was a man of perfect integrity and that his conduct had been unimpeachable; but it held that the rule must apply to all if confidence in the Stock Exchange is to be maintained, and the transactions were set aside.

Since the broker is in all circumstances obliged to act as an agent, it follows that he may make no profit save his commission. If he attempts to make such a profit, he is said to be acting as a principal, the legal consequences of which will be discussed hereafter.[10]

(*iii*) *The broker must act in obedience to his instructions*

Like any other agent, a stockbroker stands in the shoes of his principal. Having received his authority to make a transaction, he must not act outside the scope of that authority. This is a simple matter where the client has given the broker precise instructions, e.g., to purchase 500 shares in the X Co at the current market price. In *Mitchell* v. *Newhall*:[11]

> The broker was ordered to purchase "50 shares" in the Belgian Eastern Junction Railway Company. At that time no shares of that company were in the market. In fact the Belgian Government had yet to authorize its flotation. But letters of allotment for shares were commonly bought and sold in the market as shares. Accordingly the broker purchased letters of allotment.

It was held that a jury might well find that there was a good execution of the order.

Whether a broker has obeyed his client's instructions is in every

9. (1831), 5 Bli. N.S. 165.
10. See broker acting as principal, pp. 146–151, *post*.
11. (1846), 15 M. & W. 308.

case a question of fact.[12] However, a client may give his broker instructions which are vague and unprecise; and he who creates confusion cannot, in law, take advantage of it. Suppose that the instructions are capable of two *equally* reasonable interpretations, and that the broker acts, *bona fide*, upon one of them. The client cannot then repudiate the bargain as unauthorised. He cannot turn round and say: "Oh but I meant it the other way." In *Loring* v. *Davis*:[13]

> The defendant instructed his brokers, S and Co, to purchase shares in the Oriental Bank. They purchased the shares and sent him a bought-note. Before settling day, the bank went into liquidation. The defendant's solicitors thereupon wrote to S and Co repudiating the purchase on the ground that it was void under the Banking Companies (Shares) Act 1867, and gave them notice that they completed the contract at their own risk. But on the same day the defendant wrote to S, to whom he was related by marriage, as follows: "Dear James, . . . I wish you clearly to understand that whatever position you may have to assume with regard to (the shares) I consider myself fully bound to support you." Acting on the second letter, S and Co completed the purchase for the defendant. The defendant then refused to execute the transfer.

It was held that although the defendant had not executed the transfer, he had not revoked the authority of S and Co to act as his brokers either. Accordingly the court declared that he was bound in conscience to accept the shares and to indemnify the vendor.

Where a stockbroker fails, *through his own fault*, to carry out his instructions (or exceeds them) his client's remedy is in damages, measured by the actual loss which he suffers in not having the profits he would have made but for that failure. Only profits which have *in fact* been lost may be claimed, not the expected profits which the client *might* have made.[14]

It is a general rule of the law of agency that one who contracts as an agent warrants that he acts on the authority of his principal. So where a client instructs his broker to obtain shares in the P company, and the broker, by a careless mistake, obtains shares in the Q company instead, the client can repudiate the contract, and if he does so the Q Company could claim damages from the broker for breach of his warranty if they have suffered loss and expense as a result.[15]

12. See *Mitchell* v. *Newhall, (supra)*; *Lamert* v. *Heath* (1846), 15 M. & W. 486; *Aston* v. *Kelsey*, [1913] 3 K.B. 314; *Johnson* v. *Kearley*, [1908] 2 K.B. 514, C.A.
13. (1886), 32 Ch. D. 625.
14. *Salvesen* v. *Rederiaktiebolaget Nortstjerman*, [1905] A.C. 302; *Cassaboglou* v. *Gibb* (1883), 11 Q.B.D. 797, C.A. See further, Breach of Contract, Chapter 10, *post*.
15. *Re National Coffee Palace Co., ex parte Panmure* (1883), 24 Ch. D. 367.

(iv) *The broker must make the best bargain he can*

The Rules and Regulations of the Stock Exchange [16] provide in effect that a broker must execute the best bargain that he can, according to his judgment at the time of dealing. If, for example, his client instructs him to purchase at a specified price, and he is able to purchase at a lower price, the law will attribute to the client an intention to purchase at that lower price. [17] Conversely, if the broker is instructed to sell at a specified price, he must obtain a higher price if that is possible. But if he is ordered to sell when securities have reached a named limit he must sell immediately that limit is reached. He has no discretion to await a further rise even if he has good grounds for believing that it will occur. [18] Normally, where a client instructs a broker to sell at a certain price, the authority to sell terminates at the end of the current account, unless the parties have made a special arrangement of their own. [19]

(v) *The broker must make an enforceable contract*

A stockbroker has a duty to make a contract which his client can enforce: it is not enough to come to a gentlemen's agreement with another member of the exchange. In *Neilson* v. *James*: [20]

> A broker sold banking shares for his client to a jobber on the Bristol Stock Exchange. The Banking Companies (Shares) Act 1867 (now repealed) provided that all tokens of the sale and purchase of such shares should state the names of their registered proprietor. The broker and the jobber exchanged bought and sold notes which, according to the custom of the Bristol Exchange, omitted to state the proprietor's name. That made the contract void under the 1867 Act. The client claimed damages from the broker.

The Court of Appeal held that the custom, being unreasonable, did not override the statute; and also that, notwithstanding the custom, the broker had a duty to make a valid contract, and that accordingly he was in breach of his duty.

But a client may have impliedly authorised his broker to deal in such a way that a gentlemen's agreement is the best that the broker can achieve. In *Seymour* v. *Bridge* [1] the facts were similar to those of *Neilson* v. *James*, except that the client had on many previous occasions instructed the broker to deal in banking shares—and none of the contract or advice notes forwarded to him contained the distinguishing numbers required by the Act.

16. Rule 73a.
17. *Thompson* v. *Meade* (1891), 7 T.L.R. 698.
18. *Bertram, Armstrong & Co.* v. *Godfray* (1830), 1 Knapp. 381.
19. *Lawford & Co.* v. *Harris* (1896), 12 T.L.R. 275.
20. (1882), 9 Q.B.D. 546.   1. (1885), 14 Q.B.D. 460.

It was held that the client had acquiesced in the making of unenforceable contracts, and could not now refuse to indemnify his broker.

The broker must establish privity of contract between his client and the third party with whom he deals. In other words, he must make a contract which is binding on *both* parties. Subject to his duty to make the best bargain,[2] the contract must mirror his instructions as to price[3] and quantity:[4] if it does not, any bargain which he makes is no concern of his client, who cannot be sued upon it by the third party.[5] There is nothing, however, to prevent a broker from sub-dividing his order, so as to conceive a privity between his client and several third parties. Instructed to sell 1,000 shares, he may sell 400 to A, 300 to B, 200 to C and 100 to D. His client will have separate valid contracts with A, B, C and D.[6]

(vi) The broker must keep a bargain open until completion

Once a broker has made a bargain for his client, he must keep the bargain open until the agreed settling (i.e., account) day. He cannot use the bargain as a vehicle for the kind of sharp practices which were exposed in *Skelton* v. *Wood*:[7]

The plaintiff, an outside broker, was instructed to purchase shares. However (i) as to part of the order, instead of going into the market as he was instructed, he simply appropriated certain stock which he already held to his client's account, and (ii) as to another part of the order, he purchased the shares for his client; then, without his client's knowledge, he resold the shares and subsequently bought them back again—all before the time for completing the original bargain. He then sought to charge his client with the difference in the share values from one account to the next, and carrying-over commission, as if the bargains had been kept open all the time.

The Divisional Court held that the broker could not recover. Wright, J., condemned the transactions as a sham; and he expressed the opinion that two persons combining to effect such transactions would bring themselves within the reach of the criminal law of conspiracy.

B. THE BROKER'S DUTIES

The functions central to the stockbroker's role have now been considered. In addition, he has a number of duties, which though

2. See p. 130, *ante*.   3. See p. 128 *et seq.*, *ante*.
4. *Thompson* v. *Meade, supra; Johnson* v. *Kearley, supra.*
5. *Robinson* v. *Mollett* (1875), L.R. 7 H.L. 802.
6. *Beckhuson and Gibbs* v. *Hamblet,* [1901] 2 K.B., 73 C.A.; *Levitt* v. *Hamblet,* [1901] 2 K.B. 53. For the lumping of orders, see pp. 150–151, *post*.
7. (1894), 71 L.T. 616. See also *Ellis* v. *Pond* (1898), 1 Q.B. 426.

they do not go to the heart of his transaction, may, if they are not observed, entitle his client to repudiate it, or obtain some other remedy.

(i) Duty to observe the Rules, customs and usages of the Stock Exchange

Unless he has instructions to the contrary, the broker must assume that his client intends him to observe the Rules and Regulations, customs and usages of the Stock Exchange. If he deals in a manner not sanctioned by the Rules, etc., his client can disown the transaction.

Apart from the express Rules, the broker may only do what he would ordinarily be authorised to do. In *Wiltshire* v. *Sims*,[8] it was found that a selling broker is not ordinarily authorised to give credit for the price of stock, and it was held that if he does so his client will not be bound to transfer the stock.

(ii) Duty to enquire as to a purchaser's financial standing

Suppose that A wishes to sell some shares on which some calls remain unpaid. He instructs his broker, X, who sells them to M through the jobbers, Brown and Co. M cannot pay for the shares, and he is so impecunious that he cannot pay the outstanding calls. A transfer is not executed and A remains on the register, so that he is required to pay the calls. It would appear to be the law that if X takes it for granted that M is a man of substance, A can sue him in negligence if it turns out that M is a man of straw.[9]

In the above situation Rule 85 would put Brown and Co on their guard as well. The Rule provides that a firm may not, without the consent of the Council, transact business for a principal who has failed to fulfil his obligations to another firm or member. Firms must make all such enquiries as may be reasonable in the circumstances of the particular case to ascertain whether or not its principal has at any time failed to fulfil his obligation to a member or firm.

(iii) Duty to account

A broker must keep proper accounts, and if his client wants to know how his account stands at any given moment, he must be ready to state it.[10] *The client has two separate actions at common law:*

(a) An action of account

This is an action to compel an agent (such as a broker) to draw up and produce an account, and to pay the amount found to be due.

8. (1808), 1 Camp. 258.
9. See *obiter dictum* of Blackburn, J., in *Maxted* v. *Paine* (No. 2) (1871), L.R. 6 Exch. 132, at p. 149.
10. *Lord Chedworth* v. *Edwards* (1802), 3 Ves 46, at p. 48.

Where a client is suing his broker he, or his properly appointed agent,[11] have an automatic right to discovery (i.e., disclosure) of their account which is not affected by any procedural rules as to discovery.[12]

(b) An action on an account stated

The broker and his client may have agreed an account. If that is so, there is a *prima facie* acknowledgment of debt giving rise to a cause of action. But the broker might counter this by showing that no such debt ever existed, or that he and his client had agreed to set off debts due to him against his debts owing to the client, or that the accounts are settled because his client has approved them.[13]

(*iv*) Duty to give advice

As an agent, a stockbroker's overriding duty is to carry out his client's instructions. He has no implied duty to advise the client; but if his advice is sought he should give an opinion which is both honest and careful. In the past this has been regarded as a moral obligation only, the breach of which does not create a cause of action in law. In *Schweder & Co* v. *Walton and Hemingway*:[14]

> The plaintiffs, London stockbrokers, acted as agents for the defendants, stockbrokers in Halifax, in the purchase of shares in the British South Africa Company—the shares to be taken up or carried over by the defendants. S, a member of the plaintiff firm, heard from his mother-in-law that she had received a letter from her son, a farmer in Rhodesia, stating that rinderpest had broken out near Salisbury. Accordingly, the plaintiffs telephoned the defendants saying that they had confidential information that there would be a heavy fall in the price of the shares that day, and insisted that the defendants sold at once before the news broke. The defendants in Halifax agreed to the sale without consulting their clients, and the plaintiffs sold the shares for £6,400. The information was not accurate. Instead of falling, the value of the shares rose rapidly and at the end of the account were worth £7,290. The plaintiffs claimed the balance of an account for differences, and the defendants counter-claimed £890, the sum they had had to make good for their clients by buying back the shares.

Ridley, J., held that the counterclaim failed, as the defendants, by selling the shares without consulting their clients, were the authors of their own misfortune. Accordingly it was unnecessary for him to decide whether the London brokers were under a duty to investigate

11. *Bevan* v. *Webb*, [1901] 2 Ch. 59, C.A.
12. *Leitch* v. *Abbott* (1886), 31 Ch.D. 374.
13. See further, *Bowstead on Agency* (13th Edn.) pp. 159–162.
14. (1910), 27 T.L.R. 89.

the accuracy of their "confidential information": but he expressed the view, *obiter*, that no such duty lay upon them.

In the past, this case has been confidently regarded as an authority for the proposition that, if a stockbroker gives advice which he knows an ordinary client will rely on, he owes his client no duty to ensure that it is correct.[15] It is submitted, however, that it cannot be regarded as such an authority, because:

(*a*) Ridley, J.'s, remarks on the broker's duty were *obiter* only: they did not involve the ratio of his decision.

(*b*) The Halifax brokers were professional clients. Their experience in the market should have taught them the dangers of acting upon unverified information. But the lay client is in a different position: he knows less about the factors which affect share prices, and must therefore place greater reliance upon his broker.

The whole question of legal responsibility for business or professional advice was thrown wide open by the decision of the House of Lords in *Hedley Byrne & Co Ltd* v. *Heller & Partners, Ltd.*[16]

A bank enquired by telephone of the respondent merchant bankers as to the respectability and standing of E Ltd, one of their customers, and whether E Ltd would be good for an advertising contract for £8,000 to £9,000. Some months later the bank wrote to the merchant bankers again, asking whether they considered E Ltd trustworthy, in the way of business, to the extent of £100,000 per annum. The merchant bankers answered both the telephone call and the letter to the effect that E Ltd were respectably constituted and considered good for its normal business engagements. The appellants, who were advertising agents, relied on those replies and placed orders for advertising time and space for E Ltd, assuming personal responsibility for payment to the television and newspaper companies concerned. E Ltd went into liquidation and the appellants lost over £17,000 on the advertising contracts. They sued the merchant bankers for the amount of their loss, alleging that their replies to their enquiries had been given negligently, in the sense of misjudgment, by making a statement which gave a false impression as to E Ltd's credit.

The House of Lords found that the circumstances gave rise to a duty of care on the merchant bankers' part. The rule which was enunciated is stated clearly in the headnote:

"If, in the ordinary course of business or professional affairs, a person seeks information or advice from another, who is not under contractual or fiduciary obligation to give the information or advice, in circumstances in which a reasonable man so asked would know that he was being trusted, or that his skill or judgment was being relied on, and the

15. See for example 36 Halsbury's Laws of England (3rd Edn.) p. 783.
16. [1964] A.C. 465; [1963] 2 All E.R. 575, H.L.

person asked chooses to give the information or advice without clearly so qualifying his answer as to show that he does not accept responsibility, then the person replying accepts a legal duty to exercise such care as the circumstances require in making his reply; and for a failure to exercise that care an action for negligence will lie if damage results."

This is a decision of far-reaching importance, and it will be many years before its implications are fully explored in the courts. Whether it applies to stockbrokers, and if so to what extent, and in what circumstances, are questions which have yet to be decided. The stockbroker who is asked by his client to select the contents of his portfolio, or to advise on the future movement of particular share prices, is in a position very similar to the merchant bankers in the *Hedley Byrne* case. It might seem that *a fortiori* the stockbroker owes a duty of care because:

(*a*) he has a direct contractual relationship with his client. In the *Hedley Byrne* case the merchant bankers were not under any kind of contract with the advertising agents.

(*b*) there is a fiduciary element to the relationship.[17] In *Hedley Byrne* there was no fiduciary bond between the parties because the advertising agents were not customers of the bank.[18]

(*c*) he is not *obliged* to give advice. If therefore he is asked for it, there is no reason for him to doubt that his skill and judgment are being relied upon, and by whom. But in *Hedley Byrne* it was a matter for decision whether the merchant bankers could reasonably be expected to foresee that the information which they gave to the bank would be acted upon by someone else.

On the other hand it is submitted that the stockbroker is less vulnerable to liability for careless advice than it might appear. When he advises his client to invest in the X company, he is in effect making a forecast as to the future: namely that the price of its securities will rise. Admittedly his forecast must be based on the correct interpretation of a present state of affairs, e.g., the company's last report, its balance sheet and current economic trends; but even so there are many future events affecting the market which he cannot possibly foresee, such as strikes, political developments and Acts of God. Herein lies another distinction from the *Hedley Byrne* situation; in that case it was found as a fact that the merchant bank were negligent in giving their reference; and a reference can only relate to an *existing* and not a future situation.

17. See pp. 125–126, *ante.*
18. See The broker and his client's money, pp. 123–126, *ante.* For the fiduciary relationship between a bank and its customers, see *Woods* v. *Martins Bank, Ltd.,* [1959] 1 Q.B. 55; [1958] 3 All E.R. 166.

Public policy might form another objection to the liability of stockbrokers for erroneous advice. Barristers cannot be sued for professional negligence in the conduct of a case in court. This immunity is based on public policy, for obviously, if they were not so immune, "counsel would perform their duties under the peril of an action by every disappointed and angry client".[19] The stockbroker's position is, in this context, analogous. Share movements are not a subject on which it is possible to give firm advice with any great confidence, and if brokers were to be made liable for their mis-forecasts, they might all refuse to give advice in order to avoid a multiplicity of suits by every disappointed investor. Thus the public would be deprived of an important part of the service which a stockbroker provides.

There is, of course, nothing to prevent a stockbroker disclaiming liability for his advice. The merchant bankers in *Hedley Byrne and Co Ltd* v. *Heller and Partners Ltd*,[20] although they were held to have a duty of care in the circumstances, escaped liability in this way. There is no decision as to how *Hedley Byrne* applies to stockbrokers (if at all), and in view of this uncertainty they would be well advised so to disclaim. This is a rapidly developing part of the law, and the next few years will probably see a growing body of cases relevant to the interpretation of that decision.

C. THE BROKER'S AUTHORITY

As his client's representative on the floor, the stockbroker is invested with his client's *persona*. He must act in accordance with his instructions, and he must act only in accordance with those instructions. Sometimes the broker may be in doubt as to what his client wishes him to do. In those circumstances he must either take fresh instructions, or, if this is inconvenient, he must use his common sense to resolve the dilemma. In every case he must ask himself: what is my authority?

He can assume, in the first place, that he has authority to deal according to the Rules and Regulations of the Stock Exchange, and its usages. The Rules and Regulations are published by authority of the Council, and Rule 16 provides for sanctions against their violation. There is no doubt therefore that the Rules and Regulations are binding on members.

Whether a usage exists is a question of fact. Proof of a usage depends on universal acquiescence[1] and a Stock Exchange usage, as

---

19. *Swinfen* v. *Lord Chelmsford* (1860), S. M. & N. 890, at pp. 920–921. Cited with approval in *Rondel* v. *Worsley*, [1967] 3 All E.R. 993, at pp. 1038–1039.
20. See note 16, *supra*.
 1. *Strathlorne SS. Co., Ltd.* v. *Hugh Baird and Sons, Ltd.* 1916 S.C. (H.L.) 134.

part of the law merchant, may be proved by the fact that a judge has taken judicial notice of it in the past.[2] Whether a usage is binding is a question of law and depends (*inter alia*) upon its reasonableness.[3]

Does a client authorise his broker to observe rules and usages of which he the layman is ignorant? Of course, the client cannot be taken to know all the Rules and Regulations and usages himself; but when he employs a broker to buy shares for him, he impliedly authorises the broker to do all that is necessary to complete the bargain.[4]

The best view seems to be that the broker has a general blanket authority to deal according to all the Rules, Regulations and usages whether known to the client or not.[5] Rule 73 (every bargain to be fulfilled according to the Rules, Regulations and usages) means in effect, that the client has no choice in the matter; and any other view would lead to absurd results, with clients repudiating bargains almost at will. The only exception is that clients are not bound by usages which are unreasonable or which contravene an Act of Parliament, unless they are aware of the usage.[6] The dictum of Brett, M. R., in *Perry* v. *Barnett*,[7] although uttered in 1885, may nevertheless be cited as a rider to Rule 73:

> "Now the proposition that a person who directs another to deal upon a particular market is to be treated as if he knew the rules of that market, has been adopted in the law to some extent, but certainly not to this extent, that however unreasonable or illogical they may be, he is still to be treated as if he knew them."

It is a general rule of the law of agency that where a principal limits his agent's authority by making conditions as to its exercise, but in spite of that the agent deals in breach of a condition, he cannot thereby bind his principal if the third party knew[8] or ought to have known,[9] or ought to have enquired whether[10] the condition was being broken.

Clearly good faith is required of the client as much as of the broker. A client may not have authorised his broker to deal in a

2. *Brandao* v. *Barnett* (1846), 12 Cl. and Fin. 787, H.L., at p. 805, *per* Lord Campbell.
3. See, e.g., *Harker* v. *Edwards* (1887), 57 L.J.Q.B. 147, C.A.; *Reynolds* v. *Smith* (1893), 9, T.L.R. 494, H.L.
4. *Bayley* v. *Wilkins* (1849), 7 C.B. 886.
5. *Union and Rhodesian Trust, Ltd.* v. *Neville* (1917), 33 T.L.R. 245.
6. *Perry* v. *Barnett* (1885), 15 Q.B.D. 388, C.A.
7. *Ibid.,* p. 392.
8. See, e.g., *Cuthbert* v. *Robarts, Lubbock & Co.,* [1909] 2 Ch. 226, C.A.
9. See, e.g., *Morison* v. *London County and Westminster Bank, Ltd.,* [1914] 3 K.B. 356, C.A.
10. See, e.g., *A. L. Underwood, Ltd.* v. *Bank of Liverpool,* [1924] 1 K.B. 775.

particular way; if nevertheless he does deal in that way, there may be circumstances which will prevent the client from repudiating the bargain and leaving his broker in the cold. This was the case in *Seymour* v. *Bridge*,[11] where authority was implied from a previous and habitual course of dealing.

(i) *The broker's authority and contangos*

A contango, which will be discussed in its proper place,[12] is an arrangement whereby a bargain is not settled for the current account, but carried over into the next account. The broker can only carry over *by arrangement*. It follows that he has no authority to carry over without instructions from his client.[13] Such instructions must be firmly expressed *totidem verbis*—and cannot be merely implied. If a broker carries over without authority, the client remains liable on the contract as it stood at the time of the carrying-over, (i.e., the last day of the current account), but not after that.[14]

Of course, a broker who has contangoed his client's account without having express instructions to do so may be rescued from liability if the client's claim that he had no authority is unreasonable. In *Petre* v. *Sutherland*:[15]

> Petre, a broker, carried over stocks for his client on numerous occasions. The normal method of contango is for the broker to sell the stocks carried over to a jobber for the current account and re-purchase an equivalent number of stocks for the next account. But sometimes Petre found it difficult to find a jobber to contango with; accordingly, (following a recognised procedure) he contangoed stocks with himself instead of with a jobber. The defendant objected to payment on the ground that this was irregular. But it was proved (a) that it was not irregular, (b) that it was for the greater benefit of the defendant and (c) that on one occasion the defendant had been told that "Mr Petre will contango the stock himself," and had neither objected nor expressed any surprise.

It was held that, in the circumstances, the defendant had given Petre authority to contango. This decision should be compared with *Sachs* v. *Spielmann*:[16]

> In that case the brokers, who had been instructed to carry over, adopted the same recognised procedure as Mr Petre. The client, a banker in Frankfurt, claimed that he was not aware of this custom; but the brokers had furnished him with accounts and the manner in which they were set out ought, said the judge, to have given him notice of the custom if he

11. See p. 130, *ante*.   12. See pp. 151–155, *post*.
13. See *Re Overweg, Haas* v. *Durant,* [1900] 1 Ch. 209, where the broker tried to carry over after his client had died.
14. *Maxted* v. *Morris* (1869), 21 L.T. 535.
15. (1887), 3 T.L.R. 422.   16. (1889), 5 T.L.R. 487.

was not aware of it in the first place. Accordingly it was held that the client's claim for an account must fail.

In *Petre* v. *Sutherland* and *Sachs* v. *Spielmann* the clients both failed in very different circumstances. But the common ratio seems to be that a client cannot impliedly authorise his broker to deal in a particular way (e.g., to contango) and then, looking back on the transaction, put the telescope to his blind eye and pretend that it was all done without his knowledge.

The client's acts or behaviour must be exclusively referable to an authority to carry over if that authority is to be implied. Normally a carrying-over takes place because the client cannot find the money to pay for securities; but the mere fact that the client does not provide money by account day does not necessarily mean that he gives his broker an authority to carry over; a contango arrangement is only one of a number of possible explanations for his failure to pay up, and accordingly no authority will be implied.[17] The implication was, however, drawn in *Campbell and Co* v. *Brass*:[18]

> Several times the client's shares were carried over at the request of the client, who always settled the differences. On one set of differences, however, the client refused to pay on the ground that the contract notes were not stamped, but when sued for the differences he paid up. After this, the brokers continued to carry over as before. The client then claimed that they had no authority to do this.

It was held, however, that the previous course of dealing pointed to such an authority, and that the client's isolated refusal to pay differences on a ground unconnected with the broker's authority did not amount to a revocation.

(ii) *The client's position where a broker has acted without authority*

If the broker has made a bargain for which he had no authority whatsoever, the client may simply repudiate it, leaving the broker to assume liability. If the broker makes a bargain as authorised, but *carries it over* without the instructions or agreement of his client, the client may repudiate the bargain to the extent to which his position has been affected by the unauthorised carrying-over.

The above two situations present little difficulty. But suppose that a broker, instructed to carry over an account, closes it without instructions *before* the end of the *current* account. Here the broker is in breach of the contract even before the time fixed for its performance. This is referred to as anticipatory breach of contract, and the legal consequence is that the client has an option. Either he can

17. *Maxted* v. *Morris, supra.*
18. (1891), 7 T.L.R. 612.

treat the breach as a repudiation of the contract by the broker (in other words both parties regard the contract as at an end), and claim damages. Or he can compel the broker to go on with the contract (in spite of his attempted repudiation) and sue him for a decree of specific performance. If the client adopts the latter course, he may still recover damages measured by the sum of money which would be required to put him in the position he would have enjoyed had the broker kept the account open. In *Michael* v. *Hart & Co.*[19]

> The defendants, who were stockbrokers, had agreed with their client, the plaintiff, to carry over to the end of May account certain stocks which they had purchased for him, and made the necessary arrangements to that end. Before the settling day they closed the plaintiff's account, without authority, by selling the stocks. When he was informed of this, the plaintiff gave the defendants notice that he would insist on performance by them of their contract when the settling day arrived. At the time when the defendants closed the plaintiff's account, the prices of the stocks were falling, but shortly afterwards they rose again, and they were higher at the end of the May settlement, having been still higher during the interval between the closing of the plaintiff's account and the end of the May settlement. The plaintiff sued the defendants after the end of May settlement for damages for non-performance of this contract to carry over the stocks; and the defendants contended that the damages ought to be assessed with reference to the prices of the stocks when the defendants closed the plaintiff's account.

It was held that this was not so, but that the plaintiff was entitled to insist on performance of the defendants' contract at the end of May settlement, and to measure his damages with reference to the prices of the stocks at that date.

(iii) Termination of authority

A broker's authority to purchase continues until the purchase is effected. A broker's authority to sell determines at the time specified in his instructions;[1] but if a client instructs his broker to sell at a specific price, then there is a general usage that the broker's authority to sell ceases at the end of the then current account.[2] Where a broker has authority to carry over on contango from account to account, and his client dies during the currency of such an arrangement, that authority will cease as from the settling day following the death of his client.[3] And if the broker disregards his client's death and carries over on his own authority—ultimately

---

19. [1902] 1 K.B. 482, C.A.; 89 L.T. 422, H.L.

1. *Lawford & Co.* v. *Harris, supra.*

2. See note 1, *above.* In practice, however, many orders are expressed "IFTC" (in force till cancelled).

3. *Phillips* v. *Jones* (1888), 4 T.L.R. 401.

selling the securities at a loss—he and not his client's estate will have to bear that loss.[4]

(iv) Breach of warranty of authority

A broker dealing on the Stock Exchange warrants to those with whom he bargains that he possesses his client's authority so to bargain. If he does not have that authority, he is liable in damages to those who, relying on the warranty, act to their detriment. This is so whether they make a bargain with the broker or not.[5]

D. THE BROKER'S RIGHT OF INDEMNITY

When a broker purchases shares on the Stock Exchange, the member with whom he deals treats him as a principal and he is personally liable to pay for the shares.[6] In this situation the law implies a contract by the client that if the broker pays for the shares, the client will repay him.[7] The question of indemnity arose in an unusual way in *Hitchens, Harrison, Woolston & Co* v. *Jackson & Sons*:[8]

> J and Sons, a firm of solicitors, obtained a money-judgment on behalf of E against Mrs L. Execution was levied, and in order to avoid a sale of Mrs L (her mother's) furniture, Miss L offered to give J and Sons her stock in the Bristol Waterworks Co in satisfaction of the judgment, and deposited with J and Sons a stock certificate and blank transfer signed by herself. J and Sons sent these documents to H.H.W. and Co stockbrokers, with instructions to sell. H.H.W. and Co sold the shares on the Bristol Stock Exchange, and remitted the proceeds to J and Sons, who paid off E's judgment debt and costs and tendered the balance to Miss L. Miss L now changed her attitude. She refused to accept the balance and objected to registration of the transfer of her stock, on the ground that her signature had been obtained by compulsion. To resolve the impasse H.H.W. and Co had to purchase an equivalent amount of the same stock to fulfil their bargain with the purchaser on the Bristol Stock Exchange. Having sold two lots of stock for the price of one they claimed an indemnity from J and Sons.

The House of Lords held that J and Sons had an obligation to put H.H.W. and Co in a position to complete the contract of sale which they had employed H.H.W. and Co to effect; they had failed to put

---

4. *Phillips* v. *Jones* (1888), 4 T.L.R. 401.
5. *Starkey* v. *Bank of England,* [1903] A.C. 114, H.L. applying and explaining *Collen* v. *Wright* (1857), 8 E and B 647; *Re National Coffee Palace Co., ex parte Panmure* (1883), 24 Ch.D. 367, C.A.
6. Rules and Regulations of the Stock Exchange, Rule 73.
7. See *per* Lord Esher, M. R., in *Hunt, Cox & Co.* v. *Chamberlain* (1896), 12 T.L.R. 186.
8. [1943] A.C. 266, H.L.; [1943] 1 All E.R. 128.

H.H.W. and Co in such a position, and would therefore have to pay them an indemnity measured by the cost of buying the substituted stock.

The broker's right to an indemnity is anticipatory as well as retrospective, for it was held in *Stock and Share Auction and Advance Co* v. *Galmoye*[9] that a client must put his broker in funds to pay for shares *before* he can be entitled to delivery of them. In *Peppercorne* v. *Clench*[10] the clients nominated a purchaser who, in the event, was unable to pay:

> The plaintiffs, stockbrokers, were instructed by the defendants to purchase for them 200 shares in the B Co, which they did. Later the defendants nominated W as purchaser and transferee. The plaintiffs passed W's name and he was ultimately registered as the holder. Later the B Co went into liquidation and W's name was put on the list of contributories. It transpired that, unknown to the plaintiffs, W was an infant, and his name was accordingly removed from the list of contributories, and the name of B as transferor was substituted. The Committee of the Stock Exchange ordered the plaintiffs to indemnify B; the plaintiffs in turn claimed an indemnity from the defendants for (*a*) their losses to date arising out of their obligation to indemnify B, (*b*) their future liability arising out of having passed the name of W as purchaser.

It was held that the plaintiffs could recover both (*a*) *and* (*b*). However, it was held in *Dyson* v. *Peat*[11] that an agent may not claim an indemnity where there was a potential, and not an actual, claim against which he had a right to be indemnified.

The purchase price is not the only item for which the broker can be indemnified. If he has carried out his instructions properly his client is bound to indemnify him for every liability which he reasonably incurs in the execution of those instructions, or in the observance of Stock Exchange Rules which are reasonable and of which the client was aware at the time when he gave his instructions.[12] However it is part of the general law of indemnity that the person claiming indemnity must limit his expenditure or minimise his loss as far as possible. He cannot recover extravagant and unnecessary expenses which go beyond his instructions. In *Walter and Gould* v. *King*:[13]

> The defendant had instructed the plaintiffs, who were Stockbrokers, to buy cycle company shares, and the plaintiffs had done so and paid for

9. (1887), 3 T.L.R. 808.
10. (1872), 26 L.T. 656. See also *Wolmershausen* v. *Gullick,* [1893] 2 Ch. 514.
11. [1917] 1 Ch. 99.
12. See *Robinson* v. *Mollett, supra,* for a case where the client was not aware of the usage which his broker observed.   13. (1897), 13 T.L.R. 270.

them. When the defendant failed at the proper time to find the purchase money, the plaintiffs went to a jobber, had a fair price fixed for the shares and then went through the form of selling and buying back the shares at that price.

On appeal, Lord Esher, M.R., said that in this case it was the duty of the broker to give credit for the value of the shares which he had kept for himself. The time when such value ought to be fixed would, of course, vary in different cases according to the circumstances; after examining the facts, the Court of Appeal held that the value had been fixed at a reasonable time.

(i) Where the broker has no right of indemnity

The client is not however obliged to indemnify his broker against the consequences of acts done *dehors* the authority conferred upon him by the client. In *Skelton* v. *Wood*[14] for example, the broker deliberately omitted to keep the bargain open until the time for completion had arrived. This was an elementary transgression of his authority, and clearly the client was not bound to indemnify him against its results.

The client might instruct his broker to make a bargain which the broker must know is unlawful or prohibited in some other way. In *Re London, Hamburg and Continental Exchange Bank, Zulueta's Claim*:[15]

> A broker was instructed by some company directors to buy shares in that company *on behalf of the company*. As with the great majority of other companies, such a purchase of its own shares was prohibited by the memorandum and articles.

It was held that the broker, although he was only obeying his instructions, had made a bargain which was obviously *ultra vires*, and accordingly he could not claim an indemnity from the company. His position as a business man prevents a stockbroker from pleading ignorance in this and comparable situations. Giffard, L. J., said:[16]

> "Mr Henry . . . being a stockbroker, must have known that a purchase by a company of their own shares is not a legal transaction, unless there is a clear, distinct, undoubted and special authority authorising them to do so."

A broker loses his indemnity by acting outside his authority or doing something which is prohibited. *A fortiori* he loses it if he acts

---

14. See p. 131, *ante*.
15. (1870), 5 Ch. App. 444.
16. *Ibid.*, at p. 452.

unreasonably, wastefully or fraudulently: in *Clegg* v. *Townshend*[17] a broker elected unreasonably to defend an action brought against him for the price of shares bought by him on the instructions of his client. It was held that his unreasonableness debarred him from an indemnity in respect of legal costs.

Moreover, if a broker purporting to follow his client's instructions wastefully pays out money which he is not legally bound to pay, he cannot expect his client to indemnify him for such waste. In *Bowlby* v. *Bell*:[18]

> A broker, X, contracted to sell to B shares belonging to his client A. X did not offer the price of the shares to A, or tender a transfer to him for execution. Without the execution of a transfer by A, X could not make delivery to B. So B had to purchase other shares at a higher price. He claimed the difference from X, who paid it and then claimed to be recouped the difference by A.

It was held that A had not authorised X not to deliver the shares bargained for at the earlier and lower price. He had had no say in the matter, because no transfer had been tendered to him for execution. Accordingly A was not bound to indemnify X the difference.

Nor may a broker be indemnified if he has fraudulently misapplied his client's shares, as in *Solloway* v. *McLaughlin*[19] where the brokers sold shares which they had been instructed to carry over.

A broker loses his indemnity if he acts as a principal towards his client, for he is instructed *qua* broker, and is in breach of his duty if he deals not with another, but himself.[20] however, he may contango his client's open position with himself.[21]

(ii) A defaulting broker who has acted outside his authority retains his right of indemnity if the client continues to treat him as his agent

The circumstances in which a broker may lose his right to an indemnity have now been described. But he loses it only at the election of his client, who, if he prefers, may continue their relationship. In *Hartas* v. *Ribbons*[22] the client's choice of alternatives was interpreted as an election not to continue:

> A broker was employed to buy shares, but before the settling day he was declared a defaulter on the Stock Exchange and thereby ceased to be a member. The effect of this was to close the accounts which he then

---

17. (1867), 16 L.T. 180.
18. (1846), 3 C.B. 284.
19. [1938] A.C. 247; [1937] 4 All E.R. 328, P.C.
20. See broker acting as principal, pp. 146–151, *post.*
21. See contangos, pp. 151–155, *post.*
22. (1889), 22 Q.B.D. 254, C.A.

had open with the jobbers at the current prices as fixed by the Official Assignee; but such closure did not, according to the then recognised Stock Exchange practice, affect the client, who, if he wished could have the contract completed. In that case the jobber is bound to complete on settling day. Here the client preferred to accept the official "hammer" prices.

It was held that the client, having ratified the closing of the account before the settling day, was liable to indemnify the broker against the amount for which he was liable to the jobbers on the day of that closure.[1]

E. THE BROKER'S LIEN

A common law lien may be defined as the right of one person to retain possession of the goods of another until his claims are satisfied. Since a client is not entitled to delivery before he has put his broker in funds, the broker is said to have a common law general lien upon the securities of his client in his possession. A *general* lien is the right to retain securities until satisfaction of *all* claims against their owner whether those claims relate to the securities retained or not. The case of *Re London and Globe Finance Corporation*[2] is a clear illustration of this principle:

> Documents relating to shares belonging to a regular client were held by stockbrokers to secure a specific advance of £15,000. When this amount was repaid the documents were left with the brokers, and on subsequent transactions on the Stock Exchange by the client, acting through the same brokers' losses were incurred, for which the client was liable to the brokers.

It was held that, although the *specific* purpose of the deposit had been satisfied by the repayment of the £15,000, the brokers had a *general* lien on the shares for the amount due in respect of the later Stock Exchange transactions. Buckley, J. had no doubts as to the legal position:[3]

> "Here there is nothing at all to exclude the general lien, which it is not, and cannot be, disputed exists. The transactions, as between the customer and the broker, resulted in a sum owing by the customer to the broker, and there were in the possession of the broker securities which had come into his hands in the course of his business as broker of the customer. It is a well-established principle that the broker has, as against

1. But twelve years later in *Levitt* v. *Hamblet, supra*, the Court of Appeal adopted a different view of the practice. The matter was not part of the ratio, but the court proceeded on the assumption that it is not open to a client to bind a jobber to the hammer price.
2. [1902] 2 Ch. 416.   3. *Ibid.*, pp. 420–421.

the customer, the right to hold those securities for the amount due."

But of course the broker's lien takes second place behind prior claims to the securities in question, as in *Peat v. Clayton*:[4]

> The client assigned all his property—including shares—to the plaintiffs as trustees for his creditors, who, not being able to obtain the certificates, gave the company notice of the assignment. The client then sold some of his shares through his brokers on the Stock Exchange, executed a transfer, and received the purchase money. The company (which had notice of the assignment) ultimately removed the purchaser's name from its register and refused to issue certificates. The brokers provided the purchaser with a second block of shares in the same company and then claimed a lien on the first block which they had sold for their client.

It was held that any lien which the brokers might have upon the shares was subject to the prior right of the plaintiffs.

Suppose that the securities which the broker holds in his client's name do not in fact belong to his client. It was held in *Jones v. Peppercorne*[5] that if the broker is unaware that they belong to another person, he may exercise a lien over them in respect of debts owing by the client, provided that there is nothing in the circumstances to put him on enquiry (i.e., to arouse his suspicions).

D. BROKER ACTING AS PRINCIPAL

1. The broker must act as agent

The broker has a fundamental obligation to act for his client and not for himself. Otherwise their relationship would not retain the important elements of good faith and trust.[6] If, for example, a broker who has been instructed to sell buys the shares for himself, he is acting as an agent for his client, but also as a principal for himself. This is a transaction which the law will not enforce—for the broker who is instructed to deal in a market cannot make a short circuit of his obligation by taking the transaction out of that market.

If the client wishes, he can bring an action to have such a bargain rescinded (i.e., declared null and void). In *Armstrong v. Jackson*:[7]

> The plaintiff, a doctor without business experience, instructed the defendant, a broker, to purchase for him 600 shares in the Champion Gold Reefs of West Africa Ltd. The broker had helped to promote that

4. [1906] 1 Ch. 659.   5. (1858), John. 430.
6. *Per* Lord Wynford, in *Rothschild* v. *Brookman, supra.*
7. [1917] 2 K.B. 822.

company and had been allotted a large block of its shares. Instead of
going into the market, he sold the plaintiff *some of his own block*, at
nearly £3 per share, and sent the plaintiff a fictitious contract note. The
value of the shares fell heavily. However, the plaintiff did not take them
up and the broker pretended to carry them over from account to
account, charging the plaintiff a contango rate and differences on each
transaction. The value of the shares continued to diminish. The plaintiff
became worried, and eventually on the defendant's advice took up the
shares. The plaintiff became the registered proprietor and the value of
the shares fell further. Various rumours awakened the plaintiff's
suspicions, and five years after the original purchase he issued a writ
against the defendant claiming to have the purchase set aside. The value
of the shares was then about 5 shillings per share.

It was held that the transaction should be rescinded notwithstanding that the value of the shares had decreased between the date
of purchase and the date of the action for rescission. Although the
broker had apparently done the best for his client in advising him
to take up the shares before they fell further, McCardie, J., held that
this was overridden by the broker's breach of good faith, and he
said:[8]

> "It matters not that the broker sells at the market price or that
> he acts without intent to defraud . . . the prohibition of the law is
> absolute. It will not allow an agent to please himself in a situation
> which, under ordinary circumstances, would tempt a man to do that
> which is not best for his principal . . . the parties must be put *in statu
> quo*."

Brokers acting as principals have sometimes used more intricate
transactions as a smokescreen to cover their fraudulent intentions.
So in *Skelton* v. *Wood*[9] the broker, after "buying" his own shares
for a client, *resold* them without the knowledge of the client, and
subsequently bought them back again. He tried to charge the client
with the differences as though such shares had been kept open on his
account, but the court stripped the transaction of its camouflage and
held that he was not entitled to recover.

(i) The broker may act as principal with his client's consent

A client is, of course, free to conduct his business affairs in his
own way. He may be quite agreeable to his broker dealing with him
as a principal. Then if he claims to rescind the contract the broker
can say by way of defence (*a*) that he made full disclosure that he
was acting on his own behalf, and (*b*) that his client consented to
that situation. In *Ellis and Co's Trustees* v. *Watsham:*[10]

8. [1917] 2 K.B. 822, at p. 824.   9. See p. 131, *ante*.   10. (1923), 155 L.T. Jo. 363.

W purchased shares through E and Co who sold him their own shares and forwarded to W two contract notes on each of which were the words: "bought of ourselves as principals," and no commission was charged. W stated in evidence that he had not read the statement on the bought note, and had not noticed that no commission was charged. W subsequently purchased other shares through E and Co from outside persons, and in this case the bought note contained no reference to E and Co being principals, and a commission *was* charged.

On a counterclaim by W for rescission it was held that on the first occasion E and Co had made a sufficiently full and accurate disclosure to W of the fact that they were selling as principals, and that W, with full knowledge, gave his assent to their position.

Clearly the outcome of each case must depend upon its own circumstances; *Ellis and Co's Trustees* v. *Watsham* [11] shows that the courts will not rescue clients who cannot be bothered to read the documents which their brokers provide.

(ii) *The broker ought not to act for both buyer and seller*

A broker may not act for both buyer and seller without informing them both that he is so acting. [12] Rule 89 (1) provides that "a broker shall not receive brokerage from more than one principal on a transaction carried through directly between two principals". It might be submitted, however, on the authority of *Hippisley* v. *Knee Brothers* [13] that disclosure by the broker and the consent of both his principals might enable the broker to recover commission from both on the basis that neither commission was earned under the veil of secrecy: but the Rules expressly forbid this.

(iii) *Mere non-disclosure of the purchaser does not make the broker a principal*

If a broker is employed by his client to sell shares and sends his client a contract note which omits the name of a jobber or other purchaser, the broker does not *ipso facto* become a principal and liable to the client for the purchase price of the shares. [14]

2. The broker must make no profit save his commission

The scales of a broker's commission are regulated by the Rules and Regulations of the Stock Exchange. [15] If therefore a broker tries to extract a profit over and above his commission as broker he

---

11. (1923), 155 L.T. Jo. 363.   12. *Andrews* v. *Ramsay & Co.*, [1903] 2 K.B. 635.
13. [1905] 1 K.B. 1.   14. *Gill* v. *Shepherd & Co.* (1902), 19 T.L.R. 17.
15. See Chapter 7. The Stock Exchange Commission Rules provide for minimum scale only. A broker can charge a greater commission than that set out in the scales provided, of course, that it is shown as "commission" on the contract note.

becomes, to that extent, a principal in the matter and, to that extent, he is in breach of his duty to act as an agent.

There are various devices which unscrupulous brokers have adopted in order to make a forbidden profit, and although their profit was only forbidden *pro tanto*, the law has regarded the whole transaction as tainted with fraud and allowed the client to repudiate it altogether. In *Stange & Co* v. *Lowitz* [16] for example:

> The client discovered that the plaintiffs, who were stockbrokers but not members of the Stock Exchange, had, in the contract notes which they had sent him, added something to the price at which they had really bought, besides charging commission. It was held that this amounted to a sale by the broker of his own shares and the client could repudiate it *in toto*.

The broker who makes a profit over and above his commission must account for it to his client. In *Erskine Oxenford & Co* v. *Sachs* [17] the artifice was a little more subtle than in *Stange* v. *Lowitz*:

> Brokers had made a contract on behalf of their clients for the purchase of shares on the Stock Exchange. When the clients failed to provide the money for the price of the shares, the brokers decided to close the account. They went into the market, sold a like amount of shares to a jobber and, as part of the same transaction, they repurchased the shares from him on their own account. This put-through transaction enabled the brokers to repurchase the shares at a lower price than they would have had to pay if they had purchased them in the market in the ordinary way. Notwithstanding that, the brokers made up an account in which they charged their clients commission on the "sale" of the shares to the jobber.

It was held that the brokers, having acted in a fiduciary capacity in the sale of the shares, and having, by reason of the sale and the repurchase being effected as one transaction, obtained a profit for themselves, were bound to account for the profit to their clients.

Suppose, however, that a client imposes a limit on the price at which his broker is to buy shares. There is nothing to prevent him making an agreement with his broker that the broker's remuneration shall consist of the difference between the limit and any lesser price at which he succeeds in buying the shares, [18] provided that remuneration is not less than the minimum provided by the Rules.

A stockbroker (or his clerk) who acts for an estate of which he is also a trustee, must not use his business capacity as an excuse for infringing the equitable rule that trustees may not make a profit from their trusteeship. [19]

16. (1898), 14 T.L.R. 468. 17. [1901] 2 K.B. 504.
18. *Platt* v. *Rowe* (1909), 26 T.L.R. 49. 19. *Williams* v. *Barton*, [1927] 2 Ch. 9.

3. The lumping of orders

Suppose that a broker is instructed by several clients to buy or carry over shares in the same company. Since a jobber with whom he deals treats the broker as a principal, it is no concern of the jobber whether he is acting for one client or for a hundred. There is an assumption, based on usage, that the jobber appreciates that the broker may be acting for more than one client, and hence that the jobber intends to make separate contracts with every client for whom the broker happens to act.[20] But where contracts have been lumped in this way, the court will nevertheless look at one contract in isolation in order to decide whether it contains certain implied terms, and if so whether those terms are reasonable.[1]

It makes no difference to the application of the lumping rule that the broker acts for clients in some of the contracts lumped, and on his own behalf in the others.[2] In *Re Rogers, ex parte Rogers*:[3]

> A broker had purchased large amounts of stock all as a principal on his own behalf but with a view to their division among different clients from whom he had instructions to buy. One such client was a speculator, who had instructed the broker to buy and sell stocks with the intention that he should only receive or pay "differences". Admittedly he had authorised the broker to pay any losses for him but, it was argued, he was not bound to indemnify the broker on a loss where a portion of the broker's purchase had been made specifically for him.

The Court of Appeal rejected that argument and held that the broker could recover the loss.

The Scottish case of *Maffett* v. *Stewart*[4] provides an interesting contrast. In that case it was clear that the broker's purchases were *not* referable to the instructions of his client:

> On carrying over £10,000 "Trunk Thirds" stock bought for a client, the broker sent his client a continuation note stating: "I have continued for you as under, Sold 10,000 Trunk Thirds at £50, bought at £50 3s. 3d. com in a/c." Clearly, the bought price did not have any connection with the figure 10,000. In reality, the broker had bought a much larger quantity in different parcels and at different prices. These he lumped together and divided among those of his clients who had given him orders for Trunk Thirds, charging as the price *the average* of the different prices. This average price (£50 3s. 3d.) was in fact the one stated in the continuation note. It did not correspond with, and was not

20. *Scott and Horton* v. *Godfrey*, [1901] 2 K.B. 726.
1. As in *Consolidated Goldfields of South Africa, Ltd.* v. *E. Spiegel & Co.* (1909), 100 L.T. 351.
2. *Scott and Horton* v. *Godfrey* (*supra*).   3. (1880), 15 Ch. D. 207.
4. (1887), Ct. of Sess. 506.

referable to, any of the prices at which he had purchased the various parcels. The broker sued his client for payment of differences on a number of such transactions.

The Court of Session was unable to connect the broker's purchases with orders alleged to have been given by his clients: no common factor could be found. The majority of the court held that in the circumstances it had to treat the broker as having acted on his own account. Lord Shand, who concurred with the majority, gave his reasons in a hypothetical way:

"The case would have been very different if it . . . had been proved that the defender (the client) had authorised the pursuer (the broker) to speculate for him precisely in the way that the pursuer did—that is, to buy stocks in different quantities and at varying prices—to lump those and to strike an average price—and to take and hold the stocks, or rather a certain proportion of them, as allocated and as applicable to the defender's orders; or even had authorised the pursuer to carry on the whole transaction as principal himself, in his own name, though truly as agent for the defender . . . But no case of this kind is either alleged or proved. Such a course of dealing would be quite beyond the ordinary duties or powers of a broker . . . Besides . . . there is no proof that the defender agreed to make the pursuer an agent to speculate in his own name for the defender, and in the way he did, mixing up the transactions of different customers in regard to quantities and prices of stocks."

E. CONTANGOS AND RELATED ARRANGEMENTS

1. Contangos

How the expression "contango" became part of the Stock Exchange vocabulary is obscure, but there is little doubt about its origin. It is thought to have a fortuitous derivation[5] (possibly via the Spanish *contengo*), from the Latin verb *continere*, which means to contain or hold within fixed limits. In its primary sense, a contango is a customary arrangement whereby the payment for securities bought or sold for one account is held up or "carried over" until the next or a subsequent account. The word is synonymous with continuation. In its secondary sense, contango means the commission paid to the seller by the purchaser in consideration for such a postponement.

Suppose that a client requests his broker to purchase securities for which the client is unable or unwilling to pay at the time. The

5. See Murray, *A New English Dictionary*: the first record of its use is in 1853 among the stockbrokers of Liverpool.

shares will, of course, have to be paid for on the next account day, and accordingly money for that payment will have to be found by the broker instead. This arrangement gives rise to two important legal consequences which can now be regarded as well settled:

(i) The broker becomes the absolute owner of the securities purchased; and

(ii) The broker is subject to a new contract to resell to the client (known as the "giver") an equivalent number of the same securities for the agreed subsequent account.

These two principles are not mutually exclusive and should be considered together.

Continuation or contango is in form and in law a sale and repurchase, or purchase and resale as the case may be.[6] The vital point is that when a broker buys securities on contango, he is treated by the law as an out-and-out purchaser, and not a mere mortgagee or pledgee. In *Bentinck* v. *London Joint Stock Bank*:[7]

A client employed his brokers to purchase shares on contango. He authorised the brokers to hold the shares as security for their advances, and also to repledge them. Accordingly the brokers deposited the shares with their bankers as security for a bank loan. Eventually the brokers were declared defaulters on the Stock Exchange and the client claimed to redeem the securities.

It was held that there was nothing to lead the bank to suppose that the shares were not the brokers' *own* property; and since the bank was *bona fide* holder for value without notice, the client could not redeem the securities on paying to the bank the amount due from himself to the brokers; he could redeem only by paying the larger amount due from the brokers to the bank.

Although the broker becomes the absolute owner of securities purchased on contango, the law will imply a new and reciprocal contract to re-acquire similar securities for the client. The parties are not merely gaining time for the performance of the old contract: they are making a fresh contract which stands on its own.[8] The broker must acquire and retain an *equivalent* number of securities available for resale to the client. He cannot take advantage of the contango to make a secret profit at the client's expense. The position is well illustrated by the decision of the Privy Council in *Solloway* v. *McLaughlin*:[9]

6. *Bongiovanni* v. *Société Générale* (1886), 54 L.T. 320, and see Rule 107.
7. [1893] 2 Ch. 120.
8. *Levitt* v. *Hamblet, supra.*
9. [1938] A.C. 247; [1937] 4 All E.R. 328, P.C.

A client instructed his stockbrokers to buy for him on the Toronto Stock Exchange a number of shares on margin. The shares declined in value, but the brokers carried them over for him. The client deposited shares of the same class with his brokers as security. Sensing that the value of the shares would continue to drop, the brokers adopted a fraudulent device. They purported to make valid contracts of purchase for the client on contango, but *contemporaneously* sold shares of the same company and used their client's shares to complete the sales. The shares fell in value as expected. When the client closed his account the brokers repurchased the shares (now considerably cheaper), and delivered them to the client.

On appeal from the Supreme Court of Canada, the Privy Council held—

(i) as to the shares originally ordered by the client, he was entitled, on discovery of the fraud, to recover the money he had paid on the footing of an honest transaction, giving credit for the actual value of the shares at the time that he eventually closed his account and received them;

(ii) as to the shares deposited on margin, the broker never had any right to deal with them, and the client could recover damages for conversion.

Lord Atkin summarised the issues with his accustomed clarity: [10]

"A broker is not considered to be under an obligation to retain for his client the specific shares which may be delivered to him under the contract made for his client, but he has, of course, to get into his possession, and retain, an equivalent number of shares. Under the fraudulent system (the brokers) . . . were bears when their clients were bulls; they correctly anticipated the fall of the market, and when their clients demanded the shares they went into the market and bought them at the fallen price to their own substantial profit."

The authority of a broker to carry over a bargain depends upon his authority to act as his principal's agent; and so it was held that where a client who had a continuation account died, any authority, express or implied, to his broker to extend the continuation determined. [11]

A. COMMISSION ON CONTANGO, DIFFERENCES AND THE MAKING-UP PRICE

There is a clear distinction between the commission in consideration of a contango (itself known as "contango") and the difference payable when a sale and repurchase (or purchase and resale) are set off against each other. Each will be separately defined.

10. [1938] A.C. 247, at p. 256.   11. *Re Overweg, Haas* v. *Durant,* [1900] 1 Ch. 209.

(i) Commission on contango

"Contango" is the consideration which a purchaser pays to the seller through his broker for the privilege of having his bargain carried over. It may consist of a price per share or other security, or in a percentage of the value of the security. The rate which brokers may charge in respect of contango business is regulated by the Rules and Regulations of the Stock Exchange.[12]

A commission or rate of interest payable to the purchaser who wishes to contango, rather than by him, is commonly known as a backwardation.

(ii) Differences

A difference may be simply defined as the balance of sums due between a broker and his client at the end of an account.

A broker purchases shares for his client on contango. The shares rise in value, and are carried over. During a subsequent account the client calls upon the broker to deliver (i.e., re-sell to him). The client is entitled not only to the shares, but also the difference between the original purchase price and their price at the end of the subsequent account. Conversely, if the value of the shares has declined, the burden of the difference must be borne by the client: he owes it to the broker.

(iii) The making-up price

When shares are re-sold or re-purchased on the closure of a contango arrangement, such resale or repurchase is for the next settling day, and they change hands at the making-up price of the day fixed by the orders of the Council.[13] The bargains may simply be balanced in the broker's books without delivery, but if delivery takes place the original price will be charged plus or minus that difference. The commission or "contango" is independent of the difference, and charged as a separate item.

2. Giving-on

Suppose that on contango day the ultimate purchaser does not wish to take up and pay for the security which his broker has already bought. When this occurs his broker may agree to "give-on" the securities. In essence, the giver agrees to sell the securities for the *current* account and, as to the *following* account, he makes a new contract to buy the securities for *that* account. A difference is

12. Rule 192 (4).
13. Making-up prices are deemed to represent the ruling middle prices at the close of business on the last day of the dealing period. Under Rule 109, they must be published in the Stock Exchange Official List of making-up prices at 10.30 a.m. on contango day.

payable by or to the giver according to the interim fluctuation in the share values; and he will of course be charged commission or interest.

Where a broker gives-on securities for his client, and then deposits the securities with his bank as cover for an advance or an overdraft, the bank is, as was decided in *Bentinck* v. *London Joint Stock Bank*,[14] not bound to enquire into the broker's authority to deal with them.

3. Taking-in

Taking-in denotes the contango arrangement in reverse. On a sale of shares, the seller may wish to postpone *delivery* until the next account. Here too there is a new contract. The seller (known as "the taker") is obliged, under the principles enunciated above, to *repurchase* for the *current* account an *equivalent* number of similar securities, and retain them for delivery in the new account.[15] If the price of the shares alters in the meantime, the difference must be calculated and taken into account. But the seller becomes absolute owner of the shares carried over, and if he sells *them* at a profit, he can retain the profit for himself.[16]

F. LOANS, MORTGAGES AND PLEDGES

1. Loans

Members of the Stock Exchange frequently lend each other money against the deposit of securities. The period of the loan normally extends to the next account day. When the account day arrives either party may determine the loan; but there is usually an arrangement that if the loan is not so determined, it will continue from account to account.

The value of the securities lent will fluctuate from time to time. If it has fallen since the last account day, the borrower will repay to the lender part of the money borrowed. Conversely if the value has risen, the borrower might obtain a further advance or alternatively return some of the securities to the lender. Loans are no longer for the full market value of securities: they may be for less than the full value so that the lender has a "margin" or "cover" as a cushion against the borrower's possible default. When securities are transferred to secure the repayment of a loan the registration fee, and the cost of stamping the transfer and the agreement for the loan must be borne by the borrower.[17]

14. [1893] 2 Ch. 120.
15. See *Re Plumbly, ex parte Grant* (1880), 13 Ch. D. 667.
16. *Bongiovanni* v. *Société Générale* (1886), 54 L.T. 320, C.A.
17. Rule 128 (2).

If the borrower does not repay the loan when due he is declared a
defaulter and the securities are dealt with according to the Rules
applicable to default.[18] If the cover for the loan is in the form of
stocks and shares, the lender must realise his securities within three
days or such longer period as the Official Assignee may allow. Failing that, he must take them over at prices fixed by the Official
Assignee.[19] If the security proves insufficient, the deficiency may be
proved against the defaulter's general estate as a stock claim.[20]

If the loan was unsecured, any securities or payment which the
lender has received in the fourteen days prior to the declaration of
default must be returned to the Official Assignee for the benefit of
the defaulter's stock exchange creditors generally. The lender cannot prove for his claim in the stock exchange default unless it is
admitted by the Committee of Creditors, who have power to decide
whether to treat it as a stock claim or a deferred claim or partly one
and partly the other.[1]

2. Mortgages and pledges

Suppose that a purchaser of securities is unable to provide the
money to take them up, and cannot get the seller to carry them over.
He or his broker (the mortgagor) can break the deadlock by arranging that a banker or other person (the mortgagee) lends him the
money with which to pay. The mortgagee will then take the securities or the certificates representing them for himself as security for
repayment of the money which he has advanced.

The basic difference between a mortage or pledge, and a contango, is that:

(*a*) In a contango the person who carries over the securities
becomes their owner. He can dispose of them as he pleases. His
obligation is to deliver the same amount of *similar* securities on the
next account day; but

(*b*) in a mortgage or pledge the securities deposited with the
lender (the mortgagee or pledgee) remain the property of the borrower (the mortgagor). The lender's duty is to return the *identical*
securities on repayment. He cannot dispose of them himself unless
and until the mortgagor defaults in the repayment of his loan. If he
does so, he must account to the mortgagor for any profit or loss
which he has made.[2]

18. See *Ponsolle* v. *Webber*, [1908] 1 Ch. 254.
19. See Rule 184 (2). There is a right of appeal to the Council in cases of dispute.
20. *Ibid.*, and see *Re Morgan, ex parte Phillips, ex parte Marnham* (1860), 2 De G. F.
    & J. 634.
1. See Rule 182.
2. *Langton* v. *Waite* (1869), 4 Ch. App. 402.

Mortgages and pledges are distinct concepts. Where the borrower pledges his securities the lender merely has them in his *custody*; he has no title at law or in equity and is bound to return them on repayment of the loan. No pledge takes place until the thing pledged is *delivered.* A mortgage on the other hand does not depend upon possession. The borrower can deposit share certificates with the lender, who then becomes an equitable mortgagee.[3] If the share certificates are accompanied by a blank transfer the borrower thereby gives the mortgagee authority, if he defaults in repayment of the loan, to fill in the blanks and get himself registered as owner. He can then dispose of them as he pleases. On the other hand the deposit of bearer securities is treated as a pledge.[4]

LAW APPLICABLE TO BOTH MORTGAGES AND PLEDGES

The following rules apply to mortgages and pledges generally.

(*a*) A mortgagee or pledgee is in one sense the borrower's agent. He has an implied right to sub-mortgage or repledge the securities to the extent of his own interest therein,[5] i.e., to the amount of the original advance.

But suppose the mortgagee or pledgee exceeds his authority by sub-mortgaging or repledging more than his interest. What is the borrower's position *vis-à-vis* the sub-mortgagee or sub-pledgee? If the latter has been invested with the *legal* title to the securities—if, that is to say, he has become their registered owner by a transfer duly executed by the borrower, he obtains an indefeasible right of ownership. If, on the other hand, the sub-mortgagee or sub-pledgee has only an *equitable* title (as where the mortgagee or pledgee has deposited with him a share certificate and blank transfer) the borrower as true owner can deny his title and recover the securities sub-mortgaged or re-pledged on repayment of the advance.

(*b*) If there is an agreed time for repayment, and the loan is not repaid within that time, the mortgagee or pledgee may sell the securities without having an express power to do so.[6]

---

3. But see *Fuller* v. *Glyn Mills, Currie & Co.,* [1914] 2 K.B. 168, where it was held that if the owner of shares allows his brokers to *pledge* them, and the brokers leave the form of transfer in such a condition as to give pledgees from the brokers the impression that they have authority to dispose of the legal title, he cannot claim them back from a *bona fide* transferee from the brokers.
4. *Gorgier* v. *Mieville* (1824), 2 B. & C. 45; *Donald* v. *Suckling* (1866), L.R. 1 Q.B. 585; *Carter* v. *Wake* (1877), 4 Ch. D. 605.
5. *Re Tahiti Cotton Co., ex parte Sargent* (1874), L.R. 17 Eq. 273; *France* v. *Clark* (1883–4), 26 Ch. D. 257.
6. *Wilson* v. *Tooker* (1714), 5 Bro. 193; *Re Morritt, ex parte Official Receiver* (1886), 18 Q.B.D. 222 *per* Cotton, L. J., at p. 232; *Deverges* v. *Sandeman, Clark & Co.* [1902] 1 Ch. 579, C.A., *per* Stirling, L. J., at p. 592.

(*c*) Where no time is fixed for repayment, the mortgagee or pledgee may demand repayment; and he may resell if he gives reasonable notice of his intention to do so.[7]

(*d*) The borrower may redeem at any time before the actual sale.[8]

(*e*) On redemption, the mortgagee or pledgee must return the *identical* securities mortgaged or pledged, if capable of identification. If he has sold them, profits and losses must be accounted for.[9]

(*f*) Where securities have been mortgaged, and default is made in repayment, the mortgagee may obtain a decree of foreclosure and thereby make them his own. But the pledgee's only remedy is sale.[10]

G. OPTIONS

Options may be divided into two classes:

(i) a *call*, which is the privilege of being able to call for delivery of a particular security at an agreed price and within a certain period; and

(ii) a *put*, which is a similar privilege to make delivery.

A *double option* denotes the double privilege: its holder may do both. Subject to the Rules and Regulations of the Stock Exchange, options and double options may be bargained for in the same way as securities.

1. Option must be a genuine option

An option is not enforceable unless it is a genuine option. There must be nothing to prevent the buyer of the option (i.e., the giver of the option money) exercising his privilege if he decides to do so:

> A purports to sell to B the option to call for delivery of 500 shares at £20 a share on a specified settling day. There is, however, a tacit agreement between them that B will not call for delivery on the agreed day. They agree instead that if the shares are worth more than £20 on the agreed day A will pay B the difference, and if less than £20 B will pay A the difference.

This is a contract for differences, and being a mere wager, unforceable under the Gaming Act 1845. No sale has taken place, and the parties

---

7. *Re Morritt, supra; Deverges* v. *Sandeman, supra.*
8. *Ibid.*   9. *Langton* v. *Waite, supra.*
10. *Carter* v. *Wake* (1877), 4 Ch. D. 605.

are merely staking money on the outcome of a future uncertain event
—namely a possible fluctuation in the value of some shares.[11]

2. Time is of the essence in options

Where however there is a genuine option agreement, time is of
the essence of that agreement and the parties can insist on a strict
compliance with its conditions. In *Hare* v. *Nicoll*:[12]

> Under a deed, the appellant sold the respondent 50,000 shares in a
> private company with an option for himself to repurchase 25,000 for
> £4,687 10s. if the appellant should before May 1st give the respondent
> notice of his intention in writing, and before June 1st pay her that
> specified price. The appellant gave notice by a letter dated April 30th,
> but written on May 1st. The respondent accepted this as notice duly
> given, but did not receive the re-purchase money before June 1st. The
> respondent's solicitors wrote a letter, dated June 1st and posted on June
> 4th, informing the appellant that the option was terminated. On June
> 7th the appellant tendered the specified price, which the respondent
> refused as she had disposed of the shares elsewhere. The appellant
> brought an action claiming £10,937, the difference between the market
> value of the shares on June 1st and the option price specified in the
> agreement.

The claim failed and the appeal was dismissed. Willmer, L. J.,
referred to a passage in the judgment of Parker, J., in *Re
Schwabacher*:[13]

> "With regard to contracts for the sale of shares, I think that time is of
> the essence of the contract both at law and in equity. Shares continually
> vary in price from day to day, and that is precisely why courts of equity
> have considered such a contract to be one in which time is of the essence
> of the contract, and not like a contract for the sale and purchase of real
> estate, in which time is not of the essence of the contract."

3. Options carry the benefit of a takeover bid

The question whether an option carries the benefit of a takeover
bid made while the option remains open was fully explored in the
case of *Cunliffe-Owen* v. *Teather and Greenwood*:[14]

> On June 30th the plaintiff purchased, through his brokers, put options
> for 20,000 Rootes "A" shares, including an option to sell 7,000 of the
> shares to the defendants at 14s. 2¼d. The option was to remain open
> until September 24th. On August 10th Chrysler made an offer to

---

11. See *Buttenlandsche Bankvereeniging* v. *Hildeseim* (1903), 19 T.L.R. 641, C.A.
12. [1966] 2 Q.B. 130; [1966] 1 All E.R. 285.   13. (1908), 98 L.T. 127, at p. 129.
14. [1967] 3 All E.R. 561.

acquire, at 21*s*. per share, 50 per cent of any shareholder's holding of "A" shares, the offer to be open for acceptance up to September 28th. On August 11th the Stock Exchange Council, under its powers in the Deed of Settlement, issued a notice to the effect that it would treat the value of the offer for the "A" shares as 6*s*. 6*d*. per share. On September 23rd the defendants indicated that they would accept delivery only of "A" shares which had been affected by the offer. The plaintiff, on the other hand, insisted that he could make delivery of the shares ex bid. Subsequently he brought an action claiming (*inter alia*) a declaration that he had validly exercised his option on that basis.

Ungoed-Thomas, J., heard expert evidence, and found that there is a usage of the Stock Exchange under which a purchaser of shares acquires them "cum all": i.e., he takes every benefit accruing to those shares; and he held that the defendants were entitled to the benefit of the offer at the Council's valuation, provided only that the offer had been made after the option contract.

4. The regulation of option dealings
A broker firm wishing to do option business as option dealers must now, under Rule 94, apply to the Council of the Stock Exchange for annual authorisation. On the application form the brokers undertake (*inter alia*) to keep separate accounts for their option transactions. Under Rule 110 a member may not deal in options extending for a period beyond the seventh ensuing account day.

5. The price of options
When securities on which options are open are dealt in "ex rights", a valuation of those rights must be made in order to determine the price of the securities.[15] An official price for the rights will be fixed upon application to the Secretary of the Quotations Department, and this price must be taken into account in settling the option.

No option for the put or call of a security may be fixed at an ex dividend price prior to such security being officially made ex dividend.[16]

6. The procedure for exercising options
An option can be declared on any declaration day (at the election of the giver of option money) up to and including the final declaration day for which the option was effected. Under Rule 110, if no such declaration is made, the option is deemed to be abandoned.

15. Rule 115.
16. Rule 165 (2) (*d*).

H. BARGAINS: THE FORMATION
AND RECORDING OF
A STOCK EXCHANGE CONTRACT

The Stock Exchange procedure for dealing was described in the last chapter; it remains to consider how, under that system, the parties actually formulate their bargain, once made.

1. Dictum meum pactum

The motto of the Stock Exchange, London, is "My word is my bond", and there is a long-standing usage that a contract for the sale of securities may be made orally. This usage binds a broker's client because it is a well-settled rule of law that a person who employs his agent to deal in a particular market on his behalf must be taken to have authorised his agent to deal according to the usages of that market.[17] This is so even where the principal is aware that the usage is contrary to an Act of Parliament.[18]

The usage that securities may be bought and sold by word of mouth is a very powerful one. So formerly, when the Banking Companies (Shares) Act 1867 (generally known as Leeman's Act) provided that bank shares could not be sold except by a contract in writing, members of the Stock Exchange felt free to disregard the Act. The courts looked upon such disregard as unreasonable; nevertheless, they were prepared to uphold bargains based upon this irregularity unless it could be shown that the principal was unaware of it.[19] The victory of usage over statute was complete when Parliament, recognising that Leeman's Act was unnecessary, repealed it under the Statute Law Revision Act 1966.

As soon as the bargain has been made, both dealers will enter it in a small book (which they carry with them), known as a "jobbing book".

2. The marking and recording of bargains

A. MARKING

Either dealer may "mark" the bargain by filling up a marking slip appropriate to the bargain that has been done, and lodging it in the appropriate box provided at the marking boards.

17. *Sutton* v. *Tatham* (1839), 10 Ad. & El. 27.
18. *Loring* v. *Davis* (1886), 32 Ch. D. 625.
19. *Perry* v. *Barnett* (1885), 15 Q.B.D. 388.

Marking slips are compulsory in the case of the following bargains:[20]

(*a*) Broker to broker bargains other than those resulting from the exercise of an option.

(*b*) Bargains executed with non-members.

(*c*) Bargains executed with country brokers.

(*d*) Bargains put through the market.

(*e*) Delayed delivery bargains[1] and forward bargains.[2]

The marking of any bargain other than those mentioned above is optional.[3] But bargains at a price including broker's commission or done with the Buying-in and Selling-out Department may not be marked.[4]

Bargains should be marked without delay, and may be marked up to 2.15 p.m.[5] Bargains done on the previous day either after 2.15 p.m., or inadvertently omitted may be marked before 11 a.m. on the next business day.[6]

B. RECORDING

A marked bargain is recorded when the Clerks of the House enter on the marking boards, and subsequently publish in the Official List, the price shown on the marking slip. Only one mark in any security is recorded at any one price. When dealing in a security has been suspended, no mark may be recorded in respect of that security.[7] Special boards are provided for the recording of bargains in securities quoted in provincial or foreign stock exchanges.[8]

The Rules provide for the recording of bargains not marked,[9] for complaints as to marks and their adjudication,[10] and for the expunging of marks with the authority of the Chairman, a Deputy Chairman, or two members of the Quotations Committee.[11]

Special distinguishing signs are used in the recording of bargains:[12]

‡ Bargains at special prices.

△ Bargains done with or between non-members other than country brokers.

§ Bargains executed with country brokers.

∅ Bargains done on the previous day either after 2.15 p.m., or inadvertently omitted.

♣ Bargains done for delayed delivery.

20. Rule 160 (1).
1. Rule 96 (4) (*b*).
2. Rule 97 (3).
3. Rule 160 (3).
4. Rule 160 (2).
5. Rule 160 (4) (*a*).
6. Rule 160 (4) (*b*).
7. Rule 161 (1).
8. Rule 161 (2).
9. Rule 161 (3).
10. Rule 162 (1), (2) and (3).
11. Rule 162 (4).
12. Rule 161 (4).

Rule 159 (7) provides for the suspension of the recording of bargains where necessary.

3. Books
When the contracting dealers return to their respective offices, they record the bargain in their various books. All bargains must be booked in the name of a stock exchange firm.[13]

A broker, if acting for a client, enters the bargain in his "clients' ledger" (i.e., under the names of his various clients). In every case the bargain is entered in his "checking book", "journal" or "day book" (i.e., under the names of the various securities) and his "jobbers' ledger" (i.e., under the names of the various jobbers).

A jobber also enters the bargain in his "checking book", "journal" and "jobbers' ledger". In his "jobbers' ledger" he enters all bargains with other members, whether jobbers or brokers.

4. The checking of bargains
In the morning of the business day after a bargain is effected the checking books of both dealers are taken by their clerks to the Checking Room in the Stock Exchange, and each bargain is read out and checked. If the entries do not tally, and the members concerned cannot agree (which is most unusual), the matter must be referred to the arbitration of one or more other members. If arbitrators cannot be found, or are unable to come to a decision, the dispute may be referred to the Council,[14] whose decision is final.[15]

5. The contract note
Since members make their bargains orally, the entries in their jobbing books form the only contemporaneous evidence of what has taken place between them. But the broker is in a different position *vis-à-vis* his client. Statute provides that any person who effects a sale or purchase of any stock or marketable security of the value of £5 or upwards as a broker or agent, and any person (including the manager under a unit trust scheme)[16] who by way of business deals, or holds himself out as dealing as a principal in any stock or marketable security, and buys or sells any such stock or marketable security of a value of £5 or upwards, must *forthwith* make, execute and transmit a contract note to his principal, or to his vendor or purchaser as the case may be.[17] Contract notes attract *ad valorem* stamp duty on a specified scale.[18]

13. Rule 84 (1).   14. Rule 75 (1).   15. Rule 75 (2).
16. Finance Act 1946, s. 54 (6).
17. Finance (1909–10) Act 1910, s. 78 (1).
18. *Ibid.,* s. 77 (1); Finance Act 1947, s. 52 (2) (*b*) (v).

A contract note is usually in the following form.

(Broker's address and date)

Bought (or sold) for and on account of A. Client, Esq.

                                   £   p

100 Imperial Chemical Industries Ord. Shares of £1
each fully paid
Commission
Stamp Duty
Contract stamp

For July 21st 1975 Settlement
  (signed) X Y and Co.
  Members of the Stock Exchange, London.
  Subject to the Rules and Regulations of the Stock Exchange.

The wording of a contract note is not necessarily conclusive as to the subject matter. In *May and Hart* v. *Angeli*: [19]

The contract note recited: "Bought by order of A. Angeli Esq., London, 5,000 Klerksdorp Proprietary Shares at 2½." It was held that evidence was admissible to show that Mr Angeli had in fact instructed his brokers to acquire shares in a particular pool ("Pool No. 2") of a syndicate which had been formed for the purchase of the same Klerksdorp Proprietary Shares.

Where such a mistake had been made, the court has power to rectify the contract note.[20]

6. Securities forming an interest in land

The Stock Exchange usage of making an oral contract seems to be excluded in the case of securities forming an interest in land. Under section 40 of the Law of Property Act 1925 no action may be brought on a contract for the sale of land *or an interest in land* unless that contract be in writing and signed by the person to be charged. A security may form an interest in land depending upon the constitution of the body issuing the security, and upon the nature of the security itself. In *Attree* v. *Hawe*[1] it was held that debenture

19. (1898), 14 T.L.R. 551, H.L.
20. *Dails* v. *Lloyd* (1848), 12 Q.B. 531.
 1. (1878), 9 Ch. D. 337.

stock forming a charge on the undertaking of a railway company was no more an interest in land than the ordinary shares in that company.

7. Completion

This will be considered in a later chapter.[2]

2. Chapter 8.

CHAPTER 7

Commissions

A broker who makes a bargain for his client on the Stock Exchange is obliged to charge him commission at the full rate normally applicable, and he may only make such reductions as are authorised by the Rules.[1] The broker is bound on the one hand by the Rules, which forbid him to charge a rate below the stated minimum, and on the other hand by the law, which does not allow him to make any profit *save* his commission.[2]

Only brokers may charge commission; consequently a person who is instructed to act as a broker may not act as principal instead. Suppose for example that a broker is instructed to go into the market and buy 200 shares in British Petroleum, but that he sells to his client 200 of his *own* shares in British Petroleum. He is not allowed to charge his client commission in such a case, because the bargain is not a stock exchange transaction: and unless he makes it plain to his client that he acts as his own principal, the client will be entitled to repudiate the bargain.[3]

Accordingly where a broker charges his client *no* commission, there must be a *prima facie* assumption that he is acting as principal. But the assumption will not operate where the broker merely makes an unequivocal statement to that effect: he must go further and bring the fact that he acts as principal home to his client. So in the words of one learned authority:[4]

> "A mere statement at the top of a contract note as follows: 'Where no commission is charged this contract is issued by us as principals, but not as brokers or agents,' coupled with the omission of any amount opposite the item 'Commission' in the account lower down, will not be sufficient, if the words in fact escape the attention of the buyer. Nor are the words

1. Rule 200.
2. This point was well established by decisions of the late nineteenth and early twentieth century: see *Stange & Co* v. *Lowitz* (1898), 14 T.L.R. 468 C.A.; *Erskine Oxenford and Co* v. *Sachs*, [1901] 2 K.B. 504; *Cf. Re Finlay, C. S. Wilson & Co* v. *Finlay*, [1913] 1 Ch. 565; see also *Platt* v. *Rowe* (1909), 26 T.L.R. 49; *Williams* v. *Barton*, [1927] 2 Ch. 9.
3. See pp. 146–147, *ante.*
4. Hart, *Law of Banking* (4th Edn.) p. 1050.

'sold to' in place of 'bought for' sufficient to inform persons not experienced in stock exchange transactions that the broker is not acting as broker, but as principal."[5]

If in such a situation the client, having noticed or discovered the fact that the broker was acting for himself, elected to go on and adopt the transaction, it would become a contract binding on both sides. But that would not, of course, enable the broker to charge a commission—the broker cannot have it both ways. Nor, looking at the matter from another angle, may he act as a principal for the purpose of evading the commission Rules, or adopt any other procedure for a like purpose; and he cannot commute his commission for a fixed payment or salary unless he obtains the special authorisation of the Council.[6]

Except for business transacted with country brokers, in overseas markets or in Euro-Currency Bonds,[7] a broker may not execute an order with a non-member unless he can deal thereby to the greater advantage of his client than with another member.[8]

A. THE SCALES OF MINIMUM COMMISSIONS

There are three scales which set out the minimum commission which a broker may charge for given types of transaction. The first scale, which is contained in Appendix 39 of the Rules and Regulations, lays down the minimum commissions chargeable by a London broker when acting for his client directly. The second scale, contained in Appendix 40, provides for the minimum commission chargeable by the London broker to members of other federated exchanges for whom he acts. The latter commissions are generally about half the amount of the former.

The third scale, contained in Appendix 41, lays down the minimum commissions which a broker may charge when he proposes to share his commission with an agent on the Register of Banks[9] or the General Register of Agents.[10]

1. Persons chargeable and on which scale

When a broker acts between two non-members he may charge only one of them commission,[11] and that one must be the non-member who initiated the business.[12] Other Rules serve to clear up any doubt as to whom a broker is acting for, and accordingly whether the Appendix 39 scale or the Appendix 40 scale applies:

5. See also *Re Wreford, deceased, Carmichael* v. *Rudkin* (1897), 13 T.L.R. 153.
6. Rule 203 (1).   7. See p. 262, *post*.   8. Rule 88 (1).
9. See pp. 171–172, *post*.   10. See pp. 172–173, *post*.   11. Rule 89 (1).
12. Rule 89 (2).

(1) When a broker makes a bargain between a jobber and a member of the public, he is treated for the purposes of commission as acting as the agent of the member of the public.[13]

(2) When a broker makes a bargain between a member of a federated exchange and a member of the public, he is considered as acting as agent for the member of the public.[14]

(3) When a broker transacts business between a member and a member of a federated exchange he must in no case charge less than the minimum laid down in Rule 216.[15]

(4) A broker when transacting business between a jobber and an outside broker or dealer excluded from the concession Rules by the provisions of Rule 211[16] must always charge the outside broker or dealer full commission as laid down in Appendix 39.[17]

The Council keep a special list of outside brokers and dealers who are not excluded from the concession Rules by Rule 211,[18] and are therefore not chargeable with full commission under Appendix 39.

(5) A broker, when transacting business between a member of a federated exchange and one of the outside brokers or dealers excluded under Rule 211, must charge the outsider with *full* commission as provided in Appendix 39, and he may not charge *any* commission to the country broker.[19]

(6) An external member of the Stock Exchange must be charged commission on business transacted for his account in all respects as if he were a member of the general public.[20] He may not receive a

13. Rule 218 (1).   14. Rule 218 (2).   15. Rule 218 (3).
16. Those excluded by Rule 211 are any person, firm or company who: (a) advertises for stock exchange business in the U.K. or Eire except as permitted to banks on the Register of Banks, see Appendix 49, p. 171, *post*, or (b) issues circulars or business communications in the U.K. or Eire respecting stock exchange business other than to his own principals, except as permitted to banks on the Register of Banks and agents on the General Register, (see Appendix 54, p. 167, *post*) or (c) is a member of any other institution or association (other than the London Discount Market Association, the Association of Canadian Investment Dealers and Members of the Toronto and National Stock Exchanges in Great Britain, the Association of New York Stock Exchange Member firms having representation in the U.K., and the List of Exempted Dealers, e.g., bankers doing investment business, under s. 16 of the Prevention of Fraud (Investments) Act 1958) in the London postal area where or by whom dealings in stocks or shares are carried on; or (d) is the holder of either a principal's or representative's licence granted by the Board of Trade pursuant to s. 3 of the Prevention of Fraud (Investments) Act 1958; or (e) is the parent or subsidiary or a director of, or is managed or controlled by or associated with any person coming into categories (a), (b), (c) or (d), above.
17. Rule 218 (4).   18. Rule 211 (2).   19. Rule 218 (5).
20. Rule 201 (1). For external members generally, see pp. 38–40, *ante.*

share of the commission unless he is a limited partner in the broking firm transacting the business.[1]

2. When no scale applies

In certain transactions the broker is not bound by any stated minima and can use his discretion in deciding what to charge. The transactions are:

(i) The underwriting and placing of a new issue.[2]

(ii) Valuation for probate. Where a broker has prepared a valuation for probate, and charged a fee not less than that laid down in Appendix 39 of the Rules, he may to the extent that he subsequently earns commission from business received from the estate remit all or part of the fee charged.

(iii) Contangos.[3] The broker may charge or allow a rate of interest at his discretion, but such rate may not be more favourable to his client than either:

(*a*) the rate actually paid or received by the broker in the market; or

(*b*) if the contango is effected wholly or partially by the employment of the broker's own resources such a rate as is fair and reasonable.[4]

B. CONCESSIONS

The scales of minimum commissions do not apply regardless of the size of a particular transaction. Obviously one large bargain involves less work than twenty smaller bargains of the same aggregate amount, and a broker who is able to charge a reduced commission on larger bargains is likely to attract further business. The Rules permit such reductions (known as concessions), which vary with the type of security and the size of the bargain.[5]

C. WAIVER OF COMMISSION

Where two bargains have been made to effect what is in reality one transaction, a broker may waive commission on either of them, so it is provided:

(1) Where a bargain done for the account is closed by a *corresponding* bargain in the same security for the same client and

1. Rule 201 (2). 2. Rule 200 (3).
3. For commission on contangos, see p. 154, *ante*.
4. Rule 200 (5). 5. See Rules 207–209.

for the same account, a broker may at his discretion waive commission on the closing bargain.[6]

(2) Where a bargain done for cash is closed by a *corresponding* bargain in the same security made for the same client, a broker may waive commission on the closing bargain. If such a bargain is in Gilt-Edged securities,[7] the Rule will only apply if the closing bargain is done within 28 days after the original bargain. If the bargain is in new issues passing by delivery in renounceable document form (other than Gilt-Edged securities dealt in for cash) the closing bargain must be within fourteen days of the original bargain or not later than two days before the application day whichever is the earlier.[8]

The above right of waiver may not, however, be exercised by a broker who is in the *same* transaction making a concession as permitted by the Rules. The two rights must be exercised in independent transactions, and not in combination.

D. SHARING OF COMMISSION WITH AGENTS

Brokers may employ agents to introduce or carry on business on their behalf. The Rules make extensive provisions for the control of agents, and the extent to which brokers may share commission with them. The important characteristic of stock exchange agents is that they cannot be employed informally in the usual commercial way, but must be classified and registered—whether as banks, overseas representatives, attachés, retired associates or persons in the General Register of agents.

1. Persons with whom a broker may share commission
A broker may only share his commission:

(*a*) with an agent whose name appears on the Register of Banks and the General Register, provided commission has been charged at the rates laid down in Appendix 41.[9]

(*b*) with an agent whose name appears on one or other of the Registers of overseas representatives, attachés and retired associates.[10]

(*c*) at his discretion, with a clerk or employee in his own *bona fide* exclusive full time employment. The clerk or employee's share may

6. Rule 206 (1). There is no such right of waiver when the broker acts for country brokers who are principals.
7. I.e., the securities in Rule 97.
8. Rule 206 (2). There is *no* right of waiver where the broker acts for country brokers who are principals.
9. Rule 212 (1) (*a*).   10. Rule 212 (1) (*b*).

not exceed *one-third* of the net commission retained by the broker on the business of the client which he introduces.[11]

(*d*) with a stockbroker who is a member of a recognised [12] overseas stock exchange or stockbrokers' association.[13] The United Kingdom broker must *retain* not less than *three-quarters* of the minimum scale as laid down in Appendix 41.[14] He must send to the overseas broker a contract note (*not* rendered "net"), which states that the commission is so shared, and showing commission at not less than the scale laid down in Appendix 41.[15]

2. Registers of agents

The Council keep registers of agents under the following categories. They have an uncontrolled discretion to determine the qualifications necessary for entry in and retention on such registers:

A. REGISTER OF BANKS [16]

This Register has two sections:

(i) Section A contains the names of the members for the time being of the Bankers' Clearing House and/or the British Bankers' Association.

(ii) Section B is open to other banks and banking houses carrying on business in the City of London.

Banks and banking houses placed upon this Register will be notified in accordance with the form in Appendix 49. This form contains certain conditions attached to entry in the Register, including conditions that no part of the banking agent's share of commission may be returned or allowed to its principal; that the bank will not claim or share commission on transactions done for the account or benefit of other registered agents; that the bank will not advertise for business; and that the bank will observe the Rules, Regulations and usages of the Stock Exchange in so far as they affect it.

The share of commission actually retained by a broker who shares his commission with an agent included in the Register of Banks must be not less than three-quarters of the commission charged under Appendix 41.[17]

---

11. Rule 212 (1) (*c*) and Rule 213 (3).
12. I.e., recognised by Rule 217. The stock exchanges and brokers' associations recognised under this rule are: Adelaide, Auckland, Bombay, Brisbane, Calcutta, Calgary, the Canadian Stock Exchange, Christchurch, Delhi, Dunedin, Hobart, Hong Kong, Jamaica, Johannesburg, Karachi, Lagos, Madras, Melbourne, Montreal, Nairobi, Perth, Rhodesian, Sydney, Toronto, Vancouver, Wellington, Winnipeg, the Colombo Brokers' Association and Malayan Stock Exchange.
13. Rule 212 (1) (*d*).   14. Rule 217 (1).   15. Rule 217 (2).
16. Rule 212 (2) (*a*).   17. *Ibid.*

A contract note must be sent to the bank involved, naming the bank and stating that the commission is shared with the bank. The contract note must not be rendered "net".[18]

B. THE GENERAL REGISTER [19]

The General Register is open to those persons, firms and corporations, not eligible for admission to any of the other Registers maintained by the Council who satisfy the Council that they are either or both professionally and habitually engaged in handling, transmitting, collecting or introducing stock exchange business. Application for inclusion in the General Register is made in the form prescribed by Appendix 54. The form contains undertakings by the applicant not to share commission with other registered agents, not to allow or return commission to principals, not to accept a share of commission on any transaction for the account or benefit of a third party also on one of the Registers of agents, not to advertise, and to abide by and conform with the Rules, Regulations and usages of the Exchange and any directions given by the Council, in so far as they affect the applicant.

The applicant agrees in addition to inform the brokers whom he instructs if any of the business covered by his instructions is business which does not entitle him to share commission by reason of the fact that it is business for his own account or benefit, which includes:

(*i*) *if the applicant is an individual*

(*a*) Business for account of his wife and *vice versa*;

(*b*) business done for an employee for account of his or her employer;

(*c*) business done by a director, secretary or employee of a company (or by the wife of a director, secretary or employee) for account of the company;

(*d*) business done by a director, secretary or employee of a parent company or its subsidiaries (or by the wife of such director, secretary or employee) for the account of the parent company or its subsidiaries;

(*ii*) *if the applicant is a firm or company*

(*a*) Business done by a firm acting for the account of one of its partners or employees, or for the wife of a partner; or by a branch of the firm acting for the account of its head office or another branch; or by a head office for account of its branches;

(*b*) business done by a company for the account of a director, secretary or other employee of the company, or the wife of a director, secretary or other employee; or by a branch of a company

18. Rule 212 (3).   19. Rule 212 (2) (*b*).

acting for the account of its head office or another branch; or by a
head office for account of its branches;

(*c*) business done by a company for account of any of its subsidiary companies; or by a subsidiary company for account of its
parent company.

The share of commission actually retained by a broker who shares
his commission with an agent included in the General Register may
be not less than *four-fifths* of the commission charged under
Appendix 41.[20]

A broker who shares his commission with an agent included in
the General Register must render a contract note naming the agent
and stating that the commission charged is shared with that agent.
The contract note must not be rendered "net".[1]

C. REGISTER OF OVERSEAS REPRESENTATIVES[2]

A broker firm is entitled to employ for the purpose of its business
one or more overseas representatives (not to be confused with
members of overseas stock exchanges) resident outside Great
Britain and the Republic of Ireland. All such representatives must
appear on the Register kept in accordance with Appendix 50, which
provides (*inter alia*):

1. A broker firm wishing to employ an overseas representative
must apply to the Council for prior consent in the appropriate form.

2. Such consent may be revoked by the Council; it *must* be
revoked if the overseas representative divides or shares his remuneration with his principal.

3. Overseas representatives may be employed by one member firm
only, and may not do business with any other broker or broker firm
whether as agent or otherwise.

4. Overseas representatives may not advertise for stock exchange
business in the United Kingdom or the Republic of Ireland.

5. An overseas representative may not in advertisements, circulars, business letter heads, cards or other documents on which his
name appears, or on any name plate, board or sign make any reference to the fact that his name has been included in the Register of
Overseas Representatives.

6. An overseas representative may be an individual or a firm; but
if an individual he may not be a partner in a firm or in the employ of
an individual firm or company.

7. An overseas representative may not act as such for his own
personal business.

A broker may remunerate an overseas representative with a share
not exceeding *one-quarter* of the commission chargeable to the

20. Rule 212 (2) (*b*).   1. Rule 212 (3).   2. Rule 213 (2).

principal whom he introduces, where such commission is charged in accordance with Appendix 39.

Where the commission is also shared by the broker with an agent on the Register of Banks or the General Register, commission must be charged under Appendix 41 and the remuneration of the overseas representative may not exceed one-quarter of the commission actually retained by the broker.

A contract note must be sent to the overseas representative naming him and stating that he shares in the commission. The contract note must not be rendered "net".

D. REGISTER OF ATTACHÉS [3]

A Register of Attachés is kept by the Council in accordance with the provisions of Appendix 51. The proposed attaché makes a declaration to the effect that he is in the sole employment of his principals and is regularly and normally located in their office; and he undertakes: [4]

(i) not to solicit business from persons, firms or companies other than his own principals;

(ii) that no part of his share of commission will be returned or allowed to his principal or to any other person;

(iii) that he will abide by and conform with the Rules, Regulations and usages of the Stock Exchange, and any directions given by the Council of the Stock Exchange in so far as they affect him.

A broker may remunerate an attaché in his own exclusive employment with a share not exceeding *one-third* of the commission charged to the principal whom he introduces, where such commission is charged in accordance with Appendix 39.

In cases where an attaché introduces business for an agent whose name appears on the Register of Banks or upon the General Register, commission must be charged under Appendix 41 and the remuneration of the attaché may not exceed *one-third* of the net commission actually retained by the broker.

E. REGISTER OF RETIRED ASSOCIATES [5]

A Register of Retired Associates is kept by the Council in accordance with Appendix 53. The Register is open to all ex-members, ex-attachés and ex-clerks who after long association with their firm have genuinely retired from active business by reason of age or ill-health. Registration is also open to the widows of all these classes.

3. Rule 203 (2) (*b*).   4. See Appendix 51.
5. Rule 203 (2) (*c*).

The applicant will make similar undertakings as in the case of attachés, and in addition he promises "not to claim or accept a share of commission on any business which does not entitle me to share commission by reason of the fact that it is business for my own account" (this will include the business of the applicant's husband or wife).[6]

A broker may remunerate a retired associate with a share not exceeding *one-quarter* of the commission charged to the principal he introduces, where such commission is charged in accordance with Appendix 39.

In cases where a retired associate introduces business for an agent whose name appears upon the Register of Banks or upon the General Register, commission must be charged under Appendix 41 and the remuneration of the retired associate may not exceed *one-quarter* of the net commission actually retained by the broker.

3. Where sharing commission is not permitted[7]

A broker may not share his commission with an agent when:

(*a*) the agent's share is divided with or allowed to his principal or any other person;

(*b*) the commission is charged on the agent's own personal business, which includes the business disclosable by an agent on the General Register;[8]

(*c*) the agent is an agent who advertises for stock exchange business in the public press except as permitted to banks in Appendix 49.[9]

(*d*) the agent is an agent who issues circulars in Great Britain or the Republic of Ireland respecting stock exchange business to other than his own principals except as permitted in Appendices 49 and 54.[10]

6. See Appendix 53.   7. Rule 214.
8. For business disclosable by an agent on the General Register, see Appendix 54 (8) and pp. 172–173, *ante*.
9. Banks may advertise in the public press as follows: (i) if so authorised by the Prevention of Fraud (Investments) Act 1958, they may advertise within their own premises the fact that they are prepared to undertake stock exchange business, and issue circulars to company shareholders offering to acquire their shares, provided that they do not treat any shareholder so circularised as their principal; (ii) if an agent operating an investment management scheme as authorised under the Prevention of Fraud (Investments) Act 1958, they may advertise *that service*, provided that customers who use that service are given opportunity to nominate their own broker for any stock exchange transactions.
10. Agents in the General Register may issue such circulars when duly authorised under the Prevention of Fraud (Investments) Act 1958 and with the prior consent of the Council.

E. PERSONS WITH WHOM SHARING COMMISSION IS PROHIBITED

1. A jobber

A broker may not share with a jobber or a clerk to a jobber the commission which he charges, with the exception of underwriting and brokerage commissions in respect of new issues received from a brokerage house.[11]

2. An ex-member

A firm or member may not, without the permission of the Council, carry on business for or with a person who has been expelled from the Stock Exchange, or who has ceased to be a member on failure to pay subscriptions or other payments due to the Council, or who after ceasing for any reason to be a member becomes a bankrupt.[12]

F. THE RELATIONSHIP BETWEEN A BROKER AND THE AGENT SHARING HIS COMMISSION

1. The relationship must be clear

The relation between a principal and his agent is one which can give rise to numerous misunderstandings if the parties do not come to a clear initial agreement as to their respective rights. In *Bickley* v. *Browning, Todd & Co*,[13] the agent's failure to do this prejudiced his position subsequently:

> The plaintiff, a "half-commission man", and the defendants, a firm of stockbrokers, made an agreement that the plaintiff should have a share of the commission on orders introduced by the plaintiff and executed by the defendants. The plaintiff had a seat in the defendants' office, and was paid by commission, and not by salary, for helping to carry out the business in the office. Eventually the plaintiff left the defendants' service, and brought an action against them to recover a share of the commission earned by them on transactions which they, as brokers, had entered into *after* he had left their service, on behalf of persons whom he had introduced to them *during* that service.

It was held that the agreement was one which gave rise to the relationship of employment, not agency, and that, as there was no evidence that the parties had agreed that commission was to be paid for an indefinite period after that employment should cease, the plaintiff was not entitled to commission on orders given *after* the

---

11. Rule 215.   12. Rule 84*a*.   13. (1913), 30 T.L.R. 134.

termination of his employment. But it was also held that where *during* his employment orders had been given to open and carry over stocks, the plaintiff was entitled to commission on those transactions until they were closed, even though each carry-over was technically a new purchase and sale.[14]

Whether the relation is one of employment or agency is a question of fact. Some persons who share commission with a broker are loosely referred to as "agents" when in law their position is primarily that of employees. For example, an attaché must be in a broker's "own exclusive *employment*" before he may be registered and share commission;[15] and a clerk cannot unless he is in "*bona fide* exclusive full time *employment*".[16] On the other hand, retired associates approximate more closely to agents in the strict legal sense, since they must be "exclusively associated" with their sponsoring broker,[17] and on application they must declare that they "ceased to be employed" in the Stock Exchange on a particular date.[18]

2. Agents who share commissions and losses

The mere fact that a broker's agent or employee agrees to share (i) commissions earned by or paid to the broker *and* (ii) the losses which the broker incurs (*both* on the business which he, the agent or employee, has introduced) does not make him a partner of the broker. The simple reason for this is that the Rules and Regulations prohibit a member from entering into partnership with a non-member.[19]

Where the agent agrees to share losses as well as commission, he is his broker's indemnifier and not his guarantor. The distinction is important, because by section 4 of the Statute of Frauds 1677 a guarantee, i.e., "a special promise to answer for the debt or default of another person", cannot be effective unless it is in writing. But an agent's agreement is one of *indemnity*. His broker's loss is not merely the "debt or default of another person", for it arises from a transaction in which he as agent has an interest. Accordingly his agreement to share that loss is enforceable even though made orally. This was the position in *Sutton & Co* v. *Grey*,[20] where brokers orally agreed that they would divide commissions with their agent "*just as if* you were our partner and a member of the Stock Exchange", and that "if there should be a loss in respect of the transactions, you shall indemnify us against half the loss".[1]

14. See contangos, pp. 152–153, *ante.*
15. Rule 213 (2) (*b*).
16. Rule 213 (3).
17. Rule 213 (2) (*c*).
18. See Appendix 53.
19. Rule 54 (1).
20. [1894] 1 Q.B. 285, C.A.
1. *Ibid.*, at p. 287.

The stock exchange agent who agrees to share losses is not what is known as a *del credere* agent [2] (i.e., one who for *extra* commission undertakes to indemnify his principal against losses arising from the failure of persons whom he introduces to carry out their bargains). If a stock exchange agent agrees to share losses, that does *not* mean that he will do so *only* in return for an extra or a prohibited share of commission on profits.

3. Carrying-over charges

Where an agent sharing commission introduces business for his broker, who then makes a bargain and later carries it over, there is no usage by which the agent may share or participate in charges paid to the broker for carrying over. [3]

2. [1894] 1 Q.B. 285, C.A.
3. *Von Taysen* v. *Baer, Ellissen & Co* (1912), 56 Sol. Jo. 224.

CHAPTER 8

Delivery and Settlement

A. COMPLETION OF A STOCK EXCHANGE BARGAIN

1. The fortnightly account

Immediately after the conclusion of dealings for a particular settlement the broker prepares and sends to his client a statement which is known as a fortnightly account. This shows all the transactions effected on behalf of the client during the account, all purchases, sales and continuations. If the same number of each denomination of securities have been bought as sold, the fortnightly account shows the differences payable, or to be received, by the client on account day. Similarly, if securities have been bought or sold, and then carried over, the differences payable by or to the client will be stated. If, on the other hand, the client is going to take delivery or deliver, the account shows what sum he will have to pay against delivery, or what sum he will receive when he delivers or, in the case of a private investor, the net sum he is due to pay or receive.

2. Time for completion

There is an implied term in a stock exchange bargain that on the next (or an agreed) account day the buyer will either take the securities himself and indemnify the seller, or else name another buyer who is able and willing to do so. There are only two ways in which the parties can avoid this rule:[1]

(i) By agreeing to postpone settlement. Such postponement would be a new contract.

(ii) By making a bargain that on account days only differences will be payable. In reality this is no more than an arrangement for a series of bets, and debts arising from them are unenforceable in law.

The time for the completion of bargains is fixed by the Rules and Regulations. Where a bargain is done for the current account, it must be completed during the next following settlement period, and

1. See *Re Morgan, ex parte Phillips, ex parte Marnham* (1860), 2 De G. F. and J. 634.

bargains for completion in any *subsequent* settlement period are, with three exceptions, prohibited.[2] The three exceptions are:

(*i*) *"New time" bargains.* These are bargains made on the last two days of a dealing period for completion in the next but one settlement period.

(*ii*) *Delayed delivery bargains.* A selling broker may require more time for the execution and delivery of the necessary documents, or a jobber for obtaining the security which was the subject of the bargain. Members may defer to necessity and release each other from their strict obligation as to time. Thus a jobber might deal "N.T.P." (not to press) or "N.B.I." (no buying-in). But all such bargains must be marked without delay and the marking slip must be inscribed "D.D." (for delayed delivery) in the appropriate column.

(*iii*) *Bargains in new issues* for delivery in scrip form are for completion on the business day following the day of the bargain, unless otherwise arranged.

The Council may pass resolutions postponing or extending a settlement period either indefinitely or to some specified day later than its account day. Such postponement or extension may apply to all bargains or only to bargains in particular specified securities.

3. Delivery and payment

Time is deemed to be of the essence of the contract to deliver. In other words, if delivery does not take place within the time fixed by the Rules and Regulations or agreed by the parties, the buyer may refuse to accept the securities. The justification for making time of the essence was clearly enunciated in *Doloret* v. *Rothschild:*[3]

> "Where a court ... holds that time is not of the essence of the contract, it proceeds upon the principle that, having regard to the nature of the subject, time is immaterial to the value ... But that principle can have no application to a case ... where, from the nature of the subject the value is exposed to daily variation, and a contract which was disadvantageous to the plaintiff on the 1st February, and would therefore be then declined by him, might be highly advantageous to him on the 2nd February."

Even if delivery has been delayed for reasons beyond the seller's control, the seller cannot escape liability for it. So in *De Waal* v. *Adler:*[4]

---

2. Rule 96 (4).
3. (1824), 1 Sim. & St. 590, at pp. 598–599. See also *Union Corporation* v. *Charrington and Brodrick* (1902), 8 Com. Cas. 99; *Barnard* v. *Foster,* [1915] 2 K.B. 288, C.A.
4. (1886), 12 App. Cas. 141, P.C.

The seller in Natal had to send the share certificate to the company's office in London for sub-division. Mail steamer was then the quickest form of transport. At the time of sale the purchaser was under the impression that the shares were deliverable within a very short time. The seller did nothing to allay this impression.

It was held that the time which the certificate took to travel from Natal to London and back was unreasonable delay (considering that the buyer did not know that it was necessary) and that the buyer had the right to refuse to accept the shares.

A buyer is not entitled to refuse delivery of a part of the securities which he has agreed to purchase.[5]

As to *payment*, Rule 101a provides that a seller cannot demand payment against delivery before the date fixed by the contract, but subject to the other provisions of the Rules he may do so at any later date before the security has been bought-in, and the Rule adds that time shall *not* be of the essence of the bargain.

4. Registration

In the absence of any guarantee on his part the seller in a stock exchange contract does not undertake to ensure that the company will register the transfer.[6] But in *Cruse* v. *Paine*:[7]

A jobber on purchasing shares *expressly* guaranteed registration. The transferee, whose name he gave, failed to register the transfer, although he paid the purchase money. Calls continued to be made on the seller, and it was held that the jobber, because of his guarantee, was bound to indemnify him against them.

This result may seem unjust: after all it was not the jobber's fault that the transferee did nothing about becoming the registered holder. Fortunately for the jobber in *Cruse* v. *Paine*, it had been decided in a case of the previous year that he could in turn claim an indemnity from the unregistered transferee.[8] On the other hand, the seller might make it impossible for the purchaser to obtain registration, as by delivering share warrants on a bargain for the sale of registered securities: in that case, whether the seller has guaranteed registration or not, the blame falls squarely on his shoulders: the buyer can repudiate the bargain and recover his purchase money.[9]

The seller must not be too ready to assume that his buyer will be acceptable to the company. Directors usually have a power to refuse

---

5. *Benjamin* v. *Barnett* (1903), 8 Com. Cas. 244.
6. *London Founder's Association* v. *Clarke* (1880), 20 Q.B.D. 576.
7. (1869), 4 Ch. App. 441.
8. *Paine* v. *Hutchinson* (1868), 3 Ch. App. 388.
9. *Iredell* v. *General Securities Corporation, Ltd.* (1916), 33 T.L.R. 67, C.A.

registration, and if the seller conceals from the company facts which would make his buyer unacceptable, he risks an action by the company if his buyer fails to meet his obligations.[10]

5. Dealings for cash

A bargain is said to be "for cash" if the securities involved bring it into the class of bargains which, under the Rules and Regulations, are for immediate settlement on the business day following the day of the bargain. Bargains which are deemed to be for cash are:

(i) Rule 97 dealings which consist, in the main, of bargains in British and Commonwealth Gilt-Edged securities;[11] and

(ii) where a rights offer is made to the holders of old securities, all dealings in such rights until the close of business two business days before the application day.[12]

Bargains in all other kinds of security are deemed and expressed to be for the current account, but both parties may subsequently agree to carry over to the next account.

B. TICKETS

1. The trace

Securities are often sold and resold for the current account several times. The chain of bargains which connects the original seller with the ultimate buyer is known as the trace. The links in this chain are the buyers' tickets. Every buyer who purchases and takes up securities in a stock exchange transaction must issue a ticket naming himself as the payer of the purchase money.[13] Other matters which appear on the face of the ticket are the amount and denomination of the securities to be transferred, the price, the date and the name of the firm with whom the issuer of the ticket dealt.

TRANSMISSION OF TICKETS TO ORIGINAL SELLER

The buyer must issue his ticket before 3 p.m. on ticket day.[14] He passes it on to his seller. His seller transmits it to the firm from whom *he* bought, endorsing that firm's name, the date and time the ticket was passed on the back. The ticket passes via the intermediaries, with their own names appearing on the ticket so that ultimately it reaches the original seller for that account. The original

10. *Re Discoverers' Finance Corporation, Ltd., Lindlar's Case,* [1910] 1 Ch. 312, C.A.
11. Bargains which are subject to stamp duty are not deemed to be for cash. But transfers of Government stocks are exempted from stamp duty under Sched. 1 of the Stamp Act 1891.
12. Rule 114*a* (2).   13. Rule 122 (1).   14. Rule 122 (2).

seller and the ultimate buyer are thus brought together for completion, and the intermediaries drop out and settle their differences on account day without waiting for the completion of the transfer.

(i) Receipt of tickets

Every firm has to have a box in the Ticket Room for (*inter alia*) the receipt of tickets,[15] though these are permitted to simply pass between offices.[16] Members who receive tickets after 3 p.m. on the ticket day must mark the date and the precise time at which the ticket was received.[17] The purpose of this is to enable the buyer or seller to locate the blame for any delay that may have occurred in the passing of tickets, when either of them has had to apply to the Buying-in and Selling-out Department.

(ii) Antedated tickets

When a firm is passed an antedated ticket and accepts that ticket when tendered as such, the firm takes that ticket with all the liabilities which may attach to such antedating. If the firm passes the ticket on as an ordinary and not an antedated ticket, the liabilities will continue to reside with the firm as a penalty for reintroducing the offending ticket to circulation.[18] But a firm which is passed an undated ticket will not be liable for loss arising from the securities having been bought-in, unless the ticket has remained in its possession for seven days.[19]

(iii) Alteration and detention of tickets

A firm which alters or improperly detains a ticket will have to make good any loss occurring as a result.[20]

(iv) Delivery of securities

On receipt of the ticket the original seller must cause the securities to be delivered (i.e., transferred) to the ultimate buyer at the price marked upon it.[1]

2. Split tickets

A jobber has the right to divide or lump orders as he pleases. Suppose that Smith (a jobber) sells to Robinson 400 shares in British Petroleum. On ticket day Robinson's broker will issue a ticket for 400 shares and hand it to Smith. It so happens that 200 of these B.P. shares were purchased by Smith for the same account from Jones (a broker) and 200 from Brown (a broker). On receipt of Robinson's ticket, Smith will split it by issuing two new tickets for 200 shares each, adding a statement that the original ticket (which he retains)[2] has been split by him. One split ticket he hands

15. Rule 99. 16. Rule 122 (4). 17. Rule 122 (5). 18. Rule 124 (1).
19. Rule 124 (2). 20. Rule 125 (1). 1. Rule 126 (1). 2. Rule 123.

to Jones, and the other to Brown. Thus Robinson is brought into
contact with both Jones and Brown, and all the links in their respective traces have been preserved. Had Smith made no contact with
Brown, he would still have had to split Robinson's ticket for the 400
shares in order to satisfy Jones. Then if Smith failed to obtain
Robinson's remaining 200 in the market, he would become liable to
Robinson for their non-delivery.

In the converse situation, the jobber who *buys* securities from
one person and agrees to *sell* them to several, may claim a ticket
from each of the persons to whom he has agreed to sell, and
transmit the original ticket onward to the person from whom he
bought.

The splitting of tickets, and the interconnection of a number of
parties who have not contracted directly with each other does not
destroy their privity of contract. In *Bowring* v *Shepherd*:[3]

> The defendant had purchased on the Stock Exchange through his
> brokers 100 partly-paid shares from a jobber for May 15th 1866. On the
> ticket day his brokers handed a ticket with the defendant's name as buyer
> to that jobber. That original ticket was divided, and a "split" for 15
> of the 100 shares passed up, through various hands, to the brokers of
> the plaintiff. The plaintiff was the registered holder of the shares and had
> initially sold them to another jobber for delivery on May 15th. On
> receipt of the defendant's name, the plaintiff executed a transfer of the
> shares to him, and the plaintiff's broker handed the transfer and the
> certificates of the shares to the defendant's brokers, who accepted them
> on his behalf and paid the plaintiff's broker the price. The defendant's
> brokers in handing on his name acted by the express authority of the
> defendant, and in accepting the transfer and paying the price they
> acted according to the custom of the Stock Exchange, though with-
> out any *express* authority of the defendant. The company stopped
> payment on May 10th, and on May 11th a petition for a winding-
> up order was presented, and an order for winding-up was afterwards
> made. On May 18th the defendant refused to accept the shares, and
> the plaintiff was afterwards compelled to pay a call as their registered
> holder.

It was held by the Court of Exchequer Chamber that the defendant was bound by the acceptance of the transfer by his brokers on
his behalf and payment of the price, and that a contract then arose
between the plaintiff and the defendant, by which the defendant was
bound to indemnify the plaintiff.

Clearly the splitting of tickets involves additional expense. The
Rules provide that such expense must be borne by the firm which
makes the split.[4] The liability of firms for losses on split tickets

3. (1871), L.R. 6 Q.B. 309.   4. Rule 123 (3).

extends for a period of six months from the date of the ticket, but the firm splitting the ticket is liable to intermediate claimants for a period of eight months.[5]

Claims for losses on split tickets for which settlement is required in the current account must be made on or before the contango day.[6]

C. BUYING-IN AND SELLING-OUT

Where one party to a bargain fails to complete it in time the Stock Exchange has a device which the member acting for the other party can use to obtain immediate satisfaction for his client.

The machinery is known as The Buying-in and Selling-out Department. Where the seller has failed to deliver securities, the buyer can make good the deficiency by buying them in through the officials of the department. Conversely, where the seller has not received a ticket from the buyer, the seller can rid himself of the buyer-less securities by "selling them out" through the same department. Buying-in and selling-out must be done in public by officials appointed by the Council.[7]

In the last analysis, the loss occasioned by a resort to the department is borne by the defaulting party, who must be traced by its officials. They will then charge him any difference arising, and commission for their attempts, successful or unsuccessful, to find a substantive buyer or seller as the case may be.[8]

1. Buying-in
The Rules state precise times by which delivery must take place;[9] failing such delivery securities may be bought in.

(i) Buying-in days
These depend upon the nature of the security. Where the securities have been bought for the account and remain undelivered:

(a) Registered securities deliverable by transfer: ten days after the account day.

(b) Inscribed stock [10] subject to *ad valorem* stamp duty: ten days after the account day.

---

5. Rule 123 (5).   6. Rule 123 (4).   7. Rule 144.
8. Rule 145.   9. Rule 103.
10. I.e., stock for which, instead of documents being issued, the holders are inscribed in the register of the issuing authority.

(*c*) Bearer securities: three *business* days after the account day.[11] Twenty-four hours' notice of buying-in must be given.[12]

Where the securities have been bought for cash or for a specified day and not delivered by the times stated in the Rules, buying-in may be effected much more promptly:[13]

(*a*) Registered securities deliverable by transfer: the next or any subsequent day, *without notice.*

(*b*) Bearer securities: immediately or on any subsequent day, *without notice.*

(*c*) Inscribed stock subject to *ad valorem* stamp duty: on the following or any subsequent day *without notice.*

(*d*) Inscribed stock not subject to *ad valorem* stamp duty: on the following day at 11 a.m. or any subsequent day *without notice.*

(*ii*) *Instructions to buy-in*

The buyer's broker will send a simple form of instructions addressed to the Buying-in and Selling-out Official and stating:

"Please BUY-IN the following (list) against (list)."

The manager will, in due course, send either a notice stating that he has endeavoured to buy in the securities but without success, or a bought contract note stating: "Bought by order of — against —," the number and description of the securities, and the price at which they were bought-in.

(*iii*) *Loss occasioned by buying-in*

The loss, i.e., the difference between the total cost of the security bought-in (consideration plus commission) and the amount realised by the resale, must be borne by the party at whose door the responsibility for the delay or default can be laid.[14] So:

(*a*) In the case of registered securities—or inscribed stock subject to *ad valorem* stamp duty—the loss must be borne by the ultimate, that is to say the original, seller. The ultimate seller's liability can be transferred to an intermediary where undue delay can be proved.[15]

(*b*) In the case of bearer securities the loss must be borne by the firm which did not deliver the securities by 12.15 p.m. on the previous business day.[16]

(*c*) In the case of inscribed stock not subject to *ad valorem* stamp duty bought for a specified day and not delivered, the loss must be borne by the firm causing default.[17]

---

11. Rule 149 (1) (*a*).   12. Rule 149 (3).   13. Rule 149 (1) (*b*).
14. It is, of course, possible for the operation to result in a profit if the price of the security rises between the buying-in and the subsequent resale.
15. Rule 149 (5) (*a*).   16. Rule 149 (5) (*b*).   17. Rule 149 (5) (*c*).

(*iv*) *Release of intermediaries*

A buyer who issues a ticket or a scrip ticket naming himself as the purchaser and, having failed to secure delivery, does not buy-in within eleven days from the buying-in day, releases his immediate seller (and all intermediaries) from any liability.[18] The liability then falls upon the ultimate seller who has failed to deliver.

(*v*) *Failure to execute a buying-in order*

The department may not succeed in executing an order to buy-in. If so, notice of the buying-in must be posted daily, and, so long as the buying-in order is not withdrawn, the Department will make daily attempts to execute it. When so instructed, an official may bid for the security to facilitate a buying-in.[19] If after such a bid no buying-in is effected, the security must be designated by an asterisk in the daily notice.[20]

(*vi*) *Suspension and prohibition of buying-in*

The Council may suspend the buying-in of securities when it appears that a suspension is desirable in the general interest. The liability of intermediaries continues during such suspension unless otherwise determined by the Council.[1] Securities may not be bought-in when the seller knows that they have passed out of the seller's control to the extent that he is no longer liable for the payment of calls, or eligible to receive interest, dividends or bonus shares.[2]

2. Selling-out

The seller who does not receive a ticket is obviously unable to get in touch with intermediaries. Without a ticket he has no avenues of contact with them but he can nevertheless act swiftly in the only way open to him—by selling-out through the Buying-in and Selling-out Department.

(*i*) *Selling-out days*

(*a*) Where a bargain is for the account, and no ticket is received in time, the sell-out between 2.30 p.m. and 3.00 p.m. on the first intermediate day (i.e., the day after ticket day), or between 11 a.m. and 3 p.m. on any subsequent business day.[3]

(*b*) Where a bargain is for settlement on a specified day, and the seller does not receive a ticket by 2.30 p.m. on the day *before* such specified day, he may sell the securities up to 3 p.m. on that day or any subsequent day.[4]

(*c*) In the case of a bargain in inscribed stock for a specified day, the seller who does not receive a ticket by 12.30 p.m. on that

18. Rule 150.   19. Rule 153 (1).   20. Rule 153 (2).
1. Rule 146.   2. Rule 147.   3. Rule 155 (1) (*a*).
4. Rule 155 (2).

day may sell-out against the buyer, and the loss occasioned by the selling-out will be borne:[5]

(i) by the issuer if the ticket was not regularly issued before 11 a.m.; or

(ii) by the holder at 12.30 p.m. if the ticket had been regularly put into circulation.

(ii) Instructions to sell-out

The member acting for the seller will send a form of instructions addressed to the Buying-in and Selling-out Official, and stating:

"Please SELL-OUT for names for   the following securities (list)." If the Department is successful in disposing of the securities it will in due course forward the contract note to the member acting for the seller.

(iii) Loss occasioned by selling-out

Rule 122 (2) provides that the buyer must issue his ticket before 3 p.m. on the ticket day. If the seller receives no ticket, and it turns out that the reason is the buyer's simple failure to comply with Rule 122 (2), then clearly the buyer must be responsible for the loss resulting from the selling-out.[6]

Suppose, however, that the buyer has duly issued his ticket. The situation then becomes a little more complicated: the Rules provide that *the holder* of the ticket at certain specified times bears the liability. The situation can best be explained by reproducing the table of liabilities set out in Rule 155 (5).

Where the selling-out took place on:	Holder of ticket at:
first intermediate day	2 p.m. on first intermediate day
second intermediate day	12 noon on first intermediate day
third intermediate day and subsequent days	3 p.m. on day previous to selling-out

The above table will apply, unless the holder whom it fixes with liability can prove that he was the victim of undue delay in the passing of the ticket by another intermediary.

5. Rule 155 (3).   6. Rule 155 (4).

(iv) Release of intermediaries

The seller who delays his recourse to the Buying-in and Selling-out Department will (like the dilatory buyer) relieve intermediaries from a liability which they might otherwise have had to shoulder. If the seller of registered securities allows two business days from 3 p.m. on the second intermediate day to elapse without availing himself of his right to sell-out, *his buyer* will be relieved from all loss in cases where the ticket has not been passed in consequence of the declaration of any member as a defaulter.[7]

While the buyer has[8] eleven clear days from the buying-in day in which to attempt to buy-in securities—if his immediate seller is not to be released—so (conversely) if the seller does not *deliver* the securities within those eleven days, his immediate buyer from whom he received the ticket will be released.[9]

(v) Delivery of ticket after a security has been sold-out

When the Buying-in and Selling-out Department has sold a security on the instructions of the seller, the department may deliver direct to the new buyer if they do not receive his ticket within half an hour of the selling-out.[10]

(vi) Non-clearing scrip tickets

Where the bargain is for non-clearing securities[11] passing by delivery, the seller who fails to receive a scrip ticket by 12 noon on the first intermediate day should report the matter in writing to the buying-in and selling-out official who will enquire into the reason for the delay and report to two members of the Council.

(vii) Liability to fine for late issue of tickets

Issues of original tickets on and after the third intermediate day are liable to a fine in respect of each such ticket.[12]

D. DIVIDENDS, INTEREST AND RIGHTS

As a general rule, and in the absence of any express or implied term in the bargain to the contrary, the buyer will be entitled to all benefits which attach to the ownership of the shares as from the time of purchase.

1. Dividends

The buyer is entitled to all dividends declared for the period prior to the date of the bargain. The practice of the London Stock

7. Rule 156.   8. Under Rule 150.   9. Rule 156, *supra*.   10. Rule 157.
11. Non-clearing securities are all securities of which the Settlement Office (see pp. 200–201, *post*) does not undertake the settlement.
12. Rule 122 (4).

Exchange, however, is for securities to be quoted "ex" dividend in the Official List, and where they are not quoted "ex" dividend the quotation is deemed to be "cum" dividend; and it is the Official List quotation which dictates the terms of the bargain. Where there is no quotation the parties are free to agree the dates on which the securities become ex dividend.[13]

13. Some ex-dividend dealings are prohibited under Rule 165 (2):

(i) *Where registered securities are dealt in for the account,* no bargain may be done ex dividend earlier than the first day of the account immediately preceding the ex dividend date. Earlier dealings may however be sanctioned by the Council.

In the case of Appendix 39A securities (mainly British and Commonwealth Government stocks) dealt in for cash no bargain may be done ex dividend earlier than three weeks before the ex dividend date. And no bargain may be done cum dividend after the stock is officially made ex dividend without the prior consent of the Chairman or a Deputy Chairman.

(ii) *In the case of 3½ per cent War Loan,* securities issued by the International Bank for Reconstruction and Development and those securities which are, under the Rules, dealt in subject to the accrued or accruing interest being accounted for between buyer and seller, no bargain may be done ex dividend before, or cum dividend after the stock is officially made ex dividend.

(iii) No option for the put or call of a security may be fixed at an ex dividend price prior to such security being officially made ex dividend.

(iv) No bargain may be made cum dividend after the payment of the dividend.

Other ex dividend dealings require a certificate under Rule 165a.

Where Appendix 39A securities are dealt in ex dividend for cash done *during* the three-week period prior to the ex dividend date and where such transaction is part of a switching or reversing operation involving a cum dividend bargain, a broker must:

(a) *In the case of an ex dividend sale to the market* provide the jobber with an Appendix 47A certificate stating that the client for whom he is dealing has been the beneficial owner of the stock for at least one month immediately preceding the date of the sale, *or* that the client has bought the stock ex dividend previously during the three-week period.

(b) *In the case of an ex dividend purchase from the market* provide the jobber with an Appendix 47B certificate stating that the transaction neither reverses a cum dividend short sale already effected during the three-week period *nor* represents the ex dividend counterpart of a cum dividend sale yet to be effected.

In the case of an ex dividend bargain in Appendix 39A securities which are dealt in for cash done during the three-week period prior to the ex dividend date, where the ex dividend transaction is *not* part of a switching or reversing operation the broker must provide the jobber with an Appendix 47C certificate to that effect.

The Rules provide that jobbers should retain the certificates and brokers the written assurances of their clients for production, if necessary, to the Council or the Inland Revenue.

All transactions executed during the three-week period must be settled by delivery, and members may not agree to the reversal of transactions carried out during that time. Moreover, if they put stock through the market during the three-week period they are bound by the aforementioned Rules as to certificates.

A. WHEN SECURITIES BECOME EX DIVIDEND

Under the Rules[14] certain securities become ex dividend at certain times, so:

(i) Gilt-Edged securities included in Appendix 39A (other than bearer securities) on the last day on which transfers will be accepted cum dividend. Where the nominal value of such securities exceeds £10,000, notice of an ex dividend bargain effected within the three-week period before the security is officially quoted ex dividend must be given to the Council,[15] and the transfer must be lodged with the Quotations Department.[16]

(ii) Registered securities (except registered debentures) and securities which are dealt in in *both* bearer and registered form: the first dealing day of the account next but one before the account day on or following the first or only day on which transfers will be accepted for registration cum dividend.

(iii) Registered debentures and other securities to bearer: on the day on which the dividend is payable.

(iv) (*a*) American shares: on the day following the day on which they are dealt in ex dividend on the New York or other American stock exchange.

(*b*) Shares in American companies with a London register: on the day following the last day on which transfers will be accepted in London for registration cum dividend.

B. DEDUCTION OF DIVIDENDS

When payment is made for securities, a dividend may be *deducted* by the buyer if delivery is made after the last day on which transfers were accepted by the company in time for the buyer to receive the dividend direct.[17] The Rules provide for the settlement of such claims between firms and, failing such settlement, for transmission of the claim through the Central Stock Payment Office.[18]

When delivery has been effected through the Central Stock Payment Office, the buyer may not make a deduction of dividend, but he may claim through the Office or direct from the seller.[19]

C. ACCOUNTING FOR DIVIDENDS BY THE SELLER

The seller is in all cases responsible for such dividends as may be due to the buyer, unless an unreasonable time has been taken in executing and lodging the documents for registration, or the buyer has made unreasonable delay in claiming dividends.[20]

14. Rule 111.　　15. Rule 165*b*.　　16. Rule 165*c*.　　17. Rule 132(1).
18. Rule 132(2). For the Central Stock Payment Office see pp. 201–202, *post*.
19. Rule 103(4).　　20. Rule 120(3).

The seller must account to the buyer for dividends at the *net* amount receivable after deduction of income tax.[1] Where the seller has income tax deducted, he can prove the fact by producing a tax voucher[2] in one of the forms contained in Appendix 45 of the Rules and Regulations of the Stock Exchange and approved by the Board of Inland Revenue.

Jobbers may not enter into switching or reversing transactions or match an ex dividend transaction with a cum dividend transaction in the same Appendix 39A stock, dealt in for cash within the 28 days preceding the date to which they make up their accounts for tax purposes. Jobbers must furnish the Inland Revenue with a certificate that no such transaction has been effected when submitting their accounts for tax purposes. This certificate must be signed by the firm and the firm's accountants.[3]

Without the dividend coupon, bearer securities are not regarded as good delivery, unless of course the securities have before the date of delivery been made ex coupon,[4] or ex dividend.[5] Where bearer securities are bought cum dividend, but are to be made ex dividend on or before the date of settlement for which the bargain is done, and the buyer requires:

(*a*) delivery of the coupon; or
(*b*) the sterling value of the dividend in full, without deduction of income tax;
he must in either case make a special bargain.[6]

Where a dividend is payable on or before the day for the settlement of a bargain in bearer securities, the making-up price must be ex dividend.[7]

For the purpose of the seller's accounting for dividends, Appendix 39A securities (Gilt-Edged),[8] and "American"[9] securities are governed by other Rules. But the general principles are that:

(*a*) where securities become or are made ex dividend before the date of settlement, they pass ex dividend; and

1. Rule 112 (1). But in the case of $3\frac{1}{2}$ per cent War Loan and securities issued by the International Bank for Reconstruction and Development dividends are paid gross.

   Rule 165*d*(1) provides that in all bargains involving Appendix 39A Gilt-Edged securities dealt in for cash, dividends passing between the parties in consequence of such a bargain (including a jobber to jobber bargain) must be settled *gross* unless a valid tax voucher is provided.
2. The Rules define tax vouchers and make provisions for their operation. See Rules 165 *d* (2) *et seq.*
3. Rule 165*d*(7).   4. Rule 139 (1) (*a*).   5. Rule 139 (1) (*b*).   6. Rule 139 (2).
7. Rule 139*a*.   8. Rule 119.   9. Rule 139 (*c*) and (*d*). Rule 141.

(*b*) a dividend may be deducted if delivery is made after the last day on which transfers were accepted for registration cum dividend.

D. SETTLEMENT OF DIVIDENDS IN FOREIGN CURRENCY

Dividends in registered securities payable in a currency other than United Kingdom sterling must be settled temporarily at the official rate of exchange at the time of settlement, subject to adjustment in accordance with a valuation to be fixed upon application to the Head of the Quotations Department.[10]

Where dividends on bearer securities are payable abroad, or both in London and abroad, the Head of the Quotations Department will—upon application—fix the market value of the dividend or coupon in sterling. That valuation will be posted in the Stock Exchange and the dividend must be accounted for at that valuation.[11]

E. PROSPECTIVE DIVIDENDS

Bargains in prospective dividends are one of the dealings prohibited by Rule 165. Nevertheless it was held in *Marten* v. *Gibbons*[12] that such a bargain is not contrary to law, and that accordingly it could be enforced by a member of the Stock Exchange against a non-member.

2. Interest

Bargains in fixed income securities are deemed to include accrued interest in the price.[13] But,

(*a*) British Government securities and certain other Gilt-Edged securities[14] having five years or less to run; and

(*b*) such other securities as may be so designated in the Official List, must be dealt in subject to accrued or accruing interest being accounted for between buyer and seller up to but not including the day on which the bargain is due for settlement.[15] The accrued interest on these securities must be paid *without* deduction of income tax.[16]

3. Rights and capitalisation issues

A. MEANING OF A RIGHTS ISSUE

Where a company offers shares for sale to its existing members in numbers proportionate to their existing shareholding, the company is said to make a rights issue. In other words the members have the right to take up a proportionate number of the shares being issued.

---

10. Rule 133. 11. Rule 140. 12. (1875), 33 L.T. 561. 13. Rule 118 (1).
14. I.e., those specified in Rule 163 (1) (*b*). 15. Rule 118 (2). 16. Rule 112 (2).

Where the shares will be quoted on a stock exchange, the stock exchange will normally require the offer to be made by a renounceable letter or other negotiable instrument. The beneficial holder of the securities to which the rights attach is entitled to accept the new securities resulting from those rights or dispose of them by letter of renunciation.

B. RIGHTS OF BUYER

The Rules provide that the buyer of old securities "cum rights" or "cum capitalisation" is entitled to any such renounceable document or new securities issued in respect thereof.[17] Times are specified in which the buyer must claim his rights,[18] for the seller's liability in that event,[19] and for the seller's liability if the buyer makes his claim out of time.[1] Unless the buyer of the old security has informed the seller not later than 11 a.m. on the business day before acceptance day (the last day for the receipt of an acceptance of the company's offer made in its letter of rights), or payment day (the last day fixed, for the receipt of the next payment, if any, payable under the terms of the offer in the letter of rights) the seller is liable to deliver, free of stamp if applicable, and the buyer is liable to receive the new security against payment of any call or calls that the seller has paid on the buyer's behalf.[2]

C. SELLER A TRUSTEE OF THE BUYER'S RIGHTS

After a transfer of shares to which rights are attached the seller, if the rights are claimed in accordance with the Rules, becomes a trustee for the buyer of all those rights. This trust is not affected by the fact that the buyer knew about the rights attaching to himself but has been guilty of delay in exercising them. In *Rooney* v. *Stanton*:[3]

> The plaintiff, who was a shareholder in a company, had purchased further shares therein from the defendant. The transfers were duly executed and handed to the plaintiff. Shortly afterwards, and before the transfers were lodged with the company for registration, resolutions were passed to wind up voluntarily and reconstruct the company. A new company was accordingly formed, the shares in which were to be offered rateably to the shareholders in the old company, each share being credited with 18 shillings paid up. The balance of 2 shillings was to be paid by instalments. The plaintiff then sent the transfers for registration to the liquidator of the old company, but he refused to register them

17. Rule 114 (2). See also Chapter 4.   18. Rule 114 (2) (*a*).
19. Rule 114 (2) (*b*).   1. Rule 114 (2) (*c*).
2. The procedure for (*a*) making a rights offer, and (*b*) accepting or refusing it, are fully described in Chapter 9.
3. (1900), 17 T.L.R. 28, C.A. See also *Stewart* v. *Lupton* (1874), 22 W.R. 855.

except upon payment of 1 shilling per share, being the amount payable at that time on the shares in the new company. The plaintiff delayed making the payment and the transfers were not registered. The defendant then applied for the shares in the new company, paid to the liquidator the sum due on the shares, and received an allotment.

It was held that the defendant was a trustee of the shares in the new company for the plaintiff and that, on the facts, there was no equity to deprive the plaintiff of his rights as *cestui que trust*. On the other hand, the plaintiff had not paid for the shares held in trust for him, and he was bound to indemnify the defendant.

The position evinced by the Rules and the decision in *Rooney* v. *Stanton* does not, of course, preclude the seller and buyer "cum rights" from making an arrangement that the seller will be entitled to a *proportion* of the rights, or some advantage flowing from them.

E. CALLS

On a sale of securities the seller *ipso facto* becomes entitled to be indemnified by the buyer against all future liability, including the payment of calls, in respect of the shares sold. This right of indemnity depends upon the contract of sale, not upon the registration of the buyer as the new holder. So in *Evans* v. *Wood*:[4]

A had sold to N, a jobber, and B had purchased from N shares in a company. According to the usual practice, N gave to A the name of B as the purchaser. A transfer of the shares from A to B was executed by A and B, and the purchase money was paid by B to A. B was prevented by accidental absence from sending the transfer for registration until after the company had stopped making payments. The company was wound up, and the liquidators registered all transfers left at the office before the company stopped payments, but they refused to register the transfer from A to B: A was made a contributory in the liquidation, and paid a call on the shares.

It was held that A was entitled to a decree against B for repayment of the call, and indemnity against future liability in respect of the shares.

The Rules state that the seller may pay pending calls, provided that a call letter has been issued, and claim the amount of the calls from the buyer on delivery of the security.[5] But suppose that a buying jobber "names" a buyer who is unacceptable to the seller, so that no transfer is registered and the seller remains holder of the

---

4. (1867), L.R. 5 Eq. 9. See also *Shepherd* v. *Gillespie* (1868), 3 Ch. App. 764.
5. Rule 127.

shares and has to pay calls. It was held in *Allen* v. *Graves*[6] that the buying jobber will have to indemnify the seller against that continuing liability.

F. PAYMENT

1. Account day

The various members who have dealt in a particular security settle up completely on account day. Each member adjusts his account with the member with whom his bargain was made, on the footing of the making-up price (where applicable) or in other cases, the ticket price. Schwabe and Branson's *Law of the Stock Exchange*[7] explains the position with transparent simplicity:

"So a member who has bought securities from another for £100, if the securities at the making-up price are worth £90, or in cases where the adjustment is at ticket price and that price is £90, pays the other £10. If he is going to take up the shares, he will pay the £90 on tender of the transfer, so providing the £100 for which he bought the shares. If, on the other hand, he is one of the intermediate parties who dropped out, he has nothing further to do in the matter. All these payments are made by cheques on clearing house bankers. The effect of this is that each member, through the operation of the bankers' clearing house, receives or pays the balance only which he has made or lost as the result of all his transactions during the account. It also prevents any hardship resulting from the working of the practice of adjusting accounts on the footing of the making-up price or ticket price, which may have the effect of compelling a member to draw cheques for amounts greater than his actual liabilities. Each member pays into his bank cheques in his favour to meet his own cheques as they are presented, so that his account at his bankers is diminished or increased only by the balance between the two sets of cheques, which balance represents his profit or loss on the account as a whole."

2. Differences

Where securities are carried over on contango, differences which arise on such carrying-over are payable on account day.[8] Differences which arise on the passing of tickets both as between buyer and seller, and as between intermediaries, are also payable on account day.[9] When a stock exchange firm is declared a defaulter, the prices

6. (1870), L.R. 5 Q.B. 478.   7. 2nd Edn. (1914), p. 83.
8. *Davis & Co.* v. *Howard* (1890), 24 Q.B.D. 691.
9. See *Re Woodd, ex parte King* (1900), 82 L.T. 504, at p. 506.

of securities in which they have dealt and which remain undelivered are fixed by the Official Assignee.[10] It is then the duty of members having open positions with them to close their accounts. Hammer price differences are payable on the day for which the contracts were entered into.[11]

A firm cannot demand bank notes or a banker's draft in payment of differences.[12]

3. When the price becomes payable by the purchaser

The buyer of registered securities may refuse to pay for a transfer unaccompanied by the share or stock certificate, unless it be officially certified that the certificate is in fact at the office of the company.[13] But if the transfer is perfect in all other respects, the buyer must not buy-in the securities until he has allowed the seller reasonable time to obtain the certification required.[14]

Where a transfer conveys part only of the securities represented by a certificate, the seller may deposit the certificate with the Stock Exchange Certification Office, whose duty it is to forward it to the company and certify to that effect on the transfer. This amounts to good delivery and the buyer must then pay the price.[15]

The Rules make no specific provision for payment in the case of bearer securities. However Rule 101a provides that "a seller cannot demand payment against delivery before the date fixed by the contract", and it is a fair inference that the price becomes legally payable on delivery of the documents of security.

4. Manner of payment

It is a custom of the Stock Exchange, London, for a selling member to accept the crossed cheque of a buying member; and accordingly it was held in *Mocatta* v. *Bell*[16] that where such a cheque was dishonoured, that was not necessarily evidence that the selling member had been negligent. The Master of the Rolls said:[17]

"... you would put an end to all business, if it were held that before a man took a crossed cheque, it was necessary for him to go personally and inquire of the banker whether that cheque would be duly honoured or not. When you consider the enormous amount of cheques which must necessarily pass upon the Stock Exchange on the same day, such a doctrine would be practically putting an end to all business."

10. See Chapter 10.
11. See *Re Plumbly, ex parte Grant* (1880), 13 Ch. D. 667 C.A. at p. 675.
12. Rule 104 (3).
13. Rule 129 (1). For official certification, see Rule 129 (3).   14. *Ibid.*
15. Rule 129 (2) (*a*). Under Rule 129 (2) (*b*) the Council disclaim liability for the acts and omissions of the Certification Office.
16. (1857), 24 Beav. 585.   17. *Ibid.,* at p. 596.

Cheques must be drawn on a town clearing bank, or the Bank of England, Threadneedle Street, and presented for payment through a clearing bank. They must be crossed, marked "not negotiable", drawn to order, and bear the code number of the payer. They may also be marked "account payee only".[18]

A firm may if it wishes require payment to be in bank notes, a banker's draft or a cheque payable to bearer. If no such stipulation was made at the time of the bargain, the firm must give notice to the buyer of its wishes before 10.30 a.m. on the day of delivery.[19]

G. DISPOSAL OF THE PROCEEDS OF SALE

1. Payment

A broker instructed to sell always has an implied authority to receive payment on behalf of his client.[20] Payments to agents should, in the absence of a custom to the contrary, be made in cash. But the case of *Crossley* v. *Magniac*[1] shows:

(i) The customary stock exchange payment by crossed cheque may be equivalent to payment in cash if the proceeds are duly collected.[2]

(ii) Payment by uncrossed cheque which is duly honoured is also such an equivalent.[3]

(iii) But setting off a debt owed to the broker by the client's agent is not payment in cash.[4]

(iv) Nor is payment made by a bill which cannot be allocated to the transaction in question.[5]

2. Broker must account to client

When a broker receives payment for securities sold on behalf of his client he must, as agent, account to his client. Alternatively he must pay it to an agent duly authorised by his client to receive payment on his behalf. *In Blackburn* v. *Mason*:[6]

> A custom was alleged under which a member of the London Stock Exchange, who has sold shares on the instructions of a country broker acting for an undisclosed client, is entitled to set off against the price of the shares a debt due to him from the country broker in respect of previous stock exchange transactions.

18. Rule 104 (1).   19. Rule 104 (2).
20. *Magnus* v. *Queensland National Bank* (1888), 37 Ch. D. 466, C.A., at p. 474, *per* Cotton, L. J.
1. [1893] 1 Ch. 594.   2. *Ibid.*, at p. 599, *per* Romer, J.
3. See note 2, *supra*.   4. *Ibid.*, and see *Blackburn* v. *Mason*, *supra*.
5. See *ibid.*   6. (1893), 68 L.T. 510, C.A.

The Court of Appeal held that the custom, if it existed, was unreasonable, and was not binding on the country broker's client where he did not know of, or had not agreed to be bound by it.

3. Broker mistaken as to his client

Suppose that a broker gets the impression that he is instructed by one person, when he ought to realise that in reality he is acting for others. That was the position in *Pearson* v. *Scott*:[7]

> Four executors holding stock in their name had directed a solicitor to sell it. Acting in the name of his firm, the solicitor gave to a broker (whom he had previously employed in stock exchange speculations of his own) directions to sell the stock. The broker sold the stock, and the solicitor returned to him transfers of the stock, with receipts endorsed and signed by the four executors. The sale was completed. The broker, ignoring the four executors' signatures, sent the solicitor a cheque for part of the purchase money for the shares, and carried the balance of the transaction to the credit of the solicitor in the solicitor's account with him. That account was afterwards settled by a payment made to the broker.

It was held that the broker must be taken to have had notice that the shares were not the property of the solicitor. Although the solicitor had authority from the executors to receive the purchase-money, payment to him by giving him credit in his *own* account with the broker was not sufficient to discharge the broker, who remained liable to the executors for the balance.

4. Third party liability

In *Magnus* v. *Queensland National Bank*,[8] the broker knew very well for whom he was acting. He failed to account to his clients, and yet by a series of unscrupulous manoeuvres he was able to make a third party responsible in law:

> The broker, G, wore as it were two hats: he was one of three trustees and at the same time he acted as broker to the trust. He proposed to his co-trustees to sell B stock belonging to the trust and re-invest in N.E. stock. All three trustees then, on January 27th 1882, executed a transfer of the B stock for a nominal consideration to two persons who were officers of a bank of which G was a customer. G gave the transfer to the bank as security for a loan of £50,000 *to himself*, and the transfer was registered. In February 1882, G paid off the loan, and on February 15th the bank transferred the stock to purchasers from G, and *without giving any notice to G's co-trustees*, allowed him to receive the purchase-money. G invested it in N.E. stock *in his own name*. In 1883 he sold the N.E. stock and misappropriated the proceeds. Shortly after the sale of the B stock, G had given an account to his co-trustees showing the sale of B

7. (1878), 9 Ch. D. 198.   8. (1888), 37 Ch. D. 466, C.A.

stock, and a "re-investment" in N.E. stock, and in 1884 he produced another account in which he represented the N.E. stock as still forming part of the trust funds. In 1885 he absconded. The co-trustees remembered hardly anything about the transaction, but admitted the genuineness of their signatures to the deed of transfer.

The Court of Appeal held that the bank had caused the loss to the trust estate by allowing the purchase-money to come into the hands of G who had no authority to receive it. Furthermore the bank did not have sufficient reason for believing that G had such authority. Accordingly the bank were ordered to make good the purchase-money at the suit of the co-trustees, even though the co-trustees had themselves been negligent in not seeing to it that the N.E. stock was registered in the joint names of all the trustees.

It had been argued on behalf of the bank that whatever the bank's breach of duty, it was G's default which was the real cause of the loss to the trust fund. Bowen, L.J., dismissed that argument as follows:[9]

> "It is an ocular illusion to present the case in that way ... A man knocks me down in Pall Mall, and when I complain that my purse has been taken, the man says, 'Oh, but if I had handed it back again, you would have been robbed over again by somebody else in the adjoining street.' "

The co-trustees could, of course, have recovered against G. But he was no longer available, and in any case he had contrived to leave them with an even more substantial defendant in the bank.

H. THE SETTLEMENT AND CENTRAL STOCK PAYMENT OFFICE

1. The Settlement Office

The Stock Exchange Settlement Office was instituted in order to bring together takers (i.e., buyers) and deliverers (i.e., sellers) without resort to the more cumbersome method of passing tickets *inter se*. The Office has been compared with the bankers' clearing house and deals with about two hundred of the more active securities which are said to "clear". Members are obliged[10] to make daily returns[11] (known as clearing lists or sheets) of all bargains in clearing stocks (including contangos and "new time" bargains and bargains in scrip securities) to the Settlement Office.

On analysis of these lists the Office will work out the ultimate

9. (1888), 37 Ch. D. 466, C.A., at p. 480.   10. See Appendix 44 of the Rules.
11. With a few exceptions: see Appendix 44 (2).

destination of the securities. The Office will then issue to each firm a ticket passing instruction list so that ultimate buyers are brought into direct contact with original sellers. The procedure is then as follows:[12]

(*a*) When the Office has not split a bought bargain the taker must pass his ticket to the firm named as the deliverer on the ticket passing instruction list.

(*b*) When the Office splits[13] a bought bargain (which will be indicated by a serial number on the ticket passing instruction list):

(i) The taker must mark the ticket with the relevant serial number before passing it on to the Office for splitting.

(ii) If the ticket is for a lesser amount then the original bargain, the deliverers' names and their relevant amounts must also be shown on the back of the ticket.

The Settlement Office will determine the firm or firms liable for the loss of rights caused through splitting a ticket. A firm claiming loss of rights will receive a notice giving the name of the firm or firms who are responsible. Firms cannot be liable for a greater loss than that revealed by their bargains cleared.[14]

The Settlement Office has nothing to do with the price actually to be paid by any member firm, as all transactions between firms settle at the making-up price.

2. The Central Stock Payment Office

The Central Stock Payment Office of the Stock Exchange provides facilities for member firms to settle deliveries of:[15]

(*a*) registered securities except those Gilt-Edged securities included in Appendix 39A and which are dealt in for cash; and

(*b*) renounceable documents excluding:

(i) those in respect of Appendix 39A securities dealt in for cash; and

(ii) letters in settlement of rights claims.

All firms must accept delivery when made through the Central Stock Payment Office, and must pay for such deliveries.[16]

When delivery has been effected through the Central Stock Payment Office, the buyer may not make deductions for dividends,

---

12. See Appendix 44 (8).
13. The office cannot accept a ticket for splitting:

(i) if it bears more than one serial number; or
(ii) if it is passed after 12 noon on the third intermediate day. After this a firm will have to split the ticket in accordance with the ticket passing instruction list, and will be responsible for any cost incurred.

14. Appendix 44 (10).   15. Rule 103 (2).   16. Rule 103 (3).

undelivered rights or drawings as in the case of inter-office settlements. He must claim such deductions in accordance with the provisions of Appendix 44a (which regulates Central Stock Payment generally) or direct from the seller.[17]

I. INTER-FIRM DELIVERY

The delivery of all securities begins at 9.30 a.m.,[18] and

(*a*) The latest time for delivery by a broker firm to another firm's office of registered securities dealt in for the account is 12.15 p.m. A jobber firm may deliver such securities to a broker firm's office not later than 1 p.m.

(*b*) The latest time for the inter-office delivery of Appendix 39A Gilt-Edged securities dealt in for cash is 1.15 p.m.

(*c*) The latest time for delivery of renounceable certificates or renounceable letters by a broker firm to a jobber's office is 12.30 p.m. A jobber firm may deliver such renounceable documents to a broker firm's office not later than 1.15 p.m.

(*d*) The latest time for delivery by a broker firm to another firm's office of securities passing by delivery (e.g., bearer securities) is 12.30 p.m. A jobber firm may deliver such securities to a broker firm's office not later than 1 p.m.[19]

It is provided, however, that if a seller elects to settle with the firm who passed him the ticket (delivery on trace) then the securities must be delivered not later than 11 a.m., and if so the firm who passed the ticket must pay his seller not later than 11.30 a.m.[20]

The machinery for the transfer of securities between principals will be described in the next chapter.

17. Rule 103 (4).   18. Rule 103 (1).
19. Rule 103 (5).   20. Rule 103 (5) proviso.

CHAPTER 9

Transfer

A. INTRODUCTION

1. Company's register

Section 110 of the Companies Act 1948 provides that every company must keep a register of its members containing:

(1) The names and addresses of the members, a statement of the shares held by each member, distinguishing each share by its number so long as it has one, and the amount paid or agreed to be considered as paid on the shares of each member. If the company has converted into stock, the register must show the amount of stock held by each member.

(2) The date at which each person was entered in the register as a member.

(3) The date at which any person ceased to be a member. The register is to be kept at the company's registered office, but if the register is made up at another office of the company, it may be kept there, and if it is made up by an agent, it may be kept at his office. There is a fine in default. The Act also provides for inspection of the register by members during business hours.

The register of members is *prima facie* evidence of any matters directed by the Companies Acts to be inserted in it.[1] However, by section 116 of the 1948 Act if:

(1) the name of any person is, without sufficient cause, entered in or omitted from the register; or

(2) default is made or unnecessary delay takes place in entering on the register the fact of any person having ceased to be a member.

The person aggrieved, or any member of the company, or the company, may apply to the court for rectification of the register.

The matters which, by section 110, a company is obliged to enter in its register of members, form a part of the matters which it must include in its annual return to the Registrar of Companies.

---

1. Companies Act 1948, s. 118.

2. Share certificates

A share certificate is the formal documentary evidence that a person holds a specified number of shares in a particular company. The certificate is issued by the company under its common seal. If a person holds shares, he must also by section 110 of the Companies Act 1948 be entered in the register. The right to a share certificate and the right to registration are thus inextricably linked.

By section 80 of the Companies Act 1948 every company must complete share certificates and have them ready for delivery within two months after allotment or after the date on which a document of transfer (known as a "transfer") is lodged with the company for registration. The Act provides for a fine in default.

"The object of the certificate is to facilitate dealings with the shares, whether by way of sale or security, and so make them more valuable to their owner."[2] In fact transfers cannot take place without the certificate. So if a company intends that the securities should be quoted on the Stock Exchange, the certificate must have a footnote to the effect that no transfer will be registered without production of the share certificate.[3] And Rule 129 (1) of the Rules and Regulations of the Stock Exchange allows the buyer of securities to *refuse to pay* for a transfer which is unaccompanied by the certificate, unless it be officially certified on the transfer itself that the certificate is in fact at the office of the company.

The form of the certificate is governed by the company's articles, but the Stock Exchange has provided its own comprehensive requirements. The Rules and Regulations, Appendix 34, Schedule IV A 2 stipulate that the following matters must appear on the face of the certificate:

(a) The authority under which the company (or other issuing organisation) is constituted.

(b) Preferably at the top right-hand corner, the number of shares or amount of stock the certificate represents and if applicable the number and denomination of units.

(c) A footnote stating that no transfer of the security or any part thereof represented by the certificate can be registered without production of the certificate.

(d) If applicable, the minimum amount and multiples thereof in which the security is transferable.

2. See *Charlesworth's Company Law* (9th Edn.) p. 166.
3. Rules and Regulations of the Stock Exchange, Appendix 34, Sched. IV A, para. 2 (c).

Certificates must be dated and (in the absence of statutory authority for issue under signature of appropriate officials) be issued under seal.

If relating to securities other than share capital, state on the face the rate of interest payable and the interest payment dates and include on the back (preferably with reference shown on the face) a statement or summary of the conditions as to redemption or repayment and (where applicable) conversion.

If relating to share capital there is more than one class in issue, the certificates of the preferential classes must also bear (preferably on the face) a statement of the conditions conferred thereon as to capital and dividends.

A share certificate is not a negotiable instrument, and so a company's articles usually provide that if it is defaced, lost or destroyed the company will grant the owner—usually against a letter of indemnity—a new certificate on the payment of a small fee.

3. Bearer securities

Bearer securities (for example share warrants) are documents issued by a company under its common seal stating that the bearer is entitled to the shares specified therein. Unlike share certificates, bearer securities are freely transferable between non-members as negotiable instruments. So under section 83 of the Companies Act 1948 *mere delivery* of share warrants transfers ownership of the shares.[4] The current holder of the security is not, however, a member of the company and therefore delivery is not, as in the case of share certificates, accompanied by registration.

A broker who has given value for a bearer security on an exchange is a holder for value, and he is therefore personally liable upon the contract. So, where the buyer of a bearer security finds that his title to it is disputed, or that the issuers of the security fail to meet their obligations under it, he may under Rule 134 (1) (c) of the Rules and Regulations refer the matter to the Stock Exchange Council. If in the Council's opinion the circumstances warrant such action, they may require the security in question to be returned to the seller and a similar security, not subject to the same disability, to be delivered to the buyer in its place. The Council may fix the date to which this trace back shall be carried.

Coupons for dividends must be attached to bearer securities, so that when the company advertises a dividend, the holder can present

4. The following bearer securities have been held to be negotiable instruments:— bonds of a foreign government, bonds of a foreign corporation, scrip to bearer issued for debenture bonds, scrip certificates to bearer for shares in an English joint stock company, debenture bonds to bearer, shares warrants to bearer.

the appropriate coupon to the company's paying agent against payment. Without the coupon system, the paying agent, not knowing the current holder's identity (because he is not registered), would not know to whom to pay the dividend.

An exposition of the form and contents requisite for bearer securities is to be found in Appendix 34, Schedule IV B of the Rules and Regulations. They follow *mutatis mutandis* the requirements for share certificates authorised in Appendix 34, Schedule IV A.

Bearer securities are, comparative to share certificates, rare. This is the result of their disadvantages, which are: (*a*) they cannot be issued without Treasury consent, (*b*) they must be deposited with an authorised depositary, (*c*) the shares *must* be fully paid up, (*d*) the risk of loss or theft, (*e*) the heavy stamp duty payable, (*f*) the company's waste of time and expense in advertising in newspapers to establish contact with shareholders.

4. Share transfer forms and broker's transfer forms

The seller of shares has a legal duty to do (through his broker as his agent) all that is necessary on his part to enable the buyer to be registered as the new owner.[5] He must execute a valid transfer, and transmit it and the share certificate to the buyer's broker. The seller's responsibility ends there, and the purchaser must obtain registration for himself.[6] A seller must do nothing to prevent the purchaser becoming the registered owner. The purchaser can recover damages from the seller for breach of this obligation, whether the seller and the transferor are the same person,[7] or not.[8]

Shares which are the subject of a certificate must be transferred by the seller to the buyer under what section 75 of the Companies Act 1948 refers to as a "proper instrument of transfer". Formerly, the generally accepted form of transfer did not become a "proper instrument" until it had been executed by *both* the transferor and the transferee. Moreover the signature of the transferor was not effective unless it was attested.

The Stock Transfer Act 1963 made radical alterations to the requirements, and therefore the procedure, for the transfer of securities.[9] It did away with the necessity for· ·

5. *Stray* v. *Russel* (1859), 1 E. & E. 888; affirmed in *Neiisen* v. *James* (1882), 9 Q.B.D. 546, C.A.
6. *Evans* v. *Wood* (1867), L.R. 5 Eq. 9.
7. *Hooper* v. *Herts* (1906), 1 Ch. 549, C.A.
8. *Hitchens, Harrison, Woolston and Co.* v. *Jackson and Sons,* [1943] A.C. 266; [1943] 1 All E.R. 128, H.L.
9. By s. 1 (4) the reform applies to fully paid up registered securities of any description, being (*a*) Securities issued by any company within the meaning of the Companies Act 1948 except a company limited by guarantee or an unlimited

(*a*) Execution by the transferee.
(*b*) Attestation of the transferor's signature.

The Act provided that where there were several transfers out of the same holding of shares, a new broker's transfer form (to be prepared by the transferor's broker) may be used in conjunction with the stock transfer form. When therefore a client instructs his broker to sell his shares, he will have only to execute a parent stock transfer form which covers them all, leaving his broker to prepare separate broker's transfer forms if and when he delivers the shares to two or more buyers.

5. Procedure for transfer under the Stock Transfer Act 1963

If the full benefits of the new streamlined system of transfer were to be obtained, it was necessary that from the beginning there should be "an agreed uniformity of procedure not only on the part of those who register transfers but of those who prepare them and, in the case of stock exchange transactions, the selling and buyer brokers concerned".[10] Accordingly, the City Committee on the Transfer of Securities, which devised the new system and published the report which led to the passing of the Stock Transfer Act, appointed an Advisory Committee to prepare a comprehensive guide to its working in practice. The guide was published in July 1963 under the title *The New Transfer System*. In the introduction the Advisory Committee state modestly:

"We hope that in the course of time the practices which we recommend will become established by usage, but in the meantime we wish to make clear that the notes are intended only as a suggested guide to procedure. They are in no sense mandatory and should in no way be regarded as a substitute for legal advice."

That statement was contemporary with the passing of the Act, and clearly the efficiency of the procedures recommended had yet to be tested in practice. The publication of the *New Transfer System* shows that in 1963 a large number of influential people in the City

---

company. (*b*) Securities issued by any body (other than a company within the meaning of the Act) incorporated in Great Britain, but not a building society or an industrial or provident society. (*c*) Government stock (subject to exceptions). (*d*) Local authority stocks. (*e*) Units of a unit trust scheme.
10. See the *New Transfer System*, p. 5. Many of the changes in the "new" system rest on the implied indemnity and warranty of the lodging agent as to the genuineness of the transfer, and it should be noted that the *New Transfer System* alerts registrars to the possible necessity for other precautions, having regard to the limited number of transfers lodged by individuals.

agreed that it would be a good thing to have the procedures, but to
establish them as usages it must be shown that the agreement has *in
fact* been acted upon.[11] All the indications are that the *New Transfer
System* has become the accepted unchallenged authority on the
mechanics of the system introduced by the 1963 Act. If that is so, it
can be regarded as both the initiator of usage and the expression of
it. This chapter is written on the assumption that the *New Transfer
System* is such an expression of now accepted procedures, and it will
be used as a guide in their explanation.

B. THE NEW TRANSFER SYSTEM

The standard stock transfer form and broker's form are printed
in Appendices A and B. The new system applies to both stock
exchange transactions (where both forms may be employed in conjunction) and non-market transactions (where the stock transfer
form only is used). Where stock exchange transactions are dealt
with, and unless otherwise specified, the system described is the
system applicable where bargains have been done for the account.

1. Stock exchange transactions

A. STAGE 1
Preparation of stock transfer form by the transferor.
The new system allows the stock transfer form to be prepared
and signed by the transferor in advance of the sale of the security on
the market. The Advisory Committee suggested that, where the
seller is present with his agent at the time of giving selling instructions which are firm orders, his signature on a stock transfer
form can be obtained at that time. Agents, such as banks,
accountants and solicitors, who frequently pass on orders from their
clients to brokers, were especially asked to follow this suggestion.
When agents pass on selling orders either by telephone or in
writing, they should inform their brokers whether or not a stock
transfer form has been signed; if it has been signed, the stock transfer form, accompanied by the share certificate, will be sent to the selling broker, either with any written confirmation of the selling order,
or as soon as possible after the receipt of the contract note.

This procedure is not applicable to orders which are not firm, or
to large selling orders which extend over more than one account;
in such cases the stock transfer form should be completed at the end
of the account for the amount of the security sold in that account.

11. *Sea S.S. Co.* v. *Price, Walker & Co.* (1903), Com. Cas. 292, *per* Kennedy, J., at
   p. 295.

Where an agent sends a signed stock transfer form to the selling broker, he will leave the box beside the transferor's signature blank so that the selling broker may place his own stamp in the box. This does not, of course, affect the liability of the agent *vis-à-vis* the selling broker for the genuineness of the execution.

Where a stock transfer form is not signed by the seller at the time of giving the selling order, the broker carrying out the sale on the Stock Exchange will prepare and send out with the contract note, or as soon as possible thereafter, a stock transfer form for the signature of the seller. When a stock transfer form is sent through the post for signature, it is important that the seller be asked to sign and return it *immediately* (with the share certificate if still held by the seller) so that the selling broker can make delivery:

(*a*) on account day, if the security is dealt in for the account; or
(*b*) without delay if the security is dealt in for cash.

Agents are asked always to send an unaltered stock transfer form to the transferor for signature, but if any material correction or alteration has to be made in the stock transfer form before signature, the transferor should be asked to initial the amendment when he signs the form.

B. STAGE 2

Completion of the stock transfer form by the selling broker. If necessary, preparation of brokers' transfer form(s). Certification of transfer forms by the stock exchange. Their delivery to the buying broker(s).

When the stock transfer form has been executed by the transferor, the selling broker's subsequent procedure will depend on whether the security is to be transferred in a single amount or in several amounts, and whether all or part only of the security represented by the certificate(s) is being sold.

(*i*) Total share certificate(s) to one buyer

The selling broker will insert the buyer's consideration money and place his stamp and the date in the box beside the transferor's signature in the stock transfer form and, after having the stock transfer form stamped by the Inland Revenue, will deliver it and the share certificate(s) to the buying broker. As a means of identification for the buying broker, the Stock Exchange ticket will be attached to the stock transfer form and share certificate(s).

(*ii*) Part of share certificate to one buyer

The selling broker will insert the buyer's consideration money, place his stamp and the date in the box beside the transferor's signature on the stock transfer form and have the form stamped by the Inland Revenue. Certification will normally be obtained at the Stock Exchange.[12] The selling broker will complete the required form of advice,[13] and take it with the stock transfer form and the share certificate(s) to the Certification Office of the Stock Exchange which, having certified the stock transfer form and returned it to the selling broker, will send the share certificate(s) to the registrar with the advice. The selling broker will deliver the certified stock transfer form to the buying broker with the ticket attached to it.

(iii) Total or part of share certificate(s) to two or more buyers

The selling broker will insert his stamp and the date in the box beside the transferor's signature in the stock transfer form, cancelling the lower part of the form and filling in details of the several sales on the reverse of this form;[14] the form will thus serve *inter alia* as an advice of certification and no separate form of advice will be required.

The selling broker will then complete part (I) of a broker's transfer form for each of the component sales, inserting the buyer's consideration in each and placing his stamp and the date in part (I); if the transferor is a nominee company, that company's distinguishing number should also be inserted.[15] The selling broker will have the brokers' transfer forms stamped by the Inland Revenue. Certification will normally be obtained at the Stock Exchange;[16] the

---

12. As a general rule, selling brokers will use the certification facilities provided by their stock exchange except where:

    (*a*) there is no share certificate against which the stock exchange can certify; or

    (*b*) the title of the transferor to deal with the security is not evident from the share certificate.

    In the cases of (*a*) and (*b*) above, certification by the registrar is necessary. Where the share certificate is in the registrar's possession and is due to be forwarded to another agent, the selling broker lodging the stock transfer form will obtain the authority of that other agent, preferably by having the transfer receipt, balance voucher or other temporary document which that other agent will hold endorsed in his favour.

13. See Appendix F of the *New Transfer System.*

14. The right-hand column on the reverse of the stock transfer form should be used unless the number of sales exceeds the spaces in that column, when both columns should be used with a "carried forward" total at the foot of the left-hand column and a "brought forward" total at the foot of the right-hand column. If there are six or more certificates they should be listed on the reverse of the stock transfer form. If a balance certificate is not to be sent to the selling broker, instructions as to its disposal may be given on the reverse of the stock transfer form.

15. For the arrangements relating to nominee and trustee companies, and the Public Trustee, see the *New Transfer System,* paras. 24–27.

16. See note 12, *supra.*

selling broker will take the stock transfer form, all the brokers' transfer forms, and the share certificate(s) to the Certification Office which, having certified the brokers' transfer forms and returned them to the selling broker, will forward the share certificate(s) to the registrar with the stock transfer form. The selling broker will deliver the certified brokers' transfer forms to the buying brokers with the appropriate ticket attached to each.

(iv) Jobber selling his own securities

A jobber or other dealer in securities who is disposing of securities registered in his name or in the name of his nominee may either have a single stock transfer form for the total amount sold completed with a dependent brokers' transfer form for each buyer or have a separate stock transfer form completed for each buyer. If separate stock transfer forms are completed, in order to distinguish between forms for the same amount of the same security which are certified on the same day, the jobber or other dealer in securities will mark each transfer with a distinguishing number to be inserted after his name in the stock transfer form. A separate series of numbers should be used for each security, beginning at 1 when the new system of transfer came into force and starting again at 1 on January 1st of each succeeding year. If brokers' transfer forms are used the identifying number of the stock transfer form should be carried to each dependent brokers' transfer form. Jobbers should keep for their own use a record of certifications with the relative identifying numbers.

(v) Brokers' transfer forms must relate to their parent stock transfer form

It is important that brokers' transfer forms can be related with certainty to the stock transfer form from which they arise. Consequently when a selling broker is disposing of a client's holding piecemeal, and is making a number of sales during the same account, he should arrange if possible that only one stock transfer form is used for the total amount sold. Where this cannot be arranged and he has to obtain certification of brokers' transfer forms arising from two or more stock transfer forms *on the same day*, it will be necessary for the selling broker, with the agreement of the registrar, to record a distinguishing number on each stock transfer form and the same distinguishing number on the relative brokers' transfer forms. Unless the registrar is informed prior to certification that this is being done, the stock transfer forms will be returned to the selling broker, and in consequence the brokers' transfer forms will not be registered on presentation. This rule does not apply to nominee companies who adopt their own system of distinguishing numbers.

(vi) Brokers' transfer forms presented for certification

Brokers' transfer forms will not be certified by a stock exchange or by a registrar unless they are presented for certification at the same time as the relative stock transfer form is lodged; they will not be certified against a stock transfer form already lodged or against a certified stock transfer form. Brokers' transfer forms must not therefore be presented for certification, either to the Stock Exchange or the registrar, until they use up all the stock or shares to which the stock transfer form relates.

(vii) Balance certificate

Where a balance certificate is due to the selling broker and he is making or expects to make within a short while further sales on behalf of his client, he may instruct the registrar to hold the balance certificate to his order,[17] such instructions should be clearly indicated on the reverse of the stock transfer form where that form is used as the advice of certification.

(viii) Reproduction on brokers' transfer forms of matters contained in the stock transfer form

Brokers' transfer forms and the parent stock transfer form contain certain information common to both, i.e., the name of the undertaking, the name of the security and details of the transferor. This common information may be reproduced on to the printed brokers' transfer forms by carbon paper or by photographic or other similar process. Brokers using a photographic or similar method of reproduction are advised to obtain confirmation from the suppliers of the equipment that the photographic copy writing will be clear in definition and will neither fade nor deteriorate in course of handling when reproduced on to the printed brokers' transfer form. The Committee considered that in the interests of registrars they should advise brokers to use the printed brokers' transfer form itself in all cases and not take photographic copies thereof; moreover the stamps of brokers must be impressed on each form.

C. STAGE 3

The buying broker enters the names of the transferee(s) on the transfer form(s). He then sends transfer form(s) together with any share certificate to the company or other issuer for registration.

On taking delivery of a stock transfer form or a brokers' transfer form, the buying broker, in accordance with rules made by the stock exchanges, will verify that the stamp of the selling broker making

17. In the case of transfers certified by a provincial stock exchange, the instructions may include a request to hold the balance to the order of the certifying stock exchange.

delivery to him appears on the form. The buying broker will then insert particulars of the transferee and forward the form to the registrar together with any share certificate. Where by arrangement with his broker, an agent will himself be lodging the transfer for registration, the name only of the transferee need be passed to the broker. The agent, on receiving from the broker the stock transfer form or the brokers' transfer form, will insert the address and title of the transferee and, as lodging agent, will place his stamp in the box at the foot before forwarding the form to the registrar.[18]

Transfers must not remain in quasi-bearer form

Stock transfer forms and brokers' transfer forms, except for the brief period when they pass between selling and buying members of a stock exchange, must not remain in "quasi-bearer" form.[19] A buying broker taking delivery of a stock transfer form or a brokers' transfer form, if acting for another agent (e.g., a country broker), will therefore insert the name of the transferee and affix his stamp; it will then remain for that other agent to do no more than complete the form by inserting the address, etc., of the transferee and his stamp as lodging agent.

The above rule does not apply when a sale originates on a provincial stock exchange and the "takers" have dealt in the London Stock Exchange. Here the selling broker will retain the stock transfer form until his immediate buyer informs him of the amounts of the component purchases for which brokers' transfer forms will be required, and also the price of each such purchase for the calculation of stamp duty. The selling broker will then prepare the requisite brokers' transfer forms if necessary, have the form(s) stamped by the Inland Revenue in centres where this is possible, have the brokers' transfer forms, if any, certified against the signed stock transfer form, affix his own stamp as selling broker and forward the transfer form(s) to his buyer. When the transfer form(s) is received by the broker in the other exchange, that broker will have the form(s) stamped by the Inland Revenue, if this has not already been done, and will then place his own stamp to the left of that of the original selling broker before delivering it within his own market with the appropriate buying broker's ticket attached. In the event of a further delivery to another exchange this operation would be repeated. This procedure does not apply where the selling broker is able to sell to a broker on another exchange buying direct for a client. In such cases the selling broker, after obtaining certification, will have the transfer form(s)

18. See further the *New Transfer System*, para. 22.
19. See s. 67 of the Finance Act 1963, reproduced in Appendix L of the *New Transfer System*, which prohibits the circulation of blank transfers.

stamped by the Inland Revenue and insert the name of the buying broker's client before inserting his own stamp and delivering the transfer form(s) to the buying broker on the other exchange.

D. STAGE 4

The company or other issuer issues a new certificate to the buyer.

The Advisory Committee also drew up supplementary notes on the issue of certificates by registrars. This last stage in the transfer of securities was not affected by the new transfer system, but the object of the supplement was "to reduce the present lack of uniformity in practice and the inconvenience which it causes". The notes were intended for the guidance of registrars, and of agents "as it is important that they should know the procedure of registrars so that the proper documents can be submitted". In the opinion of the Advisory Committee registrars are entitled, if they so choose, to insist on the requirements of the *New Transfer System* being fully met, as it is in the interest of the certificate holder that alterations to the register should be made only on his personal instructions or on the presentation of duly authenticated legal documents. The guiding notes on the issue of certificates are reproduced below:

(i) The Committee had no doubt that the length of time which many companies allowed to elapse between the lodgment of the transfer and the issue of the new certificate caused general inconvenience and additional work. The period of two weeks now prescribed by the London Stock Exchange is not the optimum but the maximum length of time which may elapse; wherever possible certificates should be issued sooner. Some companies issue certificates within four or five days; if this period were generally adopted the investing public and their agents would benefit and companies too would gain through having to handle fewer temporary documents.

Companies were asked to re-examine their internal arrangements for the issue of certificates—in particular, audit procedure; they were asked also to consider sealing at more frequent intervals, delegating the sealing of certificates to a sealing committee, and making arrangements for certificates to be issued sealed but not signed.

(ii) Companies which issued certificates measuring more than 10 inches by 8 inches were asked to adopt a size within these limits as soon as practicable. In view of the possibility that the address of a registration office may change, it was suggested that this address be shown on the dividend warrants or counterfoils rather than on the certificate. The Committee considered that the address of a sole holder or the first named holder in a joint account should be quoted on certificates but that the addresses of second and subsequent holders in a joint account need not be shown.

(iii) As far as possible, certificates should be called in for amendment or replacement when there is a substantial change in the name of the company or the title of the security, and in other cases where confusion would arise if certificates were not amended or replaced. Certificates should also be called in for amendment when an alteration to the holder's name is made in the register, but calling in is not essential when the holder's address alters or there is some other minor alteration which does not affect the apparent title to deal.

(iv) As a general rule certificates sent by post may be dispatched by ordinary rather than by registered or recorded delivery post. The Committee considered it unnecessary for registrars to ask for receipts for certificates which are dispatched by post. Registrars were advised to satisfy themselves that their procedure prevented their being held legally responsible for the loss of certificates in course of post and that their office method afforded satisfactory evidence of posting; in such circumstances the issue of forms of receipt may even be an embarrassment. Agents too may care to consider whether they gain by asking clients to acknowledge the receipt of certificates.

(v) Where a certificate is lost or destroyed through no fault of the registrar, he should insist upon being indemnified before issuing a duplicate or permitting the stock or shares to be transferred. In the Committee's view, the protection of a continuing guarantor to the indemnity, e.g., a bank or insurance company, is necessary except where the value of the stock or shares represented by the lost certificate is trivial; as a general rule, to require the completion of a statutory declaration in addition to an indemnity is superfluous. Indemnities in respect of certificates lost while in course of post, or in the hands of agents, may, at the registrar's discretion, be given by those agents instead of by their clients but the concurrence of a continuing guarantor should still be insisted upon. Duplicate certificates should be marked "Duplicate". Agents should note that, where a duplicate certificate has been issued and the original is found, it is the original which must be surrendered for cancellation.

2. Non-market transactions

A "non-market" transaction means any transaction which is not a "stock exchange transaction" as defined in the Stock Transfer Act 1963. Under Section 4 (1) of the Act a "stock exchange transaction" is defined as:

"A sale and purchase of securities in which each of the parties is a member of a stock exchange acting in the ordinary course of his business as such or is acting through the agency of such a member."

And for the purpose of the Act "stock exchange" means the Stock Exchange, London, and any other stock exchange (whether in Great Britain or not) which is declared by order of the Treasury to be a recognised stock exchange [20] for the purposes of the Act.

Non-market transactions are effected principally by banks, accountants and solicitors acting as agents, but stockbrokers themselves do not always make bargains on an exchange.

TRANSFER PROCEDURE

The most conspicuous difference between stock exchange and non-market transfers is that the latter are always by stock transfer form only. The brokers' transfer form is not employed. The procedure is as recommended by the Advisory Committee:

(i) Where the transferor's holding is being divided into separate amounts and transferred to different transferees, a separate stock transfer form will be required for each such amount.

(ii) The stock transfer form will be completed in full (including the amount of consideration, if any, and the name and address of the transferee) and the words in italics will be deleted before the stock transfer form is sent to the transferor for execution. As the form will not be sent to the transferee for execution, and any error may not therefore come to light until after the issue of the new certificate, it is important that the particulars of the transferee should be correct and legible. The full name and title (e.g., Mr, Mrs or Miss) should be given, and the address should include the county or postal district number. If the transferee has an existing holding of the security to which the new acquisition is to be added, the particulars of the transferee must conform with those registered for the existing holding. If the new acquisition is to be kept separate from an existing holding the two amounts should be distinguished by designation or other means acceptable to the registrar. Any alteration to the form should be initialled by the transferor.

(iii) When the stock transfer form has been signed, the agent

20. By the Stock Transfer (Recognition of Stock Exchanges) Order 1966, S.I. 1966 No. 1273 the following stock exchanges were declared recognised stock exchanges:

　　Belfast, Cork, Dublin, Greenock, Midlands and Western, Northern, Scottish, Swansea and the Provincial Brokers'.

acting for the transferor will place his stamp and insert the date in the box beside the transferor's signature. The agent must assure himself of the genuineness of the execution, particular care being taken when dealing with joint holders.

(iv) Where a transfer is not stamped with *ad valorem* duty on a consideration equal to the market value (or on that value in the case of a gift) but is considered liable to the current fixed duty, agents should have detailed information as to. the circumstances in which the transfer was made given on the back of the stock transfer form and should ensure that the form bears the Inland Revenue marking officer's "transfer passed for duty" certificate. A registrar will ask for any transfer to be presented for formal adjudication of. the stamp duty.

(v) If the agent who prepares the stock transfer form lodges it for registration, he will also place his stamp in the appropriate box at the foot of the form; but where another agent is acting for the transferee and lodges the transfer for registration, it is the latter agent whose stamp will appear in this box. Under the current Exchange Control Regulations,[1] if the agent who lodges the stock transfer form is not an authorised depositary, it is necessary for an authorised depositary to give the appropriate declarations which must be lodged with the form; an authorised depositary should not place his stamp in the lodging agent's box unless he is actually lodging the stock transfer form.

(vi) Agents putting forward transfers in non-market transactions are asked always to use the stock transfer form in preference to the old form of transfer. If, because of special circumstances, an agent considers it essential to have a transfer signed for acceptance by the transferee, an acceptance clause in the form: "I, the above-named transferee, hereby accept the transfer of the above security into my name", may be written into the stock transfer form immediately below the name and address of the transferee and signed by the transferee.

3. Transfers in respect of bargains for cash

A. SAME PROCEDURE *MUTATIS MUTANDIS* AS IN BARGAINS FOR THE ACCOUNT

Transfers of securities dealt in for cash will follow the same procedure *mutatis mutandis* as those for securities dealt in for the account. Where a sale on the London Stock Exchange or a provincial stock exchange is split between two or more jobbers or other buyers, the stock transfer form may be used in conjunction with

1. See Chapter 12.

brokers' transfer forms; otherwise all transactions will be carried through on the stock transfer form alone. A jobber on the London Stock Exchange on receiving from the selling broker a stock transfer form (or brokers' transfer form) will complete the form and submit it for registration. Where a London broker is instructed to dispose of a holding piecemeal, i.e., by making sales on two or more days at frequent intervals, he will obtain from his client a separate stock transfer form to cover the sale(s) of each day; the selling broker may obtain certification of the first stock transfer form against the certificate by the Stock Exchange who will, if requested, hold the balance of the certificate to the order of the selling broker who may obtain certification against it as the subsequent sales are made. Should a selling broker have to obtain on one day certification of brokers' transfer forms which arise from two or more stock transfer forms out of the same name, it will be necessary for the registrar to be informed and for the procedure set out on p. 211, *ante*, to be adopted.

B. DISTINGUISHING NUMBERS

The stock transfer form will be used for all purchases on the London Stock Exchange of securities dealt in for cash. The "certifiable balance" facilities continue under the new system. But the names of transferees are not available at the certification stage; in order therefore to distinguish between stock transfer forms for the same amount of the same security which are certified on the same day, a jobber or other holder having "certifiable balance" facilities will mark all transfers with distinguishing numbers which will be inserted after his name in the stock transfer form. A separate series of numbers will be used for each stock, each series beginning at 1 and running in ascending numerical order until the balance for the dividend is struck. After the ex dividend date stock transfer forms will again be numbered from 1. The jobber will also insert the distinguishing number of the form on the buying broker's ticket.

The jobber and the buying broker will keep a record of the distinguishing number so that in the event of any query arising the stock transfer form can be readily identified.

For non-market transfers or lending and return of stock (two-way transfers) the stock transfer form will be used and may be lodged with the registrar for registration without prior certification. Such transfers should have the transferor's identifying number inserted.

4. General considerations applicable to all transfers under the new system

A. NEW TRANSFER SYSTEM DOES NOT AFFECT AGENTS' LIABILITY TO OTHER AGENTS OR TO REGISTRARS

The liability of agents one to the other or to the registrar remains undisturbed by the new system. Space has been set aside in both the stock transfer form and the brokers' transfer form for agents' stamps; the stamps will be of considerable assistance to those concerned in the transactions and particularly to registrars who will have on the transfer itself a record of the names and addresses of the agents who have acted in connection with the transfer. Agents are asked to arrange for their stamps to be of a size appropriate to the spaces in the forms and to show their full name and postal address and their category (e.g., "Solicitor", "Member of the Birmingham Stock Exchange" ...) It is important that the clarity of the stamps should always be maintained and that they should be renewed before becoming indistinct.

B. MISCELLANEOUS MATTERS WHICH AGENTS SHOULD HAVE IN MIND

Agents are asked to note that:

(i) Companies and other bodies corporate having a common seal should execute the stock transfer form by means of their common seal.

(ii) Where shares or units of stock have definitive numbers, the appropriate numbers should be quoted after the amount of shares or stock in stock transfer forms and brokers' transfer forms.

(iii) Where a transferor is unable to sign a stock transfer form and executes it by mark, a doctor, solicitor or other person of known position should add a certificate to the effect that the mark is that of the transferor and that the form has been read over to and appeared to be understood by the transferor.

(iv) Securities generally may not be registered in the names of firms or minors and if they are inadvertently so registered difficulty may arise when the security comes to be sold.

(v) Securities purchased on behalf of Friendly Societies, Trade Unions and other unincorporated bodies should be registered in the personal names of the trustees; securities may not be registered in the names of the bodies themselves or under the collective title of their trustees (i.e., "Trustees of ...").

(vi) Registrars do not normally open or add to accounts in which there is the name of a deceased holder.

(vii) Prior to the registration of transfers of certain securities declarations of nationality signed by the transferees are necessary.

(viii) The articles of a company may impose a limit on the number of joint holders allowed in an account.

(ix) The articles of a company may impose conditions as to membership of the company and restrictions as to the transfer of shares; in such cases the agent should ensure that his client is aware of any such conditions or restrictions.

C. SECURITIES OF OVERSEAS COMPANIES ARE NOT AFFECTED BY THE STOCK TRANSFER ACT

Securities of overseas companies or other bodies, being subject to overseas law, are not affected by the Act. But the Committee asked registrars in the United Kingdom who manage such securities to get into touch immediately with their principals advising them to take whatever action may be necessary to make the rules relating to the transfer of their securities conform with the Act. When the new system can be applied to any such security the registrar is asked to notify immediately the Secretary of the Share and Loan Department, The Stock Exchange, London, E.C.2. Securities quoted on the Stock Exchange, London, which do not come within the new system are marked with a double star in the Stock Exchange Daily Official List and monthly supplement.

C. DIVIDENDS AND RIGHTS

1. The buying broker's duties

The circumstances in which buyers acquire and lose dividends and other rights on the purchase of securities have been described elsewhere.[2] It is sufficient to note at this point that under Rule 120 (3) of the Rules and Regulations of the Stock Exchange the seller is responsible for such dividends as may be due to the buyer unless an *unreasonable* time has been taken by the transferee to (execute and) lodge the documents for registration, or there has been unreasonable delay in claiming the dividend.

It is important therefore that no delay occurs in the lodgment of transfers for registration and that wherever possible all transfers for bargains made cum dividend (or cum rights) be lodged with the company in time for the transferees to receive the dividend (or rights) from the company.

2. See pp. 189–193, *ante.*

---

2. Dividend mandates

Where the transferee wishes to have dividends paid to a bank or other person, it will assist the registrar if a dividend mandate can be lodged with him as soon as possible. Agents are therefore requested to keep a record of their clients' wishes in this respect and, where a new security is purchased for a client who wishes his dividends to be paid otherwise than to himself, to send him a mandate for completion at the earliest possible moment, or, at the latest, with the contract note. Mandates in favour of a bank should be sent to that bank for transmission to the registrar. Mandates in favour of other persons should, if possible, accompany the stock transfer forms or the brokers' transfer forms when lodged with the registrar. Specimen forms of dividend mandates are set out in Appendices C and D.

3. Guidance for registrars and agents

(i) Uniform pattern of dividend mandate

Registrars should, so far as possible, adopt a uniform pattern of dividend mandate; agents are asked to arrange that their clients complete the type of mandate acceptable to the particular registrar. Appendix C follows the pattern recommended by the Chartered Institute of Secretaries and is applicable to company securities; this mandate will cover holdings in all securities of a company. Appendix D is applicable to stock on the Bank of England register; this mandate will cover a holding in one security only. Mandates in a similar form to Appendix D will be acceptable to the registrars of other Government and local government securities, securities of public boards, etc. A mandate in the form of the appropriate specimen should always be used when dividends are to be paid to a bank,[3] and the mandate should be forwarded to the registrar through the branch of the bank concerned who should be given details of the banking account to be credited with the dividends. The banks publish a list of sorting code numbers allocated to bank branches in the United Kingdom and Republic of Ireland which includes instructions regarding dividend and interest counterfoils. Banks are now asking registrars to show their customers' account numbers in dividend counterfoils when dividend payments are made to them under new mandates—a request which had the Committee's full support. The London clearing banks have agreed to assume full legal responsibility if such account numbers are quoted incorrectly by

3. For a procedure where dividends on a holding acquired for the trustee office of a bank, or for a bank-trustee company, are to be paid to a branch of the same bank or the parent bank of the trustee company, see the *New Transfer System*, para. 26.

registrars; this is a general assurance which the Committee regarded as sufficient to cover all registrars, but they advised each registrar before he records account numbers for other banks or institutions to seek a specific indemnity [4] from the bank or institution concerned covering himself against his incorrectly quoting the account number. The Committee considered that there is some element of risk in registrars accepting instructions from holders to pay dividends to a bank or other third party for credit of a particular account. The specimen forms of mandate have been drawn in such a way that the account number is furnished to the registrar by the receiving bank as a reference to facilitate identification of the dividend and nothing more.

(ii) Lapse of joint mandate

Agents are asked to note that, where a mandate given by joint holders has lapsed, because of the death of the payee or otherwise, a registrar, in the absence of any special provisions in his company's articles, may require a further mandate from the holders; the lapsing of a mandate may not necessarily restore the right of the first holder, or first surviving holder, in a joint account to demand that dividends be paid to him.

(iii) Duplicate dividend warrants etc.

Registrars are entitled to require indemnities either from the holders or other payees (and, at their discretion, indemnity from a bank) before issuing duplicate warrants in place of those which have been lost or destroyed. Duplicate income tax vouchers may be issued on the written request of the holder or his agent. Duplicate warrants and/or vouchers must be marked "Duplicate".

(iv) Statute-barred dividend claims

The Committee considered that, in the interests of investors, companies should not, as a matter of policy, refuse valid claims to dividends, even after twelve years, unless it is the practice of their registrar to take all reasonable steps to trace the owner and effect payment before the expiry of the statutory limitation period.

(v) Advantages of the Stock Exchange's table of dividend dates

Registrars are reminded of the advantages obtained when a company is able to arrange its dividend programme in accordance with the table of suggested dates issued to companies with quoted securities each year by the Stock Exchange. The co-operation of companies in this enables early ex dividend action to be taken and permits a very high proportion of transfers relating to bargains done cum dividend to be lodged for registration before the registers or transfer books are closed or a balance is struck. Dividend claims by

4. For a specimen indemnity, see Appendix H of the *New Transfer System*.

the transferee and the consequent enquiries of registrars as to whether a transfer is registered before the closing of the books are thus considerably reduced. In the case of rights and capitalisation issues, the old securities are not normally made "ex" until the renounceable allotment letter or other document becomes available, in order to ensure that the shareholder can at all times sell the whole of his stake in the company. Claims to rights by the transferee arise because the registrar, in order to determine the persons entitled to the new securities, must close the register or strike a balance well in advance of the document of title becoming available. It should be noted, however, that a considerable reduction in claims can be effected where there is an active market if the old securities are made "ex" early after the proposals become "firm". In such a case dealings in the new securities would commence (simultaneously with making the old securities "ex") for special settlement on a date immediately following the availability of the document of title. This procedure which is conditional on the ability of the company to make an advance announcement setting out the basis of entitlement necessitates consultation and co-operation between company and Stock Exchange at an early stage in a proposed issue.

D. TEMPORARY DOCUMENTS OF TITLE

Definitive documents of title to securities must be distinguished from temporary documents of title. There is always an interval of time between the taking up of shares and the issue of a certificate to the buyer upon registration. Certificates and bearer securities are known as definitive documents of title. Before the buyer obtains his certificate, he must have other documents to evidence the contract which he has made. These are known as temporary documents.

1. Letters of allotment
Companies usually issue shares in response to a written application by the intending shareholder. In law, the application is an *offer* to take up a certain number of shares. The company *accepts* the offer by sending the applicant a letter of allotment, and the contract is then made.

A contract is valid only if the parties are *ad idem*. Accordingly it is essential that the letter of allotment does not contain qualifications: it must correspond exactly with the application. So, if the applicant requested an allotment of 500 shares and the company in reply allot him 100, he could refuse to take up any of them. Of course, issues are often oversubscribed, and the common form of application gets round the legal difficulty by saying, "I agree to accept such shares or any smaller number that may be allotted to me."

The applicant is not bound in contract to take up the shares until the decision to allot has reached him. There is no difficulty about this when communication is by an instantaneous method such as telephone or telex.[5] But if the parties use the post, communication takes place, in law, when the letter of allotment is posted. So where the letter was posted but never reached the applicant, it was held that he was a shareholder of the company.[6] Even though the company has not sent a letter of allotment, the applicant may nevertheless become a shareholder if he has implied notice of such an allotment (as where the company send a letter demanding payment of an instalment on the shares)[7] or if the applicant does something which estops (i.e., prevents) him from denying that allotment has come to his notice. In a case where the applicant himself executed a transfer of the shares, it was held that he could not successfully maintain that he did not know that they had been allotted to him.[8]

To be effective, however, a letter of allotment must be sent within a reasonable time of the application. In *Ramsgate Victoria Hotel Co., Ltd.* v. *Montefiore*[9] it was held that $4\frac{1}{2}$ months was not a reasonable time, and the applicant could refuse to take the shares. That case was decided in 1866, and what amounts to a reasonable time in law may now have diminished to meet the brisker realities of modern business.

The application can be withdrawn at any time before allotment is legally communicated.[10] "Stags" have been in the habit of taking advantage of this rule by revoking their application before allotment if it turns out that the securities could not be quickly resold at a profit. Section 50 (5) of the Companies Act 1948 partially counters this. It provides that when an application is made in response to a prospectus issued to the public at large, that application cannot be withdrawn until after the expiration of the third day after the time of the opening of the subscription lists by the company.

A. CONTENTS OF A LETTER OF ALLOTMENT

The letter will inform the applicant of the number and description of shares which he has been allotted, saying (if that is so) that

5. *Entores, Ltd.* v. *Miles Far East Corporation,* [1955] 2 Q.B. 327; [1955] 2 All E.R. 493, C.A.
6. *Household Fire Insurance Co.* v. *Grant* (1879), 4 Ex. D. 216, C.A.
7. *Forget* v. *Cement Products Co. of Canada,* [1916] W.N. 259, P.C.
8. *Crawley's Case* (1869), 4 Ch. App. 322.
9. (1866), L.R. 1 Exch. 109.
10. *Re National Savings Bank Association, Hebb's Case* (1867), L.R. 4 Eq. 9.

the shares are credited as fully paid up or giving instructions as to the payment of instalments. Usually there is a paragraph permitting the allottee to renounce the whole of the allotment by executing the "Form of Renunciation" appended to the letter. Subsequently the renounced allotment letter can be "split" on returning the letter to the company or issuing house. The letter may provide that if the allottee wishes to take up all the shares, he need do no more: and that on a fixed day he will be registered as holder of the shares and be sent a certificate. It may provide that if the allottee wishes to renounce, he should execute the " Form of Renunciation", and hand the letter of allotment to the renouncee (the person who wishes to take up the shares in his place) who will complete the registration application form appended to the letter and forward it to the company, so that he can be registered as holder and receive the share certificate.

B. LETTER OF REGRET

The issue may be oversubscribed or the company may be unwilling to make an allotment to the applicant. They are not bound to accept his offer. The usual practice in these circumstances is to send a short letter of regret signed by the company secretary.[11]

2. Rights offers and capitalisation

A. RIGHTS OFFERS

Where a company makes a rights offer and the shares will be quoted on a stock exchange, the stock exchange will normally require the offer to be made by a renounceable letter or other negotiable document.

The company will send out to its existing shareholders (i) a circular letter [12] explaining why the directors think it would be appropriate to increase the equity share capital of the company, and other relevant matters, and (ii) a provisional letter of allotment,[13] offering the holder his proportion of the new issue and giving him instructions on the manner of his acceptance. There will be provisions for renunciation and splitting; and a declaration that "the above allottee(s) or the renouncee(s) (as the case may be) is/are now entitled in accordance with the terms of the issue to be registered as the holder(s) of the shares to which the provisional allotment letter relates".

11. For form of letter of regret, see *Encyclopaedia of Forms and Precedents* (4th Edn.), Vol. 6, p. 1181.
12. Form of circular. See *ibid.*, Vol. 5, p. 727.
13. Form of provisional letter, see *ibid.*, p. 730.

Both the circular letter and the provisional letter of allotment must, before being sent to the shareholders, be delivered to the Registrar of Companies for registration, and both should state the fact that that has been done.

B. CAPITALISATION

Companies which are duly empowered by their articles to do so may, instead of distributing profits by way of dividend, effectively capitalise the same by the issue to their members of fully (or partly) paid up shares. It was held in *Dimbula Valley (Ceylon), Tea Co, Ltd.* v. *Laurie* [14] that for this purpose the profits which may be capitalised include ascertained but unrealised accretions to capital assets.

The procedure is as follows.[15] The company sends out to its shareholders (i) a letter announcing the distribution of the new shares, (ii) a form of acceptance letter to be filled up by the shareholder if he takes up the new shares, and (iii), a *renounceable* letter of allotment. The letter of allotment will contain provisions for the consolidation of shares comprised in several letters of allotment, and provisions for renunciation (with a form of renunciation) and splitting.

C. THE REGULATION OF DEALINGS CUM RIGHTS AND CUM CAPITALISATION

Rule 114 of the Rules and Regulations of the Stock Exchange provides a timetable and other rules for the above dealings.

(i) The fixed days

Where a rights offer or capitalisation issue is made by means of a renounceable document to the holders of old securities there are three important days:

(a) "The acceptance day" which is the last day fixed for the receipt of an acceptance of an offer made by a letter of rights, and

(b) "The payment day" which is the last day fixed for the receipt of the next payment payable under the terms of an offer made by a letter of rights, and

(c) "The application day" which is the last day fixed for the receipt of an application for registration as a holder of such new securities by the holder of a renounced fully paid renounceable document.

(ii) Rights of the buyer
(a) Claim made in time

The buyer of old securities "cum rights" or "cum capitalisation" is entitled to any renounceable document or new securities issued in

14. [1961] Ch. 353; [1961] 1 All E.R. 769.
15. Forms: see *Encyclopaedia of Forms and Precedents* (4th Edn.) Vol. 5, pp. 710 *et seq.*

respect thereof, if he claims them in writing not later than 4 p.m. two business days before the acceptance or application day, or before the latest time for splitting renounceable documents. The seller must then deliver the renounceable documents duly renounced not later than 1.15 p.m. on the business day preceding the acceptance day or the application day.

(*b*) Liability of seller when claim duly made

If any such claim is made not later than the time for claiming referred to above, but the seller does not make delivery, then

(i) in the case of nil paid renounceable documents the seller must take all necessary steps to prevent the rights lapsing; if they are allowed to lapse, the buyer is entitled to temporarily deduct their value (to be fixed as provided)[16] from the price paid for the old securities until delivery of the new; and

(ii) in the case of fully paid renounceable documents the buyer may require the seller to deliver new securities instead, the seller paying any *ad valorem* stamp duty payable on the transfer.

(*c*) Liability of seller when claim made late

If such claim is made after the time for claiming referred to, then,

(i) in the case of nil paid renounceable documents, provided the claim is made before the time on the acceptance day fixed for the receipt of the acceptance, the seller must do all that he reasonably can to prevent the rights lapsing and to transfer them to the buyer. If the seller sells or has sold the rights, the seller shall be liable for the proceeds of their sale; a claim made after the time fixed for the receipt of the acceptance will, however, be invalid.

(ii) in the case of fully paid renounceable documents: (*a*) if they or new securities issued in respect thereof are in the possession of the seller, he must (according to the wish of the buyer) deliver either the documents duly renounced or the new securities, the buyer paying any *ad valorem* stamp duty payable on the transfer, and (*b*) if the documents or new securities are not in the possession of the seller, he must render every assistance to the buyer in tracing them.

(*iii*) *Renunciation of rights*

If the buyer has not received delivery of nil or partly paid renounceable documents by 12.30 p.m. two business days before the acceptance day or the payment day he may at any time not later than 11 a.m. on the business day preceding the acceptance day or the payment day respectively give the seller notice that he does not wish to accept the offer or make the next payment (as the case may be). The seller having received such notice from the buyer will take no

16. See para. (4), *infra.*

further action to protect the buyer's right to the new security but the old security passing by transfer will be delivered and paid for in the normal way.

(*iv*) *Duty of seller to pay calls*

If nil paid or partly paid renounceable documents have not been delivered by the seller to the buyer at 1.15 p.m. on the business day preceding the acceptance day or payment day respectively and unless the above-mentioned notice has been given, the seller shall be bound at the request of the buyer to make all due payments on behalf of the buyer, and the buyer shall refund any such payments and be entitled to a receipt therefor. Such a request shall be implied where the buyer has duly made a claim in time.

(*v*) *Valuation of undelivered rights*

The Head of the Quotations Department will on application fix a price at which renounceable documents or the new securities to be issued in respect thereof may be settled temporarily.[17]

(*vi*) *Dealings in renounceable documents*

Where a rights offer is made to the holders of old securities all dealings in such rights until the close of business two business days before the application day must be for settlement on the business day following the day of the bargain and shall be in renounceable documents.[18]

No bargain may be made in such rights until a quotation has been granted for the underlying securities unless dealings are otherwise permitted under Rule 163.[1]

(*vii*) *Last times for delivery of renounceable documents*[2]

(*a*) The buyer of nil paid, partly paid or fully paid renounceable documents is not required to accept delivery after 1.15 p.m. on the business day preceding the acceptance day, the payment day or the application day respectively; and

(*b*) The buyer of fully paid renounceable documents is not required to accept delivery after 1.15 p.m. on the business day preceding the application day.

If delivery is not made in due time and if the buyer does not wish to accept the offer or make the next payment (as the case may be) he must, not later than 11 a.m. on the same day, give notice to the seller.

(*viii*) *Settlement of bargains*

Except as provided, bargains must, so far as possible, be settled by delivery of renounceable documents duly renounced.[3]

17. Rule 114 (4).   18. Rule 114*a* (2).   1. See pp. 118–119, *ante*.
2. Rule 114*a* (4).   3. Rule 114*a* (5).

(ix) Buying-in

Renounceable documents may not be bought-in.[4]

3. The requirements for all temporary documents of title

Before an official quotation can be obtained on the Stock Exchange, the requirements of the Rules as to temporary documents must be complied with. The requirements are set out in Appendix 34, Schedule III of the Rules and Regulations of the Stock Exchange:

(i) Documents must be serially numbered, printed on good quality paper and must be examined and autographically signed or initialled by a responsible official of the company or authorised agent. The name and address of the first holder and names of joint holders (if any) should be stated and, in the case of fixed income securities, a statement as to the amount of the next payment of interest or dividend must be included.

(ii) Where the right of renunciation is given:

(a) The form of renunciation and the registration instructions must be printed on the back of, or attached to, the document.

(b) There must be provision for splitting (without fee), and split documents must be certified by an official of the company or authorised agent. There must not be more than one clear business day between the last day for splitting and the last day for renunciation.

(c) When, at the same time as an allotment is made of shares issued for cash, shares of the same class are also allotted, credited as fully-paid, to vendors or others, the period for renunciation may be the same as, but not longer than that provided for in the case of shares issued for cash.

(d) When a security is offered in conversion of another security and is also offered for subscription in cash, the allotment letters must be marked "Conversion" and "Cash" respectively.

(e) Letters of allotment or right must be issued simultaneously; and in the event of its being impossible to issue letters of regret at the same time, a notice to that effect must be inserted in the press and appear on the morning after the allotment letters have been posted.

(f) In the absence of contrary instructions from the shareholder, all letters of right to shareholders with addresses outside the United Kingdom and the Irish Republic must be dispatched by air mail.

4. Rule 114*a* (6).

E. PROBATE AND OTHER VALUATIONS

1. Valuations for probate

When a stockholder dies, the shares which form part of his estate will have to be valued for probate. This is a task which stockbrokers (*inter alios*) customarily undertake.

Normally valuations for probate are based on the quotations of the securities concerned in the Official List. Valuation is based on the mean between the bid price and the middle price as quoted—so that if the Official List quotation is £4–£4·6 the probate valuation would be £4·15. Where the death has occurred on a day in which no quotation is available (e.g., a Saturday, Sunday or a Bank Holiday) the valuation of each individual security may be based either on the quotation on the last day before, or the first day after, the death on which a quotation was available.

Valuation is followed by distribution. When the valuation has been made, and probate has been granted or letters of administration obtained the executors or administrators can then divide the holdings into parts which *correspond in value* to the beneficiaries' interests under the will or intestacy. Under section 76 of the Companies Act 1948, a deceased person's representatives may transfer shares in pursuance of their duties without themselves becoming members of the company. But they will, of course, produce to the company the probate of the will, or, in the case of an intestacy, their letters of administration.

2. Valuation of shares transferred by gift inter vivos

Another occasion for valuing shares is when they are transferred by gifts *inter vivos*. A valuation will be necessary, because when the transfer has been drawn up *ad valorem* stamp duty becomes payable. Where shares pass *inter vivos* the valuation is based on the *middle* price in the Stock Exchange Official List at the date of the transfer. A certificate of the value must be endorsed on the back of the transfer and the broker who is instructed to prepare and stamp the transfer, and register it with the company, should *also* make himself responsible also for such endorsement.

3. Valuation of rights

When shares are transferred "cum" or "ex" rights, it is sometimes necessary to calculate the value of the rights in isolation. The calculation is done as follows:

Suppose that to have the right to buy one share of the new issue the holder must have two shares of the old. The value of two old is

£7. The cost of one new is £2. So the value of two old plus one new is £9. The *average* value of the three shares is therefore £3. The value of the rights consists of the *difference* between the average value of all three shares (£3) and the value of one old share "cum" (i.e., with) the rights to subscribe to the new (£3·50). So the *rights* are valued at 50p, and the value of the shares "ex" rights is £3·50 minus 50p = £3. The value of new shares (£2 paid) is £1 premium.

CHAPTER 10

Failures

Those who do business on the Stock Exchange may be the victims of two general categories of failure:

- A. Failure of the *parties* to a bargain to abide by its terms, in other words breach of contract.
- B. Failure of *members* to meet their obligations generally; this is known as default.

A. BREACH OF CONTRACT

1. By the broker

The stockbroker's contractual duties to his client are numerous and on occasions he may fail to observe them. Suppose he has misinterpreted his client's instructions: then his client can recover damages. Or he may have failed to account to his client: his client can claim an account. Or he may have acted as a principal and kept his client in ignorance of the fact: his client can elect to rescind the contract. The client's position, his rights and remedies in these various situations have already been explained.[1] They all amount to breaches of contract because the broker has ignored his well-accepted duties, performance of which is an implied term in any stock exchange bargain. It remains to consider the position when the broker *fails altogether* to perform his part of the transaction—when, in short, he "closes the account".

BROKER WRONGFULLY CLOSING HIS CLIENT'S ACCOUNT

In general, a broker must keep his client's account open. If he closes it without authority, he forfeits his right to be indemnified. So in *Ellis* v. *Pond*:[2]

> A broker bought stock on the Stock Exchange on behalf of his client for the next account day, and, without authority from his client and contrary to the agreement between them, sold the stock before that day at a loss.

1. See Chapter 6, *ante.*   2. [1898] 1 Q.B. 426.

It was held that the broker could not claim an indemnity from his client.

A broker who wrongfully closes his client's account will not only lose his right to an indemnity: in addition he will either have to go on and make the bargain as instructed or he will be liable to his client in the damages which his client has suffered from losing it.

The broker's fate depends upon the choice of his client. A prudent client may decide that it would be better to terminate his relation with the broker, and elect to treat the closing of the account as putting an end to the bargain. The question of damages then arises. The value of stocks and shares fluctuates daily, and it is therefore important to fix precisely the day with reference to which the client's damages are to be assessed. Damages are *not* measured by the difference between the price at the closing and the price at the end of the account—for it would always have been open to the parties to make a contango arrangement. The measure to be adopted is the difference between the price on the day that the account was wrongfully closed, and the market price at a *reasonable* time after the client was informed of the wrongful closing.[3] The client must be allowed an interval within which to decide which course—either acceptance or refusal of the closure—to adopt. But the client may not (cynically or through his own negligence) take advantage of the interval by inflating his damages during its currency. He cannot allow them to grow by standing by and doing nothing.[4] Nor may the client adopt wait and see tactics in the hope that the value of the shares—and consequently his damages—will rise. So in *Tempest* v. *Kilner*,[5] Tindal, C. J., referred to a refusal to deliver a letter of allotment:

> "There was a complete breach of the contract when the defendant, on the 12th of August, declined to perform it. He was bound *then* to deliver the document with reference to which the parties were dealing. I think the plaintiffs are not entitled to damages beyond that day: they had no right to lie by until the concern became profitable."

This dictum is in accordance with the general rule that all who claim damages at law have a duty to minimise them.

2. By the client

Circumstances can arise in which it would be intolerable and unjust for a broker to have to continue the account. The courts have acknowledged this at various times, and allowed a broker, by closing

3. See *Murray* v. *Hewitt* (1886), 2 T.L.R. 872.
4. *Samuel and Escombe* v. *Rowe* (1892), 8 T.L.R. 488.
5. (1846), 3 C.B. 249.

the account, to extricate himself from a situation in which the client has placed him against his will, and in which it is clear that he will be the only loser.

A. CIRCUMSTANCES IN WHICH THE BROKER MAY CLOSE THE ACCOUNT

(i) *When the client fails to settle*

Normally a broker will give his client notice before account day of the amount due to him from the client on account day, as that is the day on which the broker has to settle with the member(s) of the Stock Exchange with whom he dealt. A system of quick settlement is essential to the Stock Exchange's efficiency as a market, and usage permits the broker to close an account if the client's failure to put him in funds prevents him from performing the bargain which his client has instructed him to make. The broker may then sell what his client purported to buy, and buy what his client purported to sell. This usage was held to be reasonable in *Davis & Co* v. *Howard*,[6] a case which demonstrates that it is not only when the client has failed to provide funds for a *particular* bargain done for a *particular* account that the broker may close the account. In *Davis & Co* v. *Howard* a broker had been instructed by his client to carry over stock to the next settlement, and it was held that the broker might close the account if a *balance of differences* in the broker's favour had not been paid to him by his client on the account day of the current settlement, and the client had notice of such balance and had not placed at the broker's disposal funds or a collateral security sufficient to cover the amount of the balance.

In *Surman* v. *Oxenford & Co*[7] the collateral security was small in amount and had a fixed cutting limit:

> The client instructed his brokers to sell his Consols, which they did at $75\frac{1}{8}$ and $75\frac{1}{16}$. The client was a bear, speculating upon a fall in their market price and the parties arranged to keep the account open (i.e., the brokers were not to repurchase the Consols) unless and until the price *rose* to $77\frac{7}{8}$—since the client wished to limit his loss. As a security for this arrangement, the client deposited £50 and 150 shares in the Great Cobar Co Ltd. The brokers repurchased the Consols at $75\frac{25}{32}$ and the client sued them for damages and the return of his deposit.

It was held that where (as here) a client has agreed to give a security with a fixed cutting limit (here $77\frac{7}{8}$), the brokers are not entitled to close the account when that limit has not been reached, and the court awarded the client damages and the recovery of his deposit.

6. (1890), 24 Q.B.D. 691.   7. (1916), 33 T.L.R. 78.

Sometimes brokers and their clients adopt a "cover" system. A client will deposit money with his broker to cover the rise or fall in the value of shares bought or sold and carried over. There will be a condition that, whenever and as soon as the cover is exhausted by a fall in the value of the shares, the broker has an option to close the account.[8] But in *Hogan* v. *Shaw*:[9] when the cover became exhausted, the broker elected not to close the account. Later the shares rose so that once more they came within the cover. The Court of Appeal held that the broker could not then close the transaction: his option to do so had expired. Had the shares fallen a second time and re-exhausted the cover, the broker's option to close would then have revived.

A broker and his client may have an express agreement that the broker will not require settlement by or on the account day,[10] but in the absence of such an agreement, there is always an implied power in the brokers to close, and if the brokers have carried over, a power to charge reasonable remuneration for that arrangement. That was the position in *Stubbs* v. *Slater*:[11]

The plaintiff had, in November 1904, instructed brokers on the London Stock Exchange to buy certain mining shares for him. It was understood that the shares were not to be taken up on the account day, but were to be carried over. No agreement was made as to the remuneration of the brokers for arranging the carry over. The brokers bought the shares from a jobber, and in the bought-notes sent by them to the plaintiff they charged an opening commission of 1s. per share. They arranged the carry over with the jobber, and the first continuation account sent by them to the plaintiff contained a charge of "8½d. net". The shares were carried over in this way every fortnight until January 1906, the "net" rate varying with the market price of the shares. The plaintiff having failed to pay the balance against him on the mid-October 1905 carry over, they pressed for payment, and the plaintiff deposited with them as security a certificate for 390 gas shares, and signed a blank transfer of the same. The fortnightly balances continued adverse to the plaintiff, and were not paid by him. After repeated applications to the plaintiff for payment, the brokers in January 1906 closed the account with a balance of £69. 10s. against him, and sold the 390 gas shares for £162. 10s. Throughout the above transactions the plaintiff *thought* that the "net" rate charged for every carry over represented only the jobber's contango; but it *also* included a charge by the brokers for arranging the carry over—a fact which the brokers did not disclose to the plaintiff. It appeared that the "net" rate was well known on the Stock Exchange to indicate that with the jobber's contango was included the broker's remuneration. It also appeared that the brokers' charge, which amounted

8. *Ibid.*
10. *Murray* v. *Hewitt* (1886), 2 T.L.R. 872.
9. (1889), 5 T.L.R. 613, C.A.
11. [1910] 1 Ch. 632.

to £17 odd, was reasonable. The plaintiff brought an action against the brokers for an account and payment of the profit made by them in carrying over the mining shares and for damages for wrongful conversion of the gas shares. The brokers counterclaimed for payment of reasonable remuneration for carrying over the mining shares.

In the Court of Appeal, Cozens-Hardy, M. R., took the view that it was immaterial that the plaintiff, "who was not a babe in arms in respect of Stock Exchange transactions" did not know the technical meaning of the word "net". The court concurred with him and held that the brokers, not having been guilty of any breach of duty as agents, were entitled to retain the £17 as reasonable remuneration. It was also held that, in the circumstances, the implied power of sale had been reasonably exercised.

In *Deverges* v. *Sandeman Clark & Co*[12] a power to close by selling was implied where a mortgagor of shares failed to redeem the mortgage. A stockbroker was mortgagee, and it was held that he could sell the shares on default in payment of the amount due at the time for redemption, or, if no time had been fixed, then on the expiration of a reasonable notice given by him requiring payment on a day certain.

It is clear from the decisions that the courts have always been prepared to recognise that the swift settlement of bargains is even more important on the Stock Exchange than in other branches of commercial life.

(*ii*) *When the client becomes insolvent or dies*

Members of the Stock Exchange run a considerable risk of being ruined by clients who instruct them to make substantial bargains (for which they as members are personally liable) and then leave them in the cold by failing to indemnify them. A member must always be on his guard against such clients and when his business experience leads him to believe that a client is in such general financial difficulties that he is unlikely to repay him, custom permits the member to close the account immediately. In *Lacey* v. *Hill, Crowley's Claim*:[13]

On July 12th Messrs. C. bought for the current account substantial stock for Sir R.H., senior partner of a bank at Norwich. Account day was July 15th, and on the balance of his account with them Sir R.H. owed Messrs. C. some £15,000. The point had been reached at which, if Sir R.H. did not settle with them by the 15th, Messrs. C. would not be able to meet various obligations of their own and would therefore become defaulters on the Stock Exchange. So on the 12th they wrote to Sir R.H. asking for either an assurance of support or directions to close. On 13th Sir R. H. sent Messrs. C. a telegram promising to pay on the

12. [1902] 1 Ch. 579.   13. (1874), L.R. 18 Eq. 182.

15th, and instructing them to deal with the stocks as they thought best. Acting on that telegram, Messrs. C. sold part of the stock and continued part. Sir R.H. did not pay Messrs. C. on the 15th, and as a result Messrs. C. were declared defaulters on the 16th. Sir R.H. had shot himself on the afternoon of the 15th, and the bank of which he was senior partner stopped payments on the morning of the 16th. The news reached the creditors of Messrs. C. on the 16th, and they immediately sold that part of the stock which Messrs. C. had continued.

It was held that the sale was justifiable. The continuation had only been effected on Sir R.H.'s representation (which turned out to be false) that he would be able to pay on the 15th. Jessel, M.R., said that the creditors did not have to see a statement of Sir R.H.'s financial affairs before closing the account, but were entitled to use their common sense:

> "It was soon noised abroad that the bank was insolvent, and so the members of the Stock Exchange, people who were interested, were informed. This turned out to be the fact. I am asked to say that this is not evidence of the insolvency of Sir R.H. Insolvency within the Stock Exchange rule means inability to pay debts in the ordinary commercial sense and in the ordinary course of business. Then what is to be said of a bank that puts up the shutters and does not pay? Is not that evidence of insolvency? I hardly know how else a jury exercising ... ordinary common sense ... could find anybody insolvent unless he came forward and showed that the whole amount of his assets was not equal to the whole amount of his liabilities. I think there was very good evidence, and such evidence as entitled the brokers to act upon it, and therefore they had the right to sell."

In *Lacey* v. *Hill, Crowley's Claim* [14] the brokers could hardly have had firmer indications that their client was not in a position to indemnify them. This should not obscure the rule that a broker cannot without authority close his client's account without *some* concrete evidence that the client will not be able to pay: mere rumour or suspicion would not be enough.

When a client dies, his broker has no implied authority to continue the account. [15] An immediate sale in the market might, however, involve a serious loss to the client's estate. In *Re Finlay, C. S. Wilson & Co* v. *Finlay*: [16]

> The client was found drowned in the Serpentine at a time when the market for his rubber shares was in a very critical condition. His firm of brokers had as one of their members the brother of the deceased's widow, and they had a natural desire to help the widow out of her difficulties. A sale in the market was avoided by the firm having the shares valued and going through a form of selling the shares to them-

14. *Ibid.*   15. *Re Overweg, Haas* v. *Durant*, [1900] 1 Ch. 209, at p. 211.
16. [1913] 1 Ch. 565, C.A.

selves. The brokers suffered a considerable loss, but they did charge brokers' commission.

It was held that this was a transaction which the deceased client's executrix could repudiate if she wished, but that if she chose to affirm it, the brokers had no right to commission because although they were obliged to close the account, they were bound by the rule that an agent may not sell to himself.

A broker must use his judgment in deciding whether he should close the account at once. So if he exercises his right to sell immediately and then it turns out that he could have sold his deceased client's securities at a higher price had he used his judgment and waited for the end of the account before selling, it is he the broker who must bear *that* loss.[17]

A broker has a choice, on the death or insolvency of his client, as to whether he should close the account immediately or on account day. But if a client has given his broker authority to carry over a bargain, and the client dies, that authority is automatically determined, and the broker has no choice in the matter.[18]

B. MANNER OF CLOSING AN ACCOUNT

Normally an account is closed either by a purchase or sale in the open market,[19] but there is nothing to prevent a broker putting the securities through a jobber's books and buying the shares himself. If the broker adopts the latter course, the put-through price must be fixed at a time which is reasonable and a price which is fair to the client in all the circumstances.[20] In *Macoun* v. *Erskine Oxenford & Co.*,[1] Vaughan Williams, L.J., seemed to express a dislike of closing by a put-through:

> "It would be better that a broker closing a customer's account should do so by a clear sale with no concomitant bargain with the jobber on his own account".

But the Lord Justice was ready to concede that there was nothing dishonourable or unfair in the put-through in question. Given an absence of *mala fides* and the fact that this method of closing was widely accepted on the Stock Exchange he, like the rest of the Court of Appeal, was prepared to uphold the practice.

Any advantage which the broker manages to extract from a put-

17. See *Lacey* v. *Hill, Scrimgeour's Claim* (1873), 8 Ch. App. 921; and *Ellis* v. *Pond*, [1898] 1 Q.B. 426, at pp. 447 and 449.
18. *Re Overweg, Haas* v. *Durant*, [1900] 1 Ch. 209.
19. *Scott and Horton* v. *Ernest* (1900), 16 T.L.R. 498, at p. 499.
20. *Walter and Gould* v. *King* (1897), 13 T.L.R. 270, C.A.; *Macoun* v. *Erskine Oxenford & Co.*, [1901] 2 K.B. 493; *Christoforides* v. *Terry*, [1924] A.C. 566.
 1. *Supra*, at p. 502.

through is for the benefit of his client and not himself. So in
Erskine, Oxenford & Co. v. *Sachs*:[2]

> The jobber indicated that he would be content with a profit which was
> smaller than the normal jobber's turn, because in a put-through trans-
> action he did not have to wait for the opportunity of selling, or run the
> risk of losing money. The clients claimed that because of the brokers'
> fiduciary position the brokers were bound to credit them with this
> profit.

It was held that the brokers must account to their clients for the
difference between the smaller jobber's turn in fact charged, and an
ordinary jobber's turn. Vaughan Williams, L.J., anxious as always to
protect a broker's clients, inclined to the view (without however
deciding the point) that the client should have an option either to
adopt the contract and claim the profit, or to repudiate the closing
altogether.[3]

C. CLOSING PART OF AN ACCOUNT

A broker may close part of his client's account, leaving the other
part to be settled or carried over. In *Cullum* v. *Hodges*:[4]

> A broker had carried over and kept open for the December 29th
> account day some Golden Link shares and some Louisville shares. On
> December 18th the broker wrote his client a letter in which he said that,
> owing to the stringency of the money market, it would be impossible for
> him to carry over the shares at the coming settlement, and he asked the
> client either to take up the shares or to give him instructions to sell
> them. But after correspondence it was agreed that the broker should
> carry over them once again. On December 23rd (contango day) the
> broker succeeded in carrying over the Louisville shares; but he did not
> succeed in carrying over the Golden Links, and sold them.

Collins, M.R., showed that on December 23rd the broker could
have attempted any one of three things:

(i) arrange to carry them over; or
(ii) get the client to take them up; or
(iii) take them up himself.

The broker was not bound (i) to carry them over, or (iii) to take
them up himself. Since it was clear that the client could not possibly
find the money to (ii) take them up, the broker was entitled to close
that part of the account by (iii) taking up the Golden Links himself
and selling them.

Although an earlier decision[5] has to some extent cast doubt upon
the part-closure rule (simply because it was mentioned without

2. [1901] 2 K.B. 504, C.A.   3. *Ibid.*, at p. 514.   4. (1901), 18 T.L.R. 6.
5. *Samuel and Escombe* v. *Rowe, supra.*

disapproval in *Cullum* v. *Hodges*), the House of Lords in *Morten* v. *Hilton, Gibbs and Smith*[6] regarded it as:

> "quite an untenable proposition to affirm broadly that a broker cannot close part of an account and carry over the remainder when his principal is in default."

In view of that dictum the question seems hardly open to doubt.

3. Anticipatory breach

A contract is broken in anticipation when before the time for its performance one of the parties does something to indicate that he repudiates the bargain. This unilateral act does not amount to a rescission, because legally a contract cannot be rescinded except by the consent of both parties or an order of the court. Instead, the law gives the non-repudiating party a choice. Suppose that *the broker* has committed an anticipatory breach by closing his client's account without instructions. The client may either treat that as ending the bargain, and claim damages, or he can insist on the broker's performance of it and claim in addition any damages he has suffered as a result of the broker's attempted repudiation.[7] Suppose on the other hand that *the client* has committed the anticipatory breach by letting his broker know that he has no intention of indemnifying him. The broker may continue to treat the contract as binding, and sue the client for the indemnity when it has become due but remains unpaid; indeed, he could act at once by bringing an action in which he asks the court to declare that he is entitled to the indemnity when he has performed his part of the bargain.[8]

However, the broker may take the more realistic view that the client will not pay because he cannot pay. If he is right, the broker can take the alternative course of closing the account by a sale on the open market. Where this course results in a loss to himself, he can in addition recover damages from the client.

The market for the securities in question may be in a particularly bad state when the broker elects to close the account. He has a duty to mitigate his damages, and instead of selling the securities at once, he may decide to hold on to them himself for a time to await a more favourable trend. The damages which the broker may recover in such circumstances are measured by the difference between the contract price of the securities and their market price at a reasonable time after the broker's acceptance of his client's repudiation.[9]

6. (1908) reported in [1937] 2 K.B. 176. Dictum of Loreburn, L.C.
7. *Michael* v. *Hart & Co,* [1902] 1 K.B. 482, C.A.
8. *Lacey* v. *Hill, Crowley's Claim* (1874), L.R. 18 Eq. 182, *per* Jessel, M.R., at p. 191.
9. *Macoun* v. *Erskine, Oxenford & Co, supra.*

Whether a party has repudiated is in all cases a question of fact. In *Barned* v. *Hamilton*:[10]

> The client attempted to repudiate a contract under which his broker bought him some railway shares. He wrote to his broker alleging misrepresentation on the broker's part and added, "I shall consider all the contracts which you have made for me null and void, should the information above mentioned prove correct". The broker refused to accept this as a repudiation, and went on to purchase the shares. When he tendered the shares to his client, they had fallen in value and the client refused to accept them.

The court took the view that the letter was only a qualified repudiation and that the client had not substantiated his allegation of misrepresentation. Furthermore, the letter had been followed by negotiations between the parties for an amicable settlement. It was held that in the circumstances no unequivocal repudiation had been made. Tindal, C. J., said:

> ". . . it was the part of (the client) to bring matters to a final end, in a manner sufficiently precise and distinct to enable (the broker) to act upon the repudiation of the contract without hazard or difficulty."

Once a repudiation is established, whether it has been accepted as such by the other party is of itself a separate question of fact. So where the non-repudiating party brings an action for breach of contract before the date fixed for its completion, clearly he has elected to treat the contract as repudiated.[11] This is an obvious example of an unequivocal election: other courses of behaviour may not be interpreted so easily, and the negotiations of the parties will have to be looked at more closely in order to evince their real intentions.

4. Breach of contract between buyer and seller

While it is a firm rule that members of the Stock Exchange contract with each other *qua* principals, in reality they are bringing together a buyer and a seller who are not members of the Stock Exchange and probably do not know each other. A Stock Exchange bargain can involve *four* contracts: (i) the contract of the members *inter se*; (ii) the buyer's contract to indemnify the member acting on his behalf; (iii) the seller's contract to accept the securities purchased by the member acting for him; and (iv) the contract between the buyer and the seller.

Members' duties end at making contracts which comply with

10. (1841), 10 L.J.C.P. 287.
11. *Michael* v. *Hart & Co.*, [1902] 1 K.B. 482, C.A., at p. 492, *per* Collins, M.R., following *Roper* v. *Johnson* (1873), L.R. 8 C.P. 167.

their instructions, and are enforceable between the parties for whom they act. Beyond that point their clients must look to each other, as principals, for the legal performance of their bargain. In practice, members assist their clients in that performance by taking all the mechanical steps necessary to effect a valid transfer of title. It is part of the service which they provide. But a client's simple refusal or failure to perform a contract valid as made on the Stock Exchange is not the member's responsibility, although such refusal or failure may affect him in various ways.[12]

The remedies available to buyer and seller are set out below:

A. DAMAGES

The measure of damages in the breach of a contract for the sale of securities is the difference between the contract price and the market price at the date of the breach. The party affected is under a duty to mitigate his loss so far as he can; nevertheless if he keeps the securities and then cuts his losses by selling them later on a rising market, that does not prevent him from recovering the greater loss measured by their value when the breach occurred.[13]

B. INDEMNITY

The seller's right to the purchase money of securities includes a right to be indemnified in respect of calls made and paid right up to the time of completion—unless the parties agree otherwise. In *Hawkins* v. *Maltby*:[14]

> The buyer did not know that at the time of the sale a call was to be made. When the call came to his attention some time later, he did not at once object to paying it.

It was held that by his conduct he had waived any right to object which he might originally have had.

The seller's right to the purchase money is not affected by the fact that the company has gone into liquidation before account day;[15] indeed it is not affected where the company has commenced winding-up before the date of the contract.[16] But the seller cannot

---

12. For example, in stock exchange bargains the seller is responsible for the authenticity of all documents which are delivered to the buyer. So where a buyer loses his position on the register because the documents are not genuine, the loss is borne (as between members of the stock exchange) by the *member* acting for the original seller; but that member can place the burden on his client by claiming an indemnity from him—*Reynolds* v. *Smith* (1893), 9 T.L.R. 494 H.L.
13. See *Jamal* v. *Moolla Dawood Sons & Co,* [1916] 1 A.C. 175, P.C.
14. (1869), 4 Ch. App. 200.
15. *Chapman* v. *Shepherd* (1867), L.R. 2 C.P. 228.
16. *Biederman* v. *Stone* (1867), L.R. 2 C.P. 504; *Rudge* v. *Bowman* (1868), L.R. 3 Q.B. 689.

claim an indemnity where the parties were, at the time of contract, ignorant of the fact that the company had gone into liquidation.[17]

Indemnity is sometimes ordered as a second-best remedy where specific performance (see below) is in the circumstances impossible. For example, a company may have gone into liquidation—in which case the Companies Act 1948[18] forbids all transfers without the consent of the court,[19] or the directors may have refused their consent to the transfer[20]—as they generally have power to do.

C. SPECIFIC PERFORMANCE

When the buyer of shares fails to obtain them as a result of a breach on the seller's part, his normal remedy will be in damages. This is certainly the case where the bargain is for Government stock, because the securities which the seller failed to transfer are easily replaceable by others of the same type.[1] The buyer is not so fortunate, however, when he has bargained for equities, because company shares are in limited supply and he may not be able to obtain others in the market. Here the courts have recognised that damages are not an adequate compensation for the unfortunate buyer, and have compelled the seller to transfer the very shares which he contracted to sell.[2] But the court will only do this where the shares are not obtainable elsewhere in the market: so if the buyer can obtain the same shares but at a higher price, the court would refuse a suit of specific performance, but award damages measured by the difference between the contract price and the price which the buyer would have to pay if he were minded to make an alternative bargain.[3]

The remedy of specific performance is available to a seller to compel the buyer to co-operate in accepting a transfer of the shares which he has contracted to buy. But if the seller cannot make good title, he cannot obtain specific performance. In *Shaw* v. *Fisher*:[4]

Shaw wished to sell 25 Newry and Enniskillen Railway shares. His broker employed an auctioneer who sold them to Fisher. A few days

17. *London, Hamburg and Continental Bank, Re Emmerson's Case* (1866), 1 Ch. App. 433.
18. See Companies Act 1948, ss. 227, 282, 313.
19. *Chapman* v. *Shepherd* (1867), L.R. 2 C.P. 228; *Hawkins* v. *Maltby* (1869), 4 Ch. App. 200. It would appear from *Neilson* v. *James* (1882), 9 Q.B.D. 546, C.A. that where indemnity is ordered in lieu of specific performance the seller cannot be indemnified against calls in addition to the purchase price. In *Paine* v. *Hutchinson* (1868), 3 Ch. App. 388, the company had been ordered to be woundup, but *both* specific performance and indemnity were granted where the bill for specific performance was filed before the order for the winding-up of the company.
20. See *Casey* v. *Bentley* (1902), 1 I.R. 376, C.A.
1. See *Adderley* v. *Dixon* (1824), 1 Sim. & St. 607.
2. *Duncuft* v. *Albrecht* (1841), 12 Sim. 189.
3. *Re Schwabacher, Koritschoner's Claim* (1907), 98 L.T. 127, at p. 128.
4. (1855), 5 De G. M. and G. 596.

later Fisher employed the same auctioneer to resell the shares, and he resold them to Carmichael. Shaw's broker was handed the name of Carmichael for the purpose of preparing a deed of transfer, and the shares were duly transferred to him. But Carmichael refused to complete the contract by registering the shares in his own name. Carmichael absconded, and when Shaw eventually discovered that Fisher had been the original purchaser, he filed a bill claiming specific performance against him.

However it was held that Shaw had disqualified himself from proceeding against Fisher by executing a transfer to Carmichael, so that the privity between him and Fisher had been destroyed.

If the seller has only an equitable title to the shares, that can be regarded as the proper subject of a sale of which specific performance will be granted.[5]

D. AN ORDER FOR THE RETURN OF SECURITIES WRONGFULLY DETAINED

Suppose that the seller dishonestly retains securities to which the buyer is entitled as a result of a sale. The buyer can obtain an order for their return (a remedy of law) as an alternative to a decree of specific performance (a remedy of equity). The remedy is usually associated with those who deposit shares as security for a loan when (if recovery is not possible) the measure of damages is the value of the shares on the day when replacement was due or, at the depositor's option, the market price at the date of trial.[6] The question of wrongful detention arose between buyer and seller in the case of *Stewart* v. *Lupton*:[7]

The buyer purchased through his broker ten shares in the Patent Gas Company. On September 29th the seller executed a transfer to the buyer, and on October 7th left the transfer at the company's office for registration, which finally took place on October 13th. On October 4th the directors passed a resolution that existing shareholders should be issued with one new share for every share they already held, allowing them fourteen days to accept or refuse. On the same day (October 4th) a circular was sent to each shareholder on the register giving notice of the resolution. The seller received a copy because he was still on the register, though he had already divested himself of all interest in the shares in favour of the buyer on September 29th. Instead of forwarding the circular to the buyer or his brokers, the seller fraudulently kept the circular and applied for ten new shares for himself. The issue of the new shares did not come to the buyer's attention until October 26th, when the fourteen days had expired. Wanting to obtain the ten new shares to

5. *Paine* v. *Hutchinson* (1868), 3 Ch. App. 388.
6. *Harrison* v. *Harrison* (1824), 1 C. & P. 412.
7. (1874), 22 W.R. 855.

which the ten which he had already bought gave him a right, he requested the seller to hand them over. But the seller refused.

Malins, V.C., held that the seller was a trustee of the ten new shares for the buyer, that he had wrongfully detained them, and that had he not sold the shares himself, the seller ought to have handed them over to the buyer. Instead, the buyer recovered damages measured by reference to the highest market price at which he could have sold the ten shares had they been duly delivered to him.

B. DEFAULT

"Every member dealing on the Stock Exchange is, by the Rules of the House, liable for the due fulfilment of every bargain into which he enters, on pain of being immediately declared a defaulter. Any member becoming a defaulter ceases to be a member of, or capable of dealing on or entering, the Stock Exchange."[8]

There is no doubt that a member who has failed to meet his obligations under only one stock exchange contract runs the risk of being declared a defaulter, though of course that risk is very much greater when he has been guilty of numerous defaults. On a member's breach of contract, the other party (be he a client or another member) might think primarily in terms of suing the defaulting member in the courts for the common legal and equitable remedies available for such breach—although the Rules and Regulations make important restrictions upon this right.[9]

On the other hand, the member's stock exchange debts may be so numerous and widespread that the other party's best hope of obtaining satisfaction lies in the domestic procedure of the Stock Exchange under which a member who is unable to fulfil his engagements is publicly declared a defaulter in the premises of the Stock Exchange.[10] Even when a member gives his creditors a private intimation of his inability to fulfil his engagements, the creditors are forbidden to make any compromise with him, but must immediately communicate with the Chairman, a Deputy Chairman or two members of the Council so that the default can be publicly declared.[11]

On declarations, the defaulter ceases to be a member, but remains

8. *Re Plumbly, ex parte Grant* (1880), 13 Ch. D. 667, at p. 670.
9. Rule 75 restricts the rights of members to sue one another by providing that their disputes shall be referred to the arbitration of a member of the Stock Exchange. Rule 76 gives the Council power to intervene where a client proposes to sue a member on a claim which is not in accordance with the Rules, Regulations and usages of the Stock Exchange.
10. The old expression "hammered" is derived from the custom (now discontinued) of announcing the declaration by a waiter at each end of the House striking his desk with a hammer. 11. Rule 177.

bound to take all such actions as the Rules require a defaulter to take.[12] The most important of these actions is to execute and deliver a deed of arrangement [13] vesting all his assets in the Official Assignee of the Stock Exchange for distribution among his creditors in the order of precedence provided by the Rules;[14] and for this purpose to hand to the Official Assignee his books of account and other necessary documents.

1. The Official Assignee

The Rules provide for the appointment by the Council of an Official Assignee and a Deputy Official Assignee to manage the estates of defaulters. The Official Assignee's functions are administrative in nature and his principal duties are four:

(i) to obtain from the defaulter his original books of account;

(ii) to attend meetings of creditors and to summon the defaulter before such meetings if required;

(iii) to enter into a strict examination of every account and to investigate and report to the Council any bargains found to have been effected at unfair prices;

(iv) to realise and distribute the defaulter's assets in accordance with the Rules.

CONTROL OF OFFICIAL ASSIGNEE

The Official Assignee may be removed by, and is accountable to the Council.[15] Twice every year he must lay before the Council an account of the balances in his hands belonging to defaulters' estates, and once a year he must provide a statement of all dividends paid during the last year on each defaulter's estate.[16]

2. The Stock Official

Where the defaulter is a jobber and has issued or is due to issue, or holds or is due to receive a ticket in respect of a registered security on the instructions of the Settlement Office and the issuer or holder of the ticket or re-issued ticket has failed to release his immediate seller or buyer as the case may be, the Rules provide for the appointment by the Council of a Stock Official.[17]

As soon as possible after the jobber has been declared a defaulter, the Settlement Office must provide the Stock Official with lists of the bargains in registered securities returned through the Settle-

---

12. Rule 175 (4).
13. Rule 179. For a specimen deed of arrangement, see Rules and Regulations, Appendix 37.
14. Rule 170.   15. Rules 170 (1), 171 (1).   16. Rule 171 (4).   17. Rule 170 (3).

ment Office on account of that jobber. Armed with these lists, the Stock Official will assess the amounts to be paid to or received by members who bought from or sold to the jobber and still had accounts open at the declaration of his default.[18]

The Stock Official must then hand his list of assessments to the Official Assignee for settlement. Members who, on the Stock Official's assessment, are found liable for closing differences with the defaulting jobber, must open accounts with the defaulter and debit or credit those accounts with such sums as they are liable to pay or receive, the differences arising from these accounts being paid to or claimed from the Official Assignee.[19]

3. Procedure after declaration of default

A. FIXING OF THE HAMMER PRICES

After the declaration the Official Assignee must publicly fix the share prices current in the market *immediately before* the declaration.[20] The prices so fixed are called the hammer prices.

B. MEMBERS TO CLOSE THEIR ACCOUNTS WITH THE DEFAULTER

When the hammer prices have been fixed, all members having accounts open with the defaulter must close them by buying from or selling to the defaulter such securities as he may have contracted to take or deliver. If securities have been delivered on a ticket, the member making delivery should apply for payment to the member next to him on the trace, thus providing that member with evidence of default. That member and every member on the trace should act in a similar manner until the ultimate member who dealt with the defaulter is reached. This member should immediately lodge his claim with the Official Assignee.[1]

Where differences (known as hammer price differences) are owing to the other members they then claim such differences from the Official Assignee. Conversely, hammer price differences owing to the defaulter must be paid over to the Official Assignee.[2]

In the case of securities and unexpired options for which (for one reason or another) no hammer price is available, transactions must be closed at a market valuation or in the absence of a market valuation at a price determined by the Official Assignee, who must have regard to:

18. For a full description of the functions Stock Official, see Appendix 36a of the Rules.
19. Rule 172 (2).
20. *Ibid.*
1. See Appendix 36 of the Rules.
2. Rule 172 (2).

(*a*) information as to the consideration for recent transfers;

(*b*) the views of any brokers or jobbers interested in the security; and

(*c*) the prices at which the last business was done in the Stock Exchange, London or other stock exchanges.[3]

In the case of a secured loan (i.e., a *bona fide* loan between members on adequate security given either when the loan was made or not less than fourteen days prior to the default) the lender must realise his securities within three days or such longer period as the Official Assignee may allow. Failing that, he must take them over at prices fixed by the Official Assignee. If the security proves insufficient, the deficiency may be proved against the estate as a stock claim.[4]

As soon after declaration as possible all members having accounts open with the defaulter should furnish the Official Assignee with:

(*a*) a copy of the jobber's ledger for the current account;

(*b*) a statement of all bargains which have been closed at hammer prices. If there are any bargains for future dates, these must be set out on separate sheets for each account.

Where the defaulter has issued a ticket for securities which have not been paid for, a *contra* entry should be made and the original bargain closed at the hammer price.[5]

C. MEMBERS TO GET IN TOUCH WITH THE DEFAULTER'S CLIENTS

The declaration of a member's default and the consequent closing of his accounts with other members is a domestic procedure of the Stock Exchange which affects its members only. The contractual position of the defaulting member's *clients* is therefore not affected: they continue to be bound by the bargains which the defaulter has made on their behalf.[6]

Immediately on the declaration of a defaulter, members having accounts open with him should apply to the Official Assignee for the names and addresses of his clients (if any) for whom bargains are open,[7] then:

(*a*) If the client is himself in default, all bargains open for him should at once be closed by sale or purchase in the market.[8]

(*b*) If the client is not in default, the member who has a bargain open with the defaulter should immediately communicate with him.

3. Rule 172 (3).   4. Rule 184.
5. See Appendix 36 of the Rules for the full procedure.
6. *Levitt* v. *Hamblet*, [1901] 2 K.B. 53, C.A.; *Ponsolle* v. *Webber*, [1908] 1 Ch. 254; *cf. Scott and Horton* v. *Godfrey*, [1901] 2 K.B. 726.
7. Appendix 36 of the rules, para. 4.   8. *Ibid.*, para. 5.

The Official Assignee will, if requested, supply a suggested form of letter.[9]

The client is then bound to complete his transaction *at the price of the bargain*, or in the case of securities carried over, at the last making-up price and rate.[10] The member and the client may agree to treat the bargains as closed at the hammer price, but there is no usage which entitles the client to *insist* upon closing the bargain at the hammer price.[11] The client can complete direct, through his banker or other agent, or through a new broker with whom the member may (but not must) agree to "make down" the bargain (i.e., agree to his substitution as the party liable).[12]

The client may take the initiative himself and give instructions for the closing of his account; if he does this, and there is a difference between the bargain price and the closing price, that difference must be settled by himself or the member as the case may be.[13]

Where the member has duly communicated with the client, and the client has failed to give instructions for closure by 3 p.m. on the business day before the making-up day, the member is entitled to close forthwith.[14] As soon as a client has personally completed his bargain, or the member has agreed to "make down" with a new broker, a supplementary account must be furnished to the Official Assignee setting out only the bargains completed.[15]

Suppose that the client fails to complete with the member, who then claims in the liquidation of the defaulter's estate for the difference between the contract price and the hammer price, and is paid that difference in full; it was held in *Stoneham* v. *Wyman*[16] that the member is entitled to recover damages from the client in addition; but if the damages exceed the sum received by the member from the defaulter's estate, the member is bound to account to the defaulter's estate (i.e., to the Official Assignee) for that sum.

D. CREDITORS' MEETING

As soon as possible after the declaration of default the Official Assignee must call the first meeting of creditors at which he or the Deputy Official Assignee will act as chairman.[17] Notice of the meeting must be posted in the Stock Exchange not less than 24 hours in advance.[18] Written notice must be given not less than seven days in advance to every member entitled to attend a creditors' meeting:

9. Appendix 36, para. 6 (*a*).　　10. *Ibid.*, para. 6 (*b*).
11. *Levitt* v. *Hamblet*, [1901] 2 K.B. 53, *per* Collins, L.J., at p. 66.
12. Appendix 36 of the Rules, para. 6 (*c*).
13. *Ibid.*, para. 6 (*d*).　　14. *Ibid.*, para. 6 (*e*).
15. See Appendix 36 of the Rules, para. 7.　　16. (1901), 6 Com. Cas. 174.
17. Rule 173.　　18. Appendix 38, para. 1.

(*a*) whose claim has been admitted or is under consideration; or

(*b*) who has notified the Official Assignee that he has been appointed by a non-member whose claim has been admitted or is under consideration to act as his representative at meetings of creditors.[19]

Every member entitled to attend a creditors' meeting has one vote.[20] The creditors' meeting can pass resolutions by a simple majority of those entitled to vote.[1] Subsequent meetings may be convened by the Official Assignee if so requested by either the committee of creditors,[2] or in writing by creditors whose admitted claims amount to not less than one quarter in value of all claims for the time being admitted.[3]

E. LIQUIDATION OF THE DEFAULTER'S ESTATE

The Official Assignee will collect the defaulter's assets for distribution among his creditors in accordance with the Rules. Distribution will be up to 100p in the £ on the admitted claims but without interest.[4] After payment of all legal and administrative (including the Official Assignee's) expenses the proceeds of the Official Assignee's collections will be applied in the following order of priority:

(i) Allowances or payments to or for the benefit of the defaulter, his wife, widow, children or other dependants, or his clerical staff. Such allowance or payment must be authorised by the committee of creditors. In the discretion of the committee they may be charged in whole or in part against differences but subject to that they are expenses chargeable against the defaulter's general assets.[5]

(ii) Of what remains, creditors for differences have a prior claim on all differences received. If any part of the difference fund remains after the creditors for differences have been paid in full, that excess will be available for distribution among the stock creditors.[6]

(iii) From the general assets, the stock creditors are to be paid *pro rata* to their claims.[7] When they have been paid in full, the surplus must be applied to satisfy difference creditors who have not been paid in full, and after them:

19. See Appendix 38, para. 1.   20. *Ibid.*, para. 6.   1. *Ibid.*, para. 7.
2. As to the committee of creditors, see Appendix 38, paras. 8–12.
3. *Ibid.*, para. 1.   4. Rule 174 (1).   5. Rule 174 (2).
6. Rule 180 (1).
7. Rule 180 (2). Under Rule 184, where a secured loan has not been fully repaid and the security proves insufficient, the lender may prove for the deficiency as a stock creditor.

(iv) Deferred creditors,[8] who are paid *pari passu*. The following rank as deferred claims:[9]

(a) claims arising from bargains (other than options) done "out of time", i.e., for a period beyond the third ensuing account day;

(b) claims arising from differences which have been allowed to remain unpaid for more than two business days—Saturday excepted—beyond the day on which they became due.[10] Here is another instance of how the law and the Rules favour the quick settlement of bargains.

The Rules make various provisions to ensure that all creditors are, as it were, equal before the Rules and that no individual does something which will give him an unfair advantage over the general body of creditors or defeat the order of priorities above. For example, it is provided that no member shall take legal proceedings against a defaulter to enforce a claim without the consent of the committee of creditors or the Stock Exchange Council.[11]

Any surplus remaining after all classes of creditors have been paid in full must be returned to the defaulter for his own purposes.[12]

4. Default and bankruptcy

A. THE DEED OF ARRANGEMENT A *CESSIO BONORUM*

The defaulter's deed of arrangement operates as an assignment of all his assets (*cessio bonorum*) to the Official Assignee charged with the administration of his estate. One effect of this assignment is that the Official Assignee may sue and be sued in his own name in respect of these assets;[13] and where the Official Assignee recovers a sum of money in such an action, the title to that sum is *res judicata* and no other person can claim it. In *Lomas* v. *Graves & Co*;[14] an earlier action had been commenced in the name of the defaulter and the defendant in the action had paid a sum of money into court.

It was held in the present action that the Official Assignee, having a *paramount* interest in all the defaulter's assets, had a prior right to the sum over a judgment creditor of the defaulter. In *Hinde* v. *Haskew*[15] the court refused to order the nominal plaintiff to give security for costs on the ground that he was a stock exchange

8. Rule 180 (2).   9. Rule 181.
10. Rule 181 (2) further provides that differences overdue and paid previous to the day of default are not to be refunded.
11. Rule 186. See also Rules 187 and 188.   12. Rule 174 (1).
13. *Richardson* v. *Stormont, Todd & Co.*, [1900] 1 Q.B. 701, C.A.
14. [1904] 2 K.B. 557.   15. [1884] 1 T.L.R. 94.

defaulter. The plaintiff was in fact bringing an action on behalf of
the Official Assignee to recover a sum which he alleged was due to
him from the defendant in respect of differences on the Stock
Exchange. Admittedly he was a defaulter, but the Official Assignee
stood in his shoes and accordingly the court found it unnecessary to
order the plaintiff to give security for costs as well.

B. ASSIGNMENT OF THE DEFAULTER'S ASSETS AN ACT OF BANKRUPTCY

Because the Rules and Regulations provide for an assignment of
the defaulter's assets, default on the Stock Exchange is an act of
bankruptcy:[16] i.e., an act which results from the condition of his
affairs and shows him to be insolvent. Moreover, since declaration
of default is a domestic procedure of the Stock Exchange—a device
primarily for the benefit of the defaulter's stock exchange creditors
—the Rules which govern it do not affect the rights of the defaulter's general creditors outside the Stock Exchange. So if the
defaulter is adjudicated bankrupt upon a petition presented within
three months of the assignment (as the Bankruptcy Act[17] requires),
the title of his trustee in bankruptcy will relate back to the date of
the default and displace that of the Official Assignee. This was what
happened in *Tomkins* v. *Saffery*:[18]

> C had been a member of the Stock Exchange. He became unable to
> meet his stock exchange engagements and gave notice of this to the
> Secretary. The course prescribed by the Rules was then followed. C.
> made a statement at the first meeting of his creditors declaring at that
> time that he had no debts outside the Stock Exchange. His stock
> exchange creditors then consented to accept a composition; and, to
> provide for a part of it, he at the demand of the Official Assignee gave
> him a cheque for £5,000 then standing to his credit at the Bank of
> England. The Official Assignee obtained the money and apportioned it
> among his stock exchange creditors. He afterwards confessed to owing
> debts to a large amount to outside creditors, and was declared a bank-
> rupt. The trustee in bankruptcy, on behalf of the general creditors,
> claimed from the Official Assignee the £5,000.

The trustee was held entitled to recover, on the ground that what
had been done by C under the Rules of the Stock Exchange constituted an act of bankruptcy inasmuch as it amounted to a *cessio
bonorum*.

When *Tomkins* v. *Saffery* was decided non-members were not
allowed to participate in defaulters' estates. Today non-members

16. *Tomkins* v. *Saffery* (1877), 3 App. Cas. 213, H.L.; *Richardson* v. *Stormont, Todd
& Co.*, [1900] 1 Q.B. 701, C.A.; *Lomas* v. *Graves,* [1904] 2 K.B. 557, C.A.
17. Bankruptcy Act 1914, s. 4 (1) (c).
18. *Supra.*

may do so and in practice non-member creditors represent the vast majority of all creditors. It is clear that once non-member creditors have assented to the deed of assignment they may not take further steps to recover sums due.

Broker who does not suspend payments

In *Clough* v. *Samuel*[19] a broker avoided being declared a defaulter and thus avoided committing an act of bankruptcy.

> The broker, being hopelessly insolvent, told his stock exchange creditors that he would have difficulty in paying them at the approaching settlement and suggested that they should close their accounts with him, which they did. He thus avoided being declared a defaulter.

Lord Halsbury, L.C., found however that "the last thing (the broker) had in mind was a notice that he intended to suspend payment of his debts", and the House of Lords held by a majority that no act of bankruptcy had been committed. In the words of Lord Robertson:[20]

> "A man faced by a balance sheet which means certain and speedy ruin may try to arrange with his more pressing creditors or he may put off the evil day and stagger on, leaving the stoppage of his career to be brought about by the action of others. Either of these courses is different from suspending payment of his debts."

Registration of the deed of arrangement

The deed of arrangement assigning the defaulter's assets to the Official Assignee will be void against the defaulter's trustee in bankruptcy if it is not registered and stamped as provided by the Deeds of Arrangement Act 1914.[1] Unless this has been done, the defaulter's trustee in bankruptcy is entitled to the assets collected by the Official Assignee—even though the bankruptcy occurs more than three months after the notice of default.

The artificial fund

If a defaulter's bargains are closed at hammer prices the resulting differences owed by members to the defaulter, when received by the

---

19. [1905] A.C. 442.   20. *Ibid.*, at p. 448.
 1. *Ibid.*, s. 2. Under Section 3 (1) of the Deeds of Arrangement Act 1914 a deed for the benefit of a debtor's *creditors generally* will be void unless before or within twenty-one days after its registration with a registrar appointed by the Board of Trade it has received the assent of a majority in number and value of the creditors of the debtor. In *Wareham* v. *Jacobs* (12 December 1964: Milmo, J. in Q.B. Chambers, unreported) it was held that the Stock Exchange deed of arrangement was not "an instrument which is in fact for the benefit of creditors generally", and that accordingly it did not require for its validity the assent of the debtor's creditors.

Official Assignee constitutes an artificial fund arising under the Rules of the Stock Exchange. As such they do not form part of his general assets and are therefore out of the reach of his trustee in bankruptcy.[2] But ordinary differences owing to the defaulter on his accounts open at the time of his default are part of his general assets, and are therefore capable of passing into the hands of the trustee.[3]

5. Claims by non-members

Claims made by non-members (including claims for unsecured loans) may be admitted by the committee of creditors if they arise out of stock exchange transactions. The committee will have to decide whether the particular claim is to rank as a stock claim or a deferred claim, or partly one and partly the other. Where in the committee's opinion the circumstances justify it, they may decide that the whole or part of such a claim shall rank *in preference* to the stock claims.[4] Any claimant who is dissatisfied with the committee's decision can have the matter referred to the Stock Exchange Council whose determination of the matter is final.[5]

A member who is a creditor upon a defaulter's estate is forbidden to sell, assign or pledge his claim to a non-member without the concurrence of the Council; notice of such an assignment must be given immediately to the Official Assignee.[6]

6. The re-admission of defaulters

A defaulter who has not paid at least one third of the balance of any loss that has occurred on his transactions, whether on his own account or that of his clients, is not eligible for re-admission to membership.[7] A defaulter who has paid 100p in the £ may be re-admitted without notice.[8] Where the defaulter has not paid 100p in the £, but has paid one-third of the loss the Council must consider the report of a committee[9] appointed to investigate his conduct and his accounts. This committee has wide powers to investigate the defaulter's financial position before and after the declaration of default.[10] Where the defaulter has paid 100p in the £, the committee's task is confined to reporting that fact.[11]

Defaulters declared within four years of their admission as members, and defaulters who have been rejected upon two ballots can only be re-admitted by a majority of not less than three-quarters of

2. *Re Plumbly, ex parte Grant* (1880), 13 Ch. D. 667. In *Re Woodd, ex parte King,* [1900] W.N. 88, it was held that differences due to the defaulter on the passing of tickets are similarly included in the artificial fund.
3. *King* v. *Hutton,* [1900] 2 Q.B. 504, C.A.   4. Rule 182 (1).
5. Rule 182 (2).   6. Rule 185.   7. Rule 42.
8. Rule 37 (2).   9. Set up under Rule 39.   10. Rule 39 (2).
11. Rule 37 (2), *supra.*

those members of the Council who are present at a meeting of which special notice has been given and at which not less than twelve members are present.[12]

CLASSES OF RE-ADMISSION

There are two classes of re-admission:[13]

(a) *The first class*, which is for cases of failure arising from the default of clients, or from other circumstances where no bad faith or breach of the Rules and Regulations has been practised; where the operations have been in reasonable proportion to the defaulter's means or resources and where his general conduct has been irreproachable.

(b) *The second class*, for cases marked by indiscretion and by the absence of reasonable caution.

There do not appear to be any *specific* consequences of belonging to one class or the other, although it is clear that a first class re-admission is, from the defaulter's point of view, more desirable than a second class re-admission. While the first class implies an absence of moral turpitude, the second class does not provide for cases where it is present. The Rules have been so drafted that they do not make provision for the re-admission of defaulters who (in the Council's view) have been guilty of actual dishonesty.

7. Compensation funds

One of the three minimum obligations which the Federation of Stock Exchanges imposed upon the federated exchanges was to provide standard compensation funds for members of the public who have suffered loss from the default of one of their members. The Federation was careful to state that it was not conferring legal rights upon the public but that all compensation payments were to be *ex gratia* only.

A. MAINTENANCE OF COMPENSATION FUNDS

Each federated exchange must maintain a compensation fund of an amount equal to £200 in respect of each active member.[14] When compensation is paid out of the fund, the amount paid out must be restored to the fund within 30 days of payment. The compensation fund's moneys and assets must at all times be held separate and distinct from the other funds of the federated exchange. The

12. Rule 38.
13. Rule 40.
14. See generally Articles of the Federal Constitution, Appendix C.

exchanges must submit annual auditor's statements to show compliance with these provisions.

B. LIABILITY OF INDIVIDUAL MEMBERS TO CONTRIBUTE

In addition to the maintenance of the compensation fund as above, each federated exchange must either:

(*a*) incorporate in or adopt as part of its constitution a provision that every member of the exchange (other than retired members not in business and honorary members) shall be liable on demand to contribute an amount not exceeding £1,000 in respect of each default of any member of any federated exchange occurring during his membership, the contribution to be applied in payment of compensation; or

(*b*) give to the Federal Committee a legally enforceable undertaking to contribute a like sum in respect of each of its members.

C. CONSIDERATION AND PAYMENT OF CLAIMS

The Federal Constitution provides that claims are initially considered and paid by the exchange of which the defaulter was a member.[15] Where, however, claims are likely to total an amount in excess of £200 per member, provision has been made for the claims to be considered and paid by the Federal Committee who will recoup the excess from some or all of the other federated exchanges *pro rata* to their membership.

D. DEFINITION OF DEFAULT FOR COMPENSATION PURPOSES

The Federal Constitution defines default for the purposes of compensation:

(i) The default of a member or member firm means his or its failure to fulfil his or its liabilities in consequence of transacting stock exchange business.

(ii) The individual default of *each* of the partners of a firm is treated as a single default by the firm.

(iii) Subject to (ii), each default of a member or member firm will be regarded as separate and distinct, notwithstanding that it may have been contributed to or caused by the default of another member or member firm, whether of the same or any other federated exchange. The provisions for the rateable payment of balances will apply accordingly.

The Federal Committee have power to determine in relation to any default the date on which the default is deemed to have

15. There is an absolute discretion to grant or refuse compensation.

occurred, unless the date has already been fixed by any exchange committee.

E. CLAIMS ELIGIBLE FOR COMPENSATION

An application for compensation by a member of the public may be entertained on the condition that in consequence of transacting stock exchange business with or through a member or member firm of a federated exchange or of employing such a member or member firm for such business, the member of the public has, subsequent to the inception of the Federation, suffered loss through the default of such a member or member firm, provided that:

(i) as regards the member (or each of the partners of the member firm) concerned, either he has been declared a defaulter or, having ceased to be a member, he or his estate appears to be insolvent or for any other reason it appears impracticable for the claim to be satisfactorily pursued against him or his estate; and

(ii) the loss is represented by claims falling within all or any of the following categories:

(*a*) claims arising out of payments for securities not delivered by the defaulter. The loss will be assessed by reference to the amount of the contract note.

(*b*) claims arising out of securities delivered to the defaulter by the claimant or his agent but not paid for. Here too the loss will be assessed by reference to the amount of the contract note.

(*c*) claims arising out of money in the hands of the defaulter pending investment, or money in his hands which has been improperly dealt with. The assessment will be the money lost.

(*d*) claims arising out of securities in the hands of the defaulter which have been improperly dealt with. The loss will be assessed by reference to the value of the securities on the date of the default. For this purpose, the exchange committee may determine that date.

F. CONTRIBUTORY NEGLIGENCE OF APPLICANT

Contributory negligence on the part of the applicant or his agent will be taken into account. The exchange committee concerned (or the Federal Committee) is sole judge as to whether and to what extent there has been contributory negligence.

G. APPLICANT'S FINANCIAL POSITION

The financial position of the applicant is not taken into account in determining whether or not to make a grant of compensation.

H. PROCEDURE FOR APPLICATIONS

Applications must be made in such manner and should be subject to such provisions as to procedure as may be laid down from time to time by the Federal Committee.

I. SUMMING-UP

The establishment of a uniform federal system of compensation, with provisions compelling federated exchanges to assist each other in making good the defaults of their individual members, provided the public with a much more comprehensive form of insurance than hitherto. This step is in accordance with the recommendations of the Company Law Committee which reported in 1962, and which suggested that the Board of Trade should satisfy themselves, as a condition of their recognition of provincial exchanges, that such exchanges have, or will have, within a reasonable period suitable arrangements for the compensation of investors who suffer loss as a result of the default of their members.

CHAPTER 11

Business with Country and Overseas Stock Exchanges

All stock exchanges have a natural desire to protect the interests of their members: hence they try to limit the amount of business which their members take elsewhere. The Stock Exchange, London, has a Rule [1] that, except as authorised in certain cases, a broker may not execute an order with a *non-member* in quoted securities, or those in which dealings are permitted under Rule 163 (1) (*d*) [2] and (*e*), [3] unless he can deal thereby to the *greater* advantage of his client than with a fellow member. It should be emphasised that the advantage to his client must be *greater* and not merely equivalent: a proposition which the broker must (unless excused by the Chairman or Deputy-Chairman) test by offering the business in the London Exchange on the same terms as those initially proposed to or by the non-member. [4]

In the event of a broker executing an order with a non-member he must (unless excused by the Chairman or a Deputy-Chairman):

(*a*) mark the bargain without delay on the special marking slip provided for the purpose; [5] the form of the special slip appears on top of page 260.

Marks in securities in which dealings are permitted under Rule 163 (1) (*d*) [6] and (*e*) [7] are recorded on special boards provided for the purpose. Complaints and objections to the marking of bargains may be lodged with the Clerks of the House, [8] and must be in writing. [9]

1. Rule 88 (1).
2. I.e., securities quoted in the lists or supplementary lists published by the Associated Stock Exchanges.
3. I.e., securities which have been granted a primary listing on the Johannesburg Stock Exchange, or have been granted a quotation on any other stock exchange or stockbrokers' association recognised by Rule 217 or a foreign stock exchange.
4. Rule 88 (2).   5. Rule 88 (3) (*a*).   6. See p. 118, *ante*.
7. *Ibid.*   8. In accordance with Rule 162.   9. Rule 88*b* (4).

ONLY ONE SECURITY TO BE ENTERED ON EACH SLIP

DATE   /   / 19

Name of Stock or Share	*Price*	*Price if other than London terms*

Signature of jobbers to
whom the above business
was offered   ....

The above business was
offered to the jobbers   *Signature of broker:*
whose signatures appear
above before dealing
outside.   ....

The broker must also:

(*b*) state on each contract note that the bargain has been done between non-members; [10]

(*c*) in all cases be prepared to justify his actions to the Council if called upon to do so. [11]

An obvious way of evading the restrictions on dealing with non-members would be for a London broker to approach a non-member in the guise of principal (i.e., client). But the Rules provide that a broker may not act as a principal for the purpose of evading the Rules, or adopt any other procedure for a like purpose. [12] The situations in which members are authorised to deal with non-members are described below.

A. ORDERS WHICH BROKERS (OR WHERE APPROPRIATE JOBBERS) MAY EXECUTE WITH NON-MEMBERS

1. Certain orders between London and country brokers

All brokers who belong to federated stock exchanges other than the Stock Exchange, London, are known as country brokers. A

10. Rule 83 (3) (*b*).   11. Rule 88 (4).   12. Rule 88*c* (1).

London broker may not execute an order in quoted securities, or securities in which dealing is permitted,[13] with a member of any other federated stock exchange unless he can deal thereby to the *greater* advantage of his client than in London. But where the London broker deals in securities of a purely *local* nature, he may deal with a country broker in the local exchange who offers the *same* terms as he can obtain in London.[14]

When a London broker executes an order with a country broker he must:[15]

(*a*) mark the bargain without delay in the appropriate column provided on the standard marking slip.[16]

(*b*) and (*c*) as above.

Markings under this Rule must be recorded unless withheld by the authority of the Chairman, a Deputy-Chairman or two members of the Council.[17] Complaints and objections to marks under this Rule may be made in the usual way.[18]

When a London broker transacts business between a country broker and a member of the public he is considered as acting as agent of the member of the public:[19] he cannot receive commission from more than one principal.[20] Subject to that, however, a London broker may charge commission to a country broker who *initiated* a particular order.[1]

2. Certain orders executed in overseas stock exchanges

(i) Where a London broker executes an order in an overseas exchange, either directly or *through* (i.e., transmitted by) a branch office of an overseas firm.

Here there is no obligation on the broker to offer the business in the London Stock Exchange first.[2]

(ii) Where a London broker wishes to execute an order *with* a U.K. or Eire domiciled branch office of an overseas firm.

Before such an order is given, the London broker must first offer the business in the London Stock Exchange on the *same* terms as those proposed to or by the agency, branch or other intermediary of the overseas firm.[3] If the London broker does execute an order with or through such agency, etc., he must:[4]

---

13. See rule 163 (1) (*d*) and (*e*), *supra*.   14. Rule 88*a* (1).
15. Rule 88*a* (2).   16. As shown in Appendix 43 of the Rules.
17. Rule 88*a* (3).   18. I.e., under Rule 162: Rule 88*a* (4).
19. Rule 204 (2).   20. Rule 89 (1).
1. Rule 89 (2). For scale of commission, see Appendix 40 of the Rules.
2. Rule 88*b* (1).   3. Rule 88*b* (2).   4. Rule 88*b* (3).

(*a*) mark the bargain without delay on the special marking slip[5] set out above:

(*b*) and (*c*) as above.

Compliance with the above requirements for business with branch offices may be waived by the Chairman or a Deputy-Chairman. Complaints and objections to the marking of such bargains may be lodged with the Clerks of the House[6] and must be in writing.[7]

3. Orders in Euro-Currency Bonds

The Rules define Euro-Currency Bonds as "fixed income securities (excluding preferred stock and preference share capital) issued after January 1st 1963 on which capital moneys are payable in a foreign currency[8] . . . and, except in the case of Japanese issues, the interest on which is payable without deduction of tax at source".[9]

A London broker is not restricted in the execution of orders in Euro-Currency Bonds with non-members. His only particular obligation is to state that the bargain has been done between non-members in the contract note.[10]

A London jobber may deal in Euro-Currency Bonds with a non-member who is making a market in such securities provided he is specially authorised so to do by the Council.[11]

4. Business between a jobber and a unit trust

A jobber may transact business with the management company of a unit trust with the prior consent of the Council.[12] Such business is limited to the purchase from the management company of such new units of a quoted unit trust as the jobber may require for the purpose of his business as a jobber.[13]

B. ARBITRAGE

With the invention of the telephone and other means of rapid or instantaneous communication it became possible for members of

5. See Appendix 43*a* of the Rules.
6. In accordance with Rule 162.   7. Rule 88*b* (4).
8. The currencies are: U.S. dollars (external), Dutch florins, Italian lire, Deutsch marks, Sterling/Deutchmarks, French francs, Luxembourg francs, Belgian francs, Swiss francs and European Units of Account.
9. Rule 88*d* (2).   10. Rule 88*d* (1).
11. Rule 92*c*. Application for annual authorisation must be made in the form in Appendix 32*e* of the Rules. This is an exception to the Rule that jobbers may not deal with non-members (Rule 91).
12. For form of application for consent, see Appendix 32*b* of the Rules.
13. Rule 92 (2).

the Stock Exchange to buy securities in one market and almost immediately sell them at a higher price in another. When such a purchase and re-sale is effected between the Stock Exchange, London, and a *foreign* exchange, the transaction is known as arbitrage. The volume of arbitrage business has increased steadily during the twentieth century and is now very extensive.

Arbitrage is defined as

"the business of buying or selling a security *as a principal* in one centre with the intent of reversing such transaction in a centre in a country different from that in which the original transaction has taken place, in order to profit from price difference between such centres and which business is not casual but contains the element of continuity".[14]

The definition contains several salient points:

(i) The arbitrageur acts as a *principal* not as an agent. Since he deals on his own account and not for a client, he is not affected by the restrictions on dealing with non-members.

(ii) Arbitrage takes place between the Stock Exchange and a foreign market. The arbitrageur is affected by considerations which are not part of ordinary dealing in his domestic market: they include current rates of exchange where one bargain is to be settled in sterling and the other in a foreign currency, differing rates of commission, and whether dividends, interest and rights attach to a particular security when quoted in a particular foreign exchange. These and other factors can involve minute calculations; and since successful arbitrage depends upon promptly taking advantage of a temporary state of affairs, they must often be made as swiftly as possible.

(iii) Arbitrage business contains the element of continuity. The arbitrageur must ensure that there are markets in the security in *both* centres existing independently of each other; ideally, the resale should be almost contemporaneous with the purchase, so that there is no time for the price to fluctuate in the interval.

Subject to the provisions below, a broker or jobber may carry on arbitrage whether on joint account or otherwise.[15]

1. Brokers and arbitrage

In conformity with the fundamental rule of the London Stock Exchange that a broker must not make prices or otherwise act as a jobber:

14. Rule 92 (1).
15. Rule 92 (1) (*b*). Draft Rules 61 (A) (1) and 61 (C) (4) (*a*) of the Federation of Stock Exchanges (which provide for the cessation of dual capacity) prohibit broker firms from (*inter alia*) engaging in arbitrage. But the Rules are brought into force only by a confirmed special resolution of the Federal Committee, and to date no such resolution has been passed or confirmed.

(a) A broker must exclude from arbitrage (whether on joint-account with a correspondent or on non-joint account) any order received from a non-member; and if he executes such an order with a firm which is also his arbitrage correspondent he must act solely as broker and agent, and issue a contract note charging commission at a rate not less than that laid down in the commission Rules.[16]

(b) In executing an order received from an overseas arbitrage correspondent (or for that matter any correspondent), and in the making of offers or bids, a broker must not do anything to evade the commission Rules; furthermore he must where appropriate observe the Rules[17] as to sharing commission with overseas brokers.[18]

(c) A broker desiring to arbitrage on joint account with his correspondent must apply to the Council for annual authorisation.[19]

2. Jobbers and arbitrage

A jobber may not deal on non-joint account in overseas centres in securities registered solely in the United Kingdom unless specially authorised to do so by the Council in respect of a specific security or securities.[20] Furthermore he may only arbitrage in those securities in which he normally conducts business as a jobber: in no circumstances may he act as broker or agent or adopt any other procedure for a like purpose.[1]

Where stock is transferred to a jobber "in the ordinary course of his business as dealer", section 42 of the Finance Act 1920 relieves the jobber from stamp duty on the transfer in excess of ten shillings. But the Rules of the Stock Exchange forbid the jobber from applying that provision to arbitrage: in other words he is forbidden to treat arbitrage as part of his ordinary course of business for the purpose of obtaining relief from stamp duty.[2]

A jobber desiring to arbitrage whether on joint or non-joint account must apply to the Council for annual authorisation.[3]

3. Correspondents' branch offices

Neither a broker nor a jobber may transact or accept arbitrage through his arbitrage correspondent's representative or branch office in London.[4]

---

16. Rule 92 (1) (d).   17. Rule 203a.   18. Rule 92 (1) (e).
19. Rule 92 (1) (f). For form of application, see Appendix 32 of the Rules.
20. Rule 92 (1) (g).   1. Rule 92 (1) (h).   2. Rule 92 (1) (c).
3. Rule 92 (1) (j). For form of application, see Appendix 32 of the Rules.
4. Rule 92 (1) (k).

C. SHUNTING

The business of buying securities in one market and selling in another, when practised between London and country exchanges, or between two country exchanges, is known as shunting.

The London broker who engages in shunting buys or sells securities as "London correspondent" for a country firm. Shunting must be distinguished from arbitrage in that while an arbitrageur acts as a *principal* on his own behalf, a shunter always acts as an *agent* for a non-member. It follows that in the Stock Exchange, London, only *broking* firms can act as London correspondents. Country firms, on the other hand, have never been prohibited from conducting business in a dual capacity—having a broking side and a jobber–shunter side; and some firms in fact do business in both capacities.[5]

The Federation of Stock Exchanges drew up rules for the abolition of dual capacity, based on the third interim report, dated August 11th 1964, of the Federal Committee on the Co-ordination of Stock Exchanges, but the rules have not yet been brought into effect. When all the various stock exchanges in the United Kingdom are completely federated, any broker in any centre will be able to deal with any jobber in any centre. So a London broker will be able to deal with not only any London jobber but with any jobber in any other country exchange; and a country broker will be able to deal with not only any country jobber, but also any London jobber.

Control of London correspondents

A firm of brokers in London wishing to act as London correspondent of a member of a federated exchange carrying on business solely as jobbers, or in the dual capacity of brokers and jobbers, must apply to the Council for annual authorisation[6] giving such particulars as may be required, including those of any shunting line which the firm may wish to establish, maintain or use.[7] Like arbitrage, shunting has an element of continuity.

A broking firm wishing to cease acting as London correspondent of a member of a federated exchange, or to close a shunting line, must notify the Council and obtain their prior approval.[8]

A London correspondent which will act for a country jobber, or for the jobber–shunter side of a dual capacity firm must undertake:[9]

5. See Prospectus of the Federation of Stock Exchanges, Rule 61.
6. For the form of application, see Appendix 32*d* of the Rules.
7. Rule 92*b*.
8. *Ibid.*   9. *Ibid.*

(i) to disclose to a London jobber, prior to asking for a price and prior to dealing with him, the name of the country firm on whose behalf they are acting.

(ii) not to act as a principal but only as an agent in transacting such business, and to charge commission at a rate not less than that laid down in the commission Rules.[10]

It is relevant in this context that the Council may, if they in their uncontrolled discretion decide that the circumstances warrant it, declare any non-member firm to be a non-member jobber.[11] Furthermore, they have the power to prohibit or regulate the business relations of members with non-member jobbers.[12]

10. See generally, Chapter 7, *ante.*
11. Rule 92*a.*   12. *Ibid.*

CHAPTER 12

Exchange Control

INTRODUCTION

The broad objective of Exchange Control is to conserve the United Kingdom's gold and foreign currency resources and to assist the balance of payments.

Exchange Control began in the United Kingdom at the outbreak of the Second World War. The legal basis of the war-time control was the Defence (Finance) Regulations 1939[1] issued under the Emergency Powers (Defence) Acts. In October 1947 these temporary regulations were largely superseded by permanent legislation in the Exchange Control Act 1947, although certain of the original powers still remain in force under the Emergency Laws (Re-enactments and Repeals) Act 1964: these two Acts were in turn modified by section 55 of the Finance Act 1968.

The Exchange Control Act states in its preamble that it is "an Act to confer powers, and impose duties and restrictions, in relation to gold, currency, payments, securities, debts, and the import, export, transfer and settlement of property, and for purposes connected with the matters aforesaid". It is concerned not only with controlling certain types of payments but also with ensuring that funds due from abroad are properly received without delay, and are not used for any unauthorised purpose.

The powers are conferred mainly on the Treasury, including powers to make orders and give directions and permissions; and the Treasury has delegated authority to the Bank of England to administer most parts of the Act on its behalf. The Bank of England has in turn authorised most commercial banks in the United Kingdom (both British and foreign) to execute a wide range of transactions; such banks are known as "Authorised Banks". In addition, more limited authority has been given to persons such as stockbrokers and solicitors (known as "Authorised Depositaries") in connection with security transactions.

The Act distinguishes throughout between the Scheduled Territories[2] (i.e., those countries listed in the First Schedule to the

---

1. S. R. & O. 1939 No. 16ᴊ0.
2. The *Scheduled Territories* comprise the United Kingdom (including the Isle of Man and the Channel Islands), all other countries within the British Commonwealth (except Canada and Rhodesia), the Irish Republic, British Trust

Act, as amended from time to time by the Treasury) and the rest of the World. The Scheduled Territories mostly have their own exchange control laws and regulations comparable in scope to those of the United Kingdom.

United Kingdom Exchange Control does not in general impose restrictions on transactions between residents of the United Kingdom and residents of other Scheduled Territories.

Exchange Control applies mainly to financial transactions with residents of countries outside the Scheduled Territories (commonly referred to as non-residents). The currencies of such countries are "foreign currencies" for the purposes of the Act.[3] The restrictions are at present largely confined to transactions of a capital nature. Current payments are supervised but are not normally restricted. The restrictions in force are varied from time to time in accordance with Government policy and in particular in the light of the United Kingdom's balance of payments position.

A. AUTHORISED DEPOSITARIES

The Bank of England has issued authorities, on certain terms, which in general give the permissions required by persons, wherever resident, to buy and sell sterling and foreign currency securities quoted on stock exchanges in the United Kingdom and abroad. Such purchases and sales must be through an Authorised Depositary in the United Kingdom, and the list of Authorised Depositaries includes banks, stockbrokers and solicitors. Instructions have been issued by the Bank of England to Authorised Depositaries who are professional dealers in securities which enable the majority of day-to-day transactions to be carried out without delay.

As the object of control over securities is to protect the official reserves and to prevent any unauthorised transfer of United Kingdom assets to non-residents, it is essential that the rules are observed strictly at all points. To this end it is normally made a condition of all consents and permissions that an Authorised Depositary accepts the responsibility of supervising the transaction to ensure that it conforms to the terms of the relevant permission,

---

Territories, British Protectorates and Protected States, Iceland, the Hashemite Kingdom of Jordan, Kuwait, Libya, South Africa and South West Africa, the People's Republic of Southern Yemen, and Western Samoa.

3. I.e., the currencies specified by the Treasury, which include, Australian schillings, Belgian francs, Canadian dollars, Danish kroner, Deutschmarks, French francs, Italian lire, Japanese yen, Netherlands guilders, Norwegian kroner, Portuguese escudos, Spanish pesetas, Swedish kronor, Swiss francs and U.S. dollars.

that it is not excluded by any exception to that permission and that any conditions attaching to the permission are fulfilled. An Authorised Depositary who, having studied the relevant Bank of England Notices, is in any doubt about any particular deal involving securities, is advised to seek guidance from the Bank of England.

The proper administration of Exchange Control over security transactions is possible only if certain categories of securities are held with, or to the order of, an Authorised Depositary. These categories include all foreign currency securities and sterling bearer securities and the requirement applies to all such securities owned by a United Kingdom resident, wherever held, and to all such securities held in this country which are owned by a person resident outside the United Kingdom.

B. SECURITY TRANSACTIONS GOVERNED BY EXCHANGE CONTROL

1. Sterling securities

Control over dealings in sterling securities is mainly concerned with ensuring that:

(*a*) additions to non-resident holdings of such securities are paid for in sterling from an external account, in funds eligible for credit to an external account, or in sterling arising from the sale of foreign currency in the official foreign exchange market, thereby obtaining the proper balance of payments benefit from non-resident investments;

(*b*) interest, dividends and capital payments on such securities are not remitted outside the Scheduled Territories unless the holdings have been properly acquired by non-residents;

(*c*) purchases of such securities on behalf of non-residents on stock exchanges are not permitted to frustrate the rules for inward direct investments in United Kingdom companies.

Authorised Depositaries in the United Kingdom who are professional dealers in securities have been given permissions which generally enable sterling securities to be freely bought and sold on United Kingdom stock exchanges by all persons, wherever resident. These permissions are subject to certain conditions and exceptions, and it is the responsibility of the Authorised Depositary effecting a transaction to ensure that the terms of the permissions are observed, thereby enabling registrars[4] in the United Kingdom to accept

4. Registrars include all persons concerned with the keeping of any register, book, file or index in which securities are registered in the United Kingdom.

transfers lodged with them by Authorised Depositaries without question so far as Exchange Control requirements are concerned. It is of particular importance for the Authorised Depositary to establish the correct residential status of both buyer and seller. If the buyer is a non-resident, payment must be obtained by the Authorised Depositary concerned on or before the date of completion, as indicated in (a) above. If the seller is taken to be a non-resident the Authorised Depositary may normally effect the deal and lodge the transfer provided that the security has been held by him or another Authorised Depositary for account of a non-resident or it has been received from outside the Scheduled Territories in bearer form or in the form of a registered certificate which shows the holder's address to be outside the Scheduled Territories; alternatively, if the Authorised Depositary is able to satisfy himself that the beneficial owner is a non-resident who has not left a country within the Scheduled Territories with the intention of living outside the Scheduled Territories, and thereby rendered his assets liable to restriction, he may also transact the deal as being on behalf of a non-resident.

The sale proceeds of sterling securities owned by non-residents, and interest and dividends accruing on such holdings, may be credited to an external account or converted into foreign currency in the official foreign exchange market. It follows that the registration of an address outside the Scheduled Territories in respect of a security by means of a transfer or change of registered address is tantamount to authorising the remittance of funds outside the Scheduled Territories; it is the responsibility of the Authorised Depositary lodging the transfer or notifying the change of address to the registrar to ensure that the necessary permission has been given by the Bank of England either generally or specifically.

All issues of securities in the United Kingdom require permission unless it is established that neither the person to whom the security is to be issued nor the person, if any, for whom he is to be a nominee[5] is a non-resident, and a declaration to this effect is received by the person issuing the security. In addition, permissions are required for the issue of sterling bearer securities, and for any act which would result in a body corporate controlled by United Kingdom residents ceasing to be so controlled. However, a general

5. For meaning of nominee, see Exchange Control Act 1947, s. 20 (5). A person is not to be treated as a nominee simply because he holds a security or coupon as trustee if he is entitled to transfer it without permission from anyone else. Where the security or coupon is held by a body corporate, a person is not to be treated as entitled to give instructions for this purpose by reason only that he has a controlling interest in the body corporate.

authority has been given by the Bank of England allowing registrars to effect most issues of securities without formality; this authority is subject to certain exceptions and conditions and if any doubt arises registrars are advised to consult the Bank of England.

Certain sterling securities, including bearer securities and registered certificates which can be transferred to a register outside the Scheduled Territories without the consent of a registrar within the Scheduled Territories, must be kept in the custody of an Authorised Depositary if owned by United Kingdom residents or if held in the United Kingdom by non-residents. This does not, however, normally apply to any renounceable letter of allotment acceptance or rights, any renounceable certificate, or any scrip certificate to bearer which has been in existence for less than six months. Special rules apply to transfers involving securities in compulsory deposit, to ensure that unauthorised funds are not made available to non-residents.

The import and export of sterling securities may generally be effected without formality except that securities held in compulsory deposit may be exported by Authorised Depositaries only in accordance with permissions given by the Bank of England.

2. Foreign currency securities

Exchange Control in relation to foreign currency securities has four main objects:

(*a*) to ensure that foreign currency securities owned by United Kingdom residents are not disposed of without permission;

(*b*) to ensure that additions to such holdings are not financed from the official reserves;

(*c*) to secure a contribution from the United Kingdom's private holdings of foreign currency securities to the official reserves whenever a sale is made;

(*d*) to prevent persons resident outside the Scheduled Territories from selling foreign currency securities to United Kingdom residents at a premium, thereby acquiring sterling at a discount on the official rate of exchange.

All transfers of foreign currency securities in the United Kingdom and all transfers of foreign currency securities by United Kingdom residents, wherever the transfers take place, require Exchange Control permission; however, persons wishing to buy or sell such securities may do so through Authorised Depositaries who, in most cases, will be able to effect the transaction under authority issued to them by the Bank of England, but subject to certain conditions. The most important of these conditions, which are designed to achieve the objects listed in (a) to (d) above are discussed below.

In order to conserve the nation's reserves of gold and foreign currency, United Kingdom residents are not permitted to purchase foreign currency securities with official exchange or out of export receipts or other current earnings, e.g., dividends accruing in foreign currency, or by payment in sterling directly or indirectly to a non-resident. Purchases may normally be made only through Authorised Depositaries, payment being made from the proceeds of sale of other resident-owned foreign currency securities: these proceeds are known as "investment currency", and permissions have been given which enable Authorised Depositaries to buy and sell such currency on behalf of United Kingdom residents in a separate market which is known as the investment currency[6] market. Demand usually exceeds supply in this market so that investment currency normally changes hands at a premium. The sterling quotations for foreign currency securities include this premium in the price quoted.

Permissions have been given to Authorised Depositaries which allow them, subject to certain conditions, to sell foreign currency securities on behalf of residents of the United Kingdom either abroad for foreign currency or in the United Kingdom for sterling. One of these conditions has, as its objective, the transfer to the official reserves in foreign currency of part of the privately held portfolio of foreign currency securities. Thus a United Kingdom resident who sells foreign currency securities abroad is, in general, permitted to re-invest 75% of the foreign currency proceeds in other foreign currency securities, or to sell 75% of the proceeds in the investment currency market: the remaining 25% of the proceeds must be sold to an Authorised Bank at the current market rate in the official foreign exchange market, thus benefiting the official reserves. In order that an equivalent benefit shall accrue to the reserves from transactions which take place in sterling, the rules require a United Kingdom resident who sells his foreign currency securities for sterling on a United Kingdom stock exchange to buy, in the investment currency market, an amount of investment currency equivalent to 25% of the sale proceeds and to sell it to an Authorised Bank at the current market rate in the official foreign exchange market.

Transactions in foreign currency securities or in investment currency by or on behalf of residents of the Scheduled Territories other than the United Kingdom, and which fall within the scope of United Kingdom Exchange Control are, broadly, subject to the same rules as

---

6. Investment currency is often referred to loosely as "premium dollars".

apply to those carried out by residents of the United Kingdom; but in the case of sales much depends on the date and circumstances of acquisition. Foreign currency accruing to residents of the Scheduled Territories other than the United Kingdom cannot be sold as investment currency except with the specific permission of the Bank of England, nor may foreign currency securities be sold through an Authorised Depositary on their behalf unless such permission has been obtained.

Foreign currency belonging to non-residents is never investment currency and foreign currency securities held by or on behalf of such persons can never be sold in the investment currency market. A non-resident who wishes to acquire sterling in the United Kingdom must do so by selling foreign currency in the official foreign exchange market, thereby bringing a direct benefit to the reserves: any sterling so acquired is known as External Sterling.

As an essential safeguard against infringement of the rules in respect of foreign currency securities, it is required that all such securities held in the United Kingdom, or held abroad by residents of the United Kingdom, must be placed in the custody or held to the order of an Authorised Depositary. Securities which have not been deposited in this manner may not be dealt with in any way without reference to the Bank of England.

Control is exercised over the import and export of foreign currency securities, but Authorised Depositaries may normally undertake this provided that they only export such securities in settlement of permitted transactions.

STOCK TRANSFER FORM

(Above this line for Registrars only)

Certificate lodged with the Registrar

Consideration Money £ ....

(For completion by the Registrar/Stock Exchange)

Full name of Undertaking.	
Full description of Security.	
Number or amount of Shares, Stock or other security and, in figures column only, number and denomination of units, if any.	Words

Figures

(units of)

Name(s) of registered holder(s) should be given in full; the address should be given where there is only one holder.

If the transfer is not made by the registered holder(s) insert also the name(s) and capacity (e.g., Executor(s)) of the person(s) making the transfer.

In the name(s) of

I/We hereby transfer the above security out of the name(s) aforesaid to the person(s) named below *or to the several persons named in Parts 2 of Brokers Transfer Forms relating to the above security :*

Delete words in italics except for stock exchange transactions.

Signature(s) of transferor(s)

Stamp of Selling Broker(s) or, for transactions which are not stock exchange transactions, of Agent(s), if any, acting for the Transferor(s)

1...

2...

3...

4...

Bodies corporate should execute under their common seal.

Date...

Full name(s) and full postal address(es) (including County or, if applicable, Postal District number) of the person(s) to whom the security is transferred.

Please state title, if any, or whether Mr., Mrs. or Miss.

Please complete in typewriting or in Block Capitals.

I/we request that such entries be made in the register as are necessary to give effect to this transfer.

Stamp of Buying Broker(s) (if any)	Stamp or name and address of person lodging this form (if other than the Buying Broker(s))

The security represented by the transfer overleaf has been sold as follows :—

..............................Shares/Stock	..............................Shares/Stock
..............................Shares/Stock	..............................Shares/Stock
..............................Shares/Stock	..............................Shares/Stock
..............................Shares/Stock	..............................Shares/Stock
..............................Shares/Stock	..............................Shares/Stock
..............................Shares/Stock	..............................Shares/Stock
.... Shares/Stock	..............................Shares/Stock
..............................Shares/Stock	..............................Shares/Stock
..............................Shares/Stock	..............................Shares/Stock
..............................Shares/Stock	.... Shares/Stock

Balance (if any) due to Selling Broker(s)   ....

Amount of Certificate(s)

Brokers Transfer Forms for above amounts certified
    Stamp of certifying Stock Exchange   *Stamp of Selling Broker(s)*

BROKERS TRANSFER FORM

(Above this line for Registrars only)

Certificate lodged with the Registrar

Consideration Money £..

(For completion by the Registrar/Stock Exchange)

Part 1

Full name of Undertaking.	
Full description of Security.	

	Words		Figures
Number or amount of Shares, Stock or other security and, in figures column only, number and denomination of units, if any.			
			(units of)

	In the name(s) of
Name(s) of registered holder(s) should be given in full; the address should be given where there is only one holder.	
If the transfer is not made by the registered holder(s) insert also the name(s) and capacity (e.g., Executor(s)) of the person(s) making the transfer.	

I/We confirm that the Stock Transfer Form relating to the security set out above has been lodged with the Registrar, and that the said security has been sold by me/us by a stock exchange transaction within the meaning of the Stock Transfer Act 1963.

Date and Stamp of Selling Broker(s)

Part 2

Full name(s) and full postal address(es) (including County or, if applicable, Postal District number) of the person(s) to whom the security is transferred.	
Please state title, if any, or whether Mr., Mrs. or Miss.	
Please complete in typewriting or in Block Capitals.	

I/We confirm that the security set out in Part 1 above has been purchased by a stock exchange transaction within the meaning of the Stock Transfer Act 1963, and I/we request that such entries be made in the register as are necessary to give effect to this transfer.

Stamp of Buying Broker(s)	Stamp of Lodging Agent (if other than the Buying Broker(s))

SPECIMEN FORM OF DIVIDEND MANDATE

COMPANY SECURITIES

For Company's use Only

REQUEST for PAYMENT of INTEREST or DIVIDENDS

To : The Secretary or Registrar   *Date*......................................*19*........

Insert name and address
of Company.

....

....

Please forward, until further notice, all Interest and Dividends that may from time to time become due on any Stock or Shares now standing, or which may hereafter stand, in my (our) name(s) or in the name(s) of the survivor(s) of us in the Company's books to :—

Full name and address
of the Bank, Firm or
Person to whom Interest
and Dividends are to
be sent.

....

....

....

or, where payment is to be made to a Bank, to such other Branch of that Bank as the Bank may from time to time request. Your compliance with this request shall discharge the Company's liability in respect of such interest or dividends.

This form must be signed
by ALL the Registered
Holders, Executors or
Administrators as the
case may be.

(1) *Signature*..   (3) *Signature*...

Name in full......................................   *Name in full*...................................
(BLOCK CAPITALS)   (BLOCK CAPITALS)

Address...   *Address*..

....

Any change of address
may be notified by
quoting former and
present address.

(2) *Signature*..   (4) *Signature*...

Name in full......................................   *Name in full*...................................
(BLOCK CAPITALS)   (BLOCK CAPITALS)

Address...   *Address*..

....

NOTE   (i) Directions to credit a particular account MUST be given to the Bank direct and NOT INCLUDED in this form.

(ii) Where the stock is in the name of a deceased Holder, instructions signed by Executor(s) or Administrator(s) should indicate the name of the deceased.

Where the instructions are in favour of a Bank, this form should be sent to the Bank branch concerned for the insertion of the following details :—

Bank's Reference Numbers and Details :—

(1) Sorting Code No...

(2) Name of Bank and
     Title of Branch...

(3) Account Number (if any)...

STAMP OF BANK BRANCH

APPENDIX D

SPECIMEN FORM OF DIVIDEND MANDATE

SECURITIES ON BANK OF ENGLAND REGISTER

A SEPARATE FORM MUST BE USED FOR EACH ACCOUNT.

Please use BLOCK CAPITALS.

REQUEST FOR PAYMENT OF DIVIDENDS

To the Chief Accountant, Bank of England, New Change, London, E.C.4.

Name of Stock ....
(TITLE IN FULL)

Amount of Stock £ ....

STOCK ACCOUNT No.
(Please quote if known)

standing in the name(s) of—

For Sole Account :— FULL NAME AND ADDRESS (any change of address may be notified by quoting former and present address).

For Joint Account :— FULL NAMES ONLY required : addresses need not be given.

....

....

....

....

Please forward all Dividend Warrants due, † and to become due, and payable on the sum of Stock mentioned above, or on the amount for the time being so standing, to—
✱ (*See footnote*)

Full name of the Bank, Firm or Person to whom Dividends are to be sent.

....

at ....

....

....

This form must be signed by all the Stockholders, Executors or Administrators, as the case may be.

Signature(s)

....

....

....

....

Date 19

✱ If a Bank is nominated to receive the dividends—
  (a) details of the banking account to be credited must be given to the branch concerned and must not be included in this form.
  (b) this form should be sent to the branch concerned who will insert, where necessary, their reference number(s) in the box below.
† If instructions are received less than one month before a dividend date it may not be possible to apply the instructions to that dividend.

FOR USE BY BANK NOMINATED TO RECEIVE DIVIDENDS

Reference Numbers :—	Stamp of Bank Branch
(1) Sorting Code No.	
(2) Account No. (if any)	

278

Index

BROKERS—*continued*
defaulter, avoidance of declaration as, 253
duties as to Stock Exchange rules, 132
expenses of, 142
fiduciary position of, 126
function of, 103, 124
gentleman's agreement by, 130
indemnity of,
    anticipatory, 142
    defaulting broker, 144
    entitlement to, 25
    expenses, 142
    purchase price, 142
    right of, 141
    where none, 143
instructions to, 128
jobber, dealing with more than one, 112
jobbers, partnerships with, 47
liability of, 136
lien of, 145
non-members, orders executed with, 259
obedience of, 128
orders, lumping of, 150
overseas stock exchanges, orders executed in, 261
payment, authority to receive, 198
principal, acting as, 146
profit of, 148
purchaser, duty as to financial standing of, 132
    non-disclosure of, 148
solvency of, 66
Stock Exchange, duty to, 104
transfer forms of, 206
    See also TRANSFER
trustee, as, 149

BREACH OF CONTRACT. *See* CONTRACT

BUILDING SOCIETIES,
investment by, 23

BULL,
meaning, 24

BUYING-IN,
generally, 185
instructions as to, 186
intermediates, release of, 187
loss occasioned by, 186
order, failure to execute, 187
prohibition of, 187
suspension of, 187

C

CALL,
meaning, 158
payment of, 195

CAPITAL,
authorised, increase of, 78
clauses of, 12
issued, 12
limited company, of, 52
loan, 14
management and ownership, historical background, 2
nominal, 12
partnerships, of, 43
reserve, 12

CAPITALISATION,
profits, of, 226

CARE,
duty of, 135

CASH,
bargain for, 182

CENSURE,
Council, by, 31

CENTRAL STOCK PAYMENT OFFICE,
functions of, 201

CESSIO BONORUM,
deed of arrangement, 251

CHARGE,
equitable floating, 15

CHEQUES,
payment by, 197

CITY CODE,
generally, 91
nature, 93
panel, 96, 97
principles, 94
sanctions on breach, 95

CLERKS,
authorised, 68
bankrupts or defaulters as, 68
deceased members, of, 69
rules as to, 69
unauthorised, 68

CLIENT,
account, closing of, 238
    closing of part of, 239
action of account by, 132

NOMINEE COMPANIES,
rules relating to, 55

O

OFFICIAL ASSIGNEE,
functions of, 246

OPTIONS,
call, 158
dealings, regulation of, 160
double, 158
ex rights, securities dealt in, 160
genuine, to be, 158
price of, 160
procedure for exercising, 160
put, 158
take-over bid, benefit of, 159
time of the essence in, 159

OPTION DEALERS,
accountant, report of, 64

OVERSEAS BRANCHES,
rules as to, 57

OVERSEAS COMPANIES,
transfer of securities of, 220

OVERSEAS REPRESENTATIVES,
commissions, 173

OVERSEAS STOCK EXCHANGES,
arbitrage, 262
Euro-Currency Bonds, orders in, 262
orders executed in, 261

P

PARTNERSHIPS,
advantages of, 41
balance sheets. *See* BALANCE SHEETS
brokers and jobbers, between 47
capital, working, 43
companies, contrasted with, 41
corporate members, 48 *et seq.*
definition, 41
disadvantages of, 42
dissolution of, 44
external members and, 39
failure of, 45
formation of, 44
liability, 45
limited, 43
assignment, 46
censure, suspension and expulsion, 46
conduct of business, 46

PARTNERSHIPS—*continued*
limited—*continued*
contract notes, 46
correspondence, 46
default, 46
returns, 46
stake, restriction on, 67
lists, 44
market, 47
dissolution of, 48
notification of, 47
permitted, 47
what constitutes, 48
notices, 44
posting of, 45
prohibited, 47
rules, general, 44
solvency, 66
succession, 42
undisclosed, 45
unlimited companies, formation of, 48
what constitutes, 48

PAYMENT,
account day, 196
broker, authority to receive, 198
cheques, by, 197
differences, 196
manner of, 197
price, when payable, 197

PLACING,
meaning, 73
quotation, requirements as to, 78

PLEDGE,
contango, compared with, 156
law applicable to, 157
mortgage, compared with, 157

POOL,
shares, of, 9

PREVENTION OF FRAUD (INVESTMENTS) ACT 1958,
offences under, 10

PRINCIPAL. *See* AGENT

PROBATE,
valuations for, 230

PROFIT,
broker, of, 148

PROSPECTUS,
definition of, 71
stock exchange, 76

PROVINCIAL BROKERS' STOCK EXCHANGE,
formation of, 6

SETTLEMENT OFFICE,
function of, 200

SHARES,
bonus, 73
certificates, 204
limited corporate member, issue or
transfer of shares in, 55
ordinary, 13
non-voting, 14
preference, 13
redemption of, 14
transfer forms, 206
See also TRANSFER

SHAREHOLDERS,
company, of, 11

SIIUNTING,
meaning, 265

SOLVENCY,
client, of, 236
limited corporate members, 67
margin of, minimum, 66
partnerships, 66
unlimited corporate members, 66

SOUTH SEA BUBBLE,
history of, 3

SPECIFIC PERFORMANCE,
breach of contract, remedy for, 243

SPECULATION,
investment, 24

STERLING SECURITIES,
dealing in, 269

STOCK,
Government, 16
issue of, 16
local authorities, of, 18
Stock Transfer Act 1963...207

STOCK EXCHANGE, LONDON.
See also ASSOCIATED STOCK EX-
CHANGES
advertising, prohibition of, 10
bargains, protection of, 10
constitution, 8
Council. *See* COUNCIL
Deed of Settlement 1875...8
development, 5
fair market, provision of, 8
false market, prevention of, 9
federation, 6
formation of, 1
function of, 8
historical background, 1
investors, types of, 20

STOCK EXCHANGE, LONDON—
continued
membership of. *See* MEMBERSHIP OF
STOCK EXCHANGE
nature, 1
origin of, 4
partnerships. *See* PARTNERSHIPS
securities dealt in,
company securities, 13
debentures, 15
Dominion, Colonial and foreign,
17
Government stock, 16
loan capital, 14
local authority loans, 18
shares, 13
stock, 16
unit trusts, sub-units of, 19
shunting, 265
speculation, 24
stock and share dealing, growth of, 1
wagering contracts, 25

STOCK OFFICIAL,
functions of, 246

SUSPENSION,
Council, by, 31

T

TAKE-OVER,
circulars, 92
City Code, 91
nature, 93
panel, 96, 97
principles, 94
sanctions on breach, 95
control of, 91
options and, 159

TAKING-IN,
contangos, 155

TENDER,
offer by, 73

THEFT ACT 1968,
appropriation, 127

TICKETS,
alteration of, 183
antedated, 183
detention of, 183
issue of, fine for late, 189
non-clearing scrip, 189
receipt of, 183
securities, delivery of, 183
selling-out, delivery of after, 189
loss occasioned by, 188